African Arguments

African Arguments is a series of short books about Africa today. Aimed at the growing number of students and general readers who want to know more about the African continent, these books highlight many of the longer-term strategic as well as immediate political issues. They will get to the heart of why Africa is the way it is and how it is changing. The books are scholarly but engaged, substantive as well as topical.

Series editors

D0066998

Titles already published

Forthcoming

Published by Zed Books and the IAI with the support of the following organisations:

International African Institute The International African Institute's principal aim is to promote scholarly understanding of Africa, notably its changing societies, cultures and languages. Founded in 1926 and based in London, it supports a range of seminars and publications including the journal *Africa*.

www.internationalafricaninstitute.org

Royal African Society Now more than a hundred years old, the Royal African Society today is Britain's leading organization promoting Africa's cause. Through its journal, *African Affairs*, and by organizing meetings, discussions and other activities, the society strengthens links between Africa and Britain and encourages understanding of Africa and its relations with the rest of the world.

www.royalafricansociety.org

The World Peace Foundation, founded in 1910, is located at the Fletcher School, Tufts University. The Foundation's mission is to promote innovative research and teaching, believing that these are critical to the challenges of making peace around the world, and should go hand in hand with advocacy and practical engagement with the toughest issues. Its central theme is 'reinventing peace' for the twenty-first century.

www.worldpeacefoundation.org

About the author

Celeste Hicks is a freelance journalist and former BBC correspondent in Chad, who has lived and worked across the Sahel and in Somalia.

CELESTE HICKS

Africa's New Oil

Power, pipelines and future fortunes

Zed Books
LONDON

in association with

International African Institute
Royal African Society
World Peace Foundation

Africa's New Oil: Power, pipelines and future fortunes was first published in association with the International African Institute, the Royal African Society and the World Peace Foundation in 2015 by Zed Books Ltd, 7 Cynthia Street, London N1 9JF, UK

www.zedbooks.co.uk
www.internationalafricaninstitute.org
www.royalafricansociety.org
www.worldpeacefoundation.org

Set in OurType Arnhem and Futura Bold by Ewan Smith, London
Index: <ed.emery@thefreeuniversity.net>
Cover designed by www.roguefour.co.uk

A catalogue record for this book is available from the British Library

ISBN 978-1-78360-113-4 hb
ISBN 978-1-78360-112-7 pb
ISBN 978-1-78360-114-1 pdf
ISBN 978-1-78360-115-8 epub
ISBN 978-1-78360-116-5 mobi

Printed and bound by CPI Group (UK) Ltd, Croydon, CR0 4YY

Contents

Maps and figures

Acknowledgements

Thanks to Alex de Waal for your first brave suggestion for a book on Chad, and to Richard Dowden for your support throughout. Thanks to my editors Ken Barlow and Stephanie Kitchen who provided limitless moral support and patience throughout the editing process. Thanks to Miles Irving for some beautifully clear maps.

In Chad, thanks to Rita and Najikomo Benoudjita for your help with logistics and to Rim Nassingar from PWYP. To Tim Muddiman, thanks for sticking your neck out for me, and to Dr Dou Lirong from CNPCIC for facilitating my trip to Ronier and Zeng-Jie for looking after me so well. In Niger, thanks to Idy Baraou as always, Mahaman Laouan Gaya for being open and approachable, and Vigno Houngkali at WFP for your help with logistics again! In Ghana, thanks to Carrie Fox, Alberto Wilde and Mohammed from Global Communities for making my trip to Sekondi-Takoradi worthwhile. In Uganda, my eternal thanks to Judith Whiteley and Issa at Safer World for reaching out to a stranger when my phone and laptop were stolen in the middle of the night, and to Catherine Byaruhanga for your help weeks before your baby was due!

To Alice Powell from PWYP, thanks for answering my barrage of questions, likewise to George Cazenove at Tullow Oil. To Stephanie Hancock for being the only other person who knows how hard it is to get anything done in Chad. Thanks also for your ideas and answers: Jane Guyer, Géraud Magrin, George Boden, Rebecca Ponton, Bady Mamadou Balde, Dan Jones, Rosie Pinnington, Ann Pettitt, Mauricio Villafuerte, and to Steve Coll for convincing me that I had a book in me.

The original research in this book would not have been possible without the support of Joanna and Dominic Black – thank you so very much.

Finally, thank you to my husband David Allan for tirelessly reading through my drafts and being a rock when things got too much; and to Laurence, I'm sorry that for the first six weeks of your life the only sound you heard was tapping on a keyboard.

Note on quotations from interviews

Unless indicated otherwise, all the interviews from which I quote in the book were conducted by me in the period between July 2013 and October 2014 as I was carrying out research for this book. Specific in-country interviews were carried out on the following dates: 5–25 July 2013 (Chad), 21–29 January 2014 (Ghana), 20 February to 3 March 2014 (Niger), 15–20 April 2014 (Kenya), and 20–28 April (Uganda).

Abbreviations and acronyms

ACEP	Africa Centre for Energy Policy
ACODE	Advocates Coalition for Development and Environment (Uganda)
AFIEGO	Africa Institute for Energy Governance
ANT	Armée Nationale du Tchad / Chad National Army
APP	Africa Progress Panel
AQIM	al-Qaeda in the Islamic Maghreb
BEAC	Banque des États de l'Afrique Centrale / Bank of Central African States
bpd	barrels per day
CAO	Compliance Advisor Ombudsman
CAR	Central African Republic
CCDP	Chad–Cameroon Development Project
CCSRP	Collège de Contrôle et de Surveillance des Ressources Pétrolières / Petroleum Revenue Oversight and Control Committee (Chad)
CDB	Chinese Development Bank
CEO	Chief Executive Officer
CFA	Central African Franc
CGT	capital gains tax
CNOOC	China National Offshore Oil Corporation
CNPC	China National Petroleum Company (in Niger or Beijing HQ)
CNPCIC	China National Petroleum Company in Chad
COTCO	Cameroon Oil Transportation Company
CPF	central processing facility
CPPN	Commission Permanente Pétrole N'Djaména / Permanent Oil Commission, N'Djaména
CSR	corporate social responsibility
DAO	*dépense avant ordonnancement* / extraordinary budgetary procedure

DEDICATED TO THE LATE
MICHEL BONNARDEAUX

Introduction

The midday sun was beating down on the scrublands of the eastern Sahel region. Spiky black acacia trees poked out from the blinding sand, a hazy line on the horizon the only indication of where earth met sky. A fly buzzed in the stifling air, it was close to 45° Celsius. One of the dead rebel's eyes was open above a deep gash on his face, the blood congealed and dark. The eye stared up at the bleached sky. Around his crumpled body was the evidence of a hasty retreat: a few bullet casings, burnt grass, a toothbrush and one lonely boot. It was an awful place to die.

This was the Am Dam battlefield in eastern Chad in May 2009. The image of Chadian rebels skidding off across the desert on pick-up trucks complete with rocket-propelled grenades splayed like juggling clubs had been a favourite with newsrooms across the world since their first attack in 2005. These were real rebels. Twice before they had driven unopposed in a matter of days from Chad's east to west – a distance of well over 1,000 km with no paved roads. In 2006 and again in 2008 they turned up at the gates of the presidential palace in N'Djaména, threw grenades over the walls and fought face-to-face brutal combat with the presidential guard. President Idriss Déby Itno had been so scared by the threat they posed that he had actually built a moat around the entire city to protect himself. Observers started to see rebellions in Chad as a fact of life – President Déby himself came to office through similar means in 1990 and the country had never had a peaceful handover of power. It seemed only a matter of time before another rebel attack or an internal 'palace' coup would unseat him too.

However, the rebels at this battle of Am Dam in 2009 suffered a terrible defeat, and they have never posed the same kind of threat offshore, making it easier to export and reducing the potential for internal civil strife to disrupt production.

Current world energy consumption trends are also in Africa's favour. Despite efforts to increase energy production from alternative and renewable sources, the global thirst for oil is still strong. BP's *Energy Outlook 2035*, published in January 2014, predicts that global energy consumption is expected to rise 41 per cent between 2012 and 2035, and 95 per cent of that demand is expected to be from emerging economies (BP 2014). While the growth rate in consumption is slowing compared with the last twenty years, oil is still expected to make up 27 per cent of the total mix of energy by 2035, with the bulk of that being used in transportation. The BP analysis expects global demand to be 19 million bpd higher in 2035 than in 2012.

As many major sources of oil have been challenged by conflict in recent years (Iraq and Libya, for example), sub-Saharan Africa has begun to look more attractive. The figures are huge – since 1990 the petroleum industry has invested an estimated US$25 billion in exploration and production activity in Africa, around one-third of that from the US (Ghazvinian 2007: 7). Africa accounts for 10 per cent of all US oil imports, and 20 per cent of the world's total exports of crude (KPMG 2013: 4). According to figures from the US Energy Information Administration, Africa's proven oil reserves have grown by nearly 120 per cent in the past thirty years or so, from 57 billion barrels in 1980 to 124 billion barrels in 2012.

The real issue is potential. As more companies arrive and technology improves, it is likely that more deposits and discoveries will be considered to be commercially viable, thereby allowing more African countries to join the exclusive oil producers' club. The export value of those hydrocarbons is crucial to promoting economic development, argues Paul Collier, Oxford academic, co-director of the Centre for the Study of African Economies and a key commentator on natural resource issues: 'The revenues they [African countries] could get from natural resources are enormous, dwarfing any conceivable flows of aid. They could be

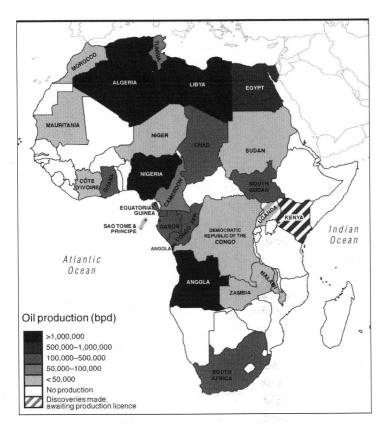

Map o.1 Africa's current production of oil

transformative' (Collier 2010: 38). The Africa Progress Panel (APP) – a group of ten individuals from the private and public sector, chaired by former UN Secretary General Kofi Annan, who advocate for equitable and sustainable development for Africa – estimated that, if the development costs of African oil remain low (at US$6 to US$10 per barrel) and the world price is US$80 per barrel, 'just the 15 million barrel increase in proven oil reserves in Africa between 2010 and 2011 could increase government revenues by $18obn, or 15% of regional GDP' (APP 2013: 44). While the problem of a notoriously volatile world oil price (when this book went to press it had dropped from US$100 in May 2014 to below US$50 a barrel) makes any attempt at reliable calculations difficult, oil will continue to contribute to African economic development. As the APP recognises, Africa's population is expected to rise to over 2 billion by the middle of the twenty-first century (ibid.: 44), and the panel shares a similar view to Collier's: that is, that the effective harnessing of natural resource revenues could provide one of the best opportunities the continent has had in the last fifty years to lift millions out of poverty.

Africa's new oil: where's the catch?

Despite these promising statistics, a number of challenges stand in the way of Africa's newest oil producers – countries such as Ghana and Uganda – effectively harnessing this once-in-a-generation opportunity. As the APP report concluded: 'The challenge is whether these temporary windfalls can be converted into a permanent breakthrough in development' (ibid.: 8). Mention oil and Africa to most people and the impression is likely to be negative. Many have argued that African oil should stay in the ground lest it lead to conflict and environmental devastation. The stories of how oil has wrecked some African nations through war and egregious corruption are well known and quite horrifying.

Old oil giants

In Nigeria – Africa's biggest oil producer – an estimated US$400 billion in oil export earnings (Shaxson 2008: 11) from the 1950s onwards has made little difference to the staggering poverty experienced by most Nigerians, while simultaneously creating a super-rich class of people associated with politics and the oil industry. The country now has an estimated twenty billionaires, many of whom made their money in oil,[1] but it is still ranked 153rd in the UN Human Development Index 2013, with 68 per cent of the population living on less than a dollar a day. Many billions of dollars have been lost through corruption and the country has become a byword for government embezzlement. As John Ghazvinian writes: 'Today in Nigeria, 80 per cent of oil and gas revenue accrues to just 1% of the population' (Ghazvinian 2007: 68).

The establishment of oil production by the British firm Shell in the 1960s led to years of protests in the oil-producing Delta region, where thousands have seen their livelihoods destroyed by pollution and oil spills. The story of Ken Saro-Wiwa, a firebrand activist who advocated for the rights of the Ogoni people who live in the Niger Delta, brought the plight of the region to the world. Under their Movement for the Survival of the Ogoni People (MOSOP) grouping, the Ogonis launched a bill of rights in 1990 seeking compensation for pollution of their lands. In 1993, a series of protests broke out against the oil companies, and in the subsequent months Saro-Wiwa and his followers alleged that hundreds had been beaten, killed or forced from their homes by the Nigerian security forces.[2] Saro-Wiwa was later charged with the murder of four conservative Ogoni leaders and executed to worldwide condemnation, and Shell eventually had to close its Ogoni operations. After Saro-Wiwa's death, other groups in the Delta region rose up in protest, including in 2006 the Movement for the Emancipation of the Niger Delta (MEND), led by Alhaji Mujahid Dokubo-Asari. Sabotage and kidnapping of oil workers by a number of groups have led to chaos and shut-downs for the oil industry, with an estimated 5 per cent of Nigeria's daily oil output (100,000 bpd) being lost in so-called 'bunkering' activities – attacks on pipelines to siphon off the oil for private sale (Katsouris and Sayne 2013).

Angola has also entered popular imagination as a resource-cursed nation. The country was devastated by civil war in the 1970s and 1980s, but thanks to offshore discoveries brought into production by ExxonMobil and Total, it is now the continent's second-biggest producer with an estimated 1.8 million bpd (IEA 2013). Again, the revenues that the country has earned should have been transformative but instead have largely disappeared down a black hole of corruption. A report by Global Witness in 2004 estimated that US$4.2 billion a year was not being accounted for – more than half the country's annual gross domestic product (GDP). The money has allowed the Angolan political elite to retain its grip on power, with President Eduardo dos Santos now the

7

al. 2007: 65), arguing that in poorer countries with fewer effective governance institutions, the 'contract' between the people and their leaders fails; resource-rich governments are able to govern without consulting the population because they have large potential revenue streams from oil at their disposal. In other words, such governments are free from the responsibilities of taxation.

One solution is simply not to extract the resource at all; Karl has argued for *not* developing oilfields until political institutions have matured sufficiently to withstand the pressures caused by a sudden influx of revenue. While this might have seemed like a potential solution in the light of early expositions of the resource curse, which suggested that the process was almost inevitable (ibid.: 95), this conclusion has been questioned by more recent research. Michael L. Ross, for example, argues that more up-to-date economic figures from the 2000s show a different pattern: 'Economic growth in the oil states has been erratic, but neither faster nor slower than economic growth in other states' (Ross 2012: 189). He suggests instead that the real question should be why such natural wealth did not lead to *above average* rates of growth.

Whatever the truth of the figures, it is clear that with such high global demand for oil, arguments for not developing oilfields in Africa are not likely to be popular in the medium term. The key question then becomes how best to deal with the challenges posed by oil. A substantial body of work has been developed to identify best practice on developing oil resources, some of it proposed by campaign groups and NGOs such as Publish What You Pay (PWYP) and the Natural Resource Governance Institute (NRGI, formerly Revenue Watch), and some of it by academics. For example, Paul Collier's 'Natural Resource Charter' initiative is a 'set of principles to guide governments and society's use of natural resources so these economic opportunities result in maximum and sustained returns for a country's citizens'.[4] These principles are: the development of natural resources to maximise the benefit for the population; government accountability; robust contracts; competitive tenders for contracts; environmental and social clauses in contracts; the development of transparent and commercially viable national oil companies; resource revenues invested sustainably; domestic spending 'smoothed out' to take into account price volatility (an issue that became of enormous importance in early 2015 as the world oil price dipped below US$50 a barrel for the first time since 2009); efficient public spending; the promotion of private sector investment; the enforcement of international rules by home governments of oil companies; and, finally, the IOCs themselves should follow best practice in contracting, operations and payments. Other organisations have developed similar decision-making chains, including PWYP's 'Chain for Change' and the NRGI's 'Value Chain'.

None of the five countries profiled in this book – Chad, Niger, Ghana, Uganda and Kenya – has adopted any of these approaches wholesale. In fact, what is most interesting is how each of these countries has essentially developed its own 'home-grown' approach to managing oil, choosing whichever aspects of the solutions for breaking the resource curse best suit them. Nevertheless, a number of key themes have emerged, and I will use some or all of them as a way to organise my approach to each country. These are: exploration and production rights and contract transparency; revenue management and sharing; local content; environmental and social protection; and transparency and accountability.

The case of Chad

This book was inspired by my experience of living and working in Chad as a BBC correspondent from 2008 to 2010. This was a pivotal moment in the country's history as it struggled to get back on its feet after several devastating rebellions spawned by the crisis in neighbouring Darfur. The attempt to rebuild the country coincided with the arrival of billions of dollars of oil revenue into the state budgets from the Komé oilfields developed in the south of the country by a consortium led by Esso.

The history of Chad's oil and of the country's attempts to beat the curse is unique. In the early 2000s, the development of the Komé fields was the subject of a controversial World Bank project to try to ensure that the revenues from natural resource

11

extraction would be used for development. The CCDP aimed to create a system of trackable and transparent payments from the oil companies involved, and to commit the government to legally enshrined poverty reduction spending priorities. Furthermore, it aimed to establish a system of civil society monitoring of government spending, and clear high environmental standards. In short, it was the first real attempt to draw up a practical 'cradle-to-grave' approach to managing natural resource extraction, with the explicit aim of avoiding the devastation of the resource curse seen in places such as Nigeria and Angola. I was struck by how little information generally is available on the whole of Chad's oil project from 2000 to the present day, and so my intention is to show that many of the current debates on transparency, accountability and breaking the resource curse that are being discussed today were actually tested 'in the laboratory' of Chad, as Columbia Law School academic Peter Rosenblum puts it.[5]

In Chapter 1, this book will tell the full story of how the World Bank project was conceived, shedding light on the thinking behind its stringent restrictions on spending that ultimately proved too much for Chad's President Idriss Déby Itno. He ripped up the original agreements and used oil money to buy weapons, which were used to defeat the rebels. After detailing this embarrassing defeat for the World Bank, Chapter 2 will examine what elements of that 'cradle-to-grave' approach survive today and how effective they are. I will then look at how useful Chad's experience has been for campaign groups and activists in other parts of Africa.

Chapter 3 will introduce the role of China, examining how the China National Petroleum Company (CNPC) moved into production in Chad as the World Bank pulled out. China has offered a system of investment that is very different to the 'best practice', transparent approach developed in response to the resource curse; the Chinese system involves opaque contracts, promises to build infrastructure and a 'no strings' approach to issues of human rights. But the process of turning east has not been easy and Chad has been disappointed with the results. Communities have been locked out of consultations over their future as large-scale projects open up on their doorsteps; there have been shocking cases of environmental damage; and an oil refinery has not met local expectations. Chad has dealt with these confrontations in a typically pugnacious manner. In Chapter 4 I will also examine the little-known case of Niger, which became a small-scale producer in 2011 in partnership with the CNPC. While Nigerien civil society has come on in leaps and bounds in recent years to meet the challenges posed by the natural resource curse, the country's government has so far been found wanting in its responsibility to stand up to the CNPC and ensure the best deal for all.

Chapter 5 will analyse the case of Ghana, which has gained a reputation for managing its oil production fairly well. The country has passed a number of important laws that deal with all aspects of the resource curse, from guaranteeing transparency of revenue flows and spending to increasing the participation of Ghanaians in the expanding sector. It also has a vibrant civil society community and a number of well-trained journalists who have worked hard to track the development of the oil project on behalf of the population. However, there are still some areas of concern when it comes to ensuring that the law is followed to the letter, and in developing and compensating the producing region.

Chapter 6 looks at East Africa. Although it is early days and not a drop of oil has been produced in either Uganda or Kenya, both countries are deeply involved in trying to design a policy and legislative framework that will help guarantee the transparent flow of revenues from oil companies and that this money is used for national development. Much of what I have written is based on a number of excellent civil society reports that aim to put East Africa's oil industry into the theoretical framework of combating the resource curse. Both countries are seeking to protect their environments, as well as designing policies whereby local people can benefit from increased jobs and opportunities. However, the development of the sector is currently being held back by the lack of action on building an export pipeline and by Uganda's somewhat controversial insistence on the construction of a refinery to produce fuel for local consumption.

13

This is not an academic book. My methodology is based on first-hand journalistic investigation and interviews, much of which was carried out during my time in Chad and in subsequent visits over the last six years. I also completed four research trips to Uganda, Kenya, Ghana and Niger during 2013–14 when I was able to meet and interview a wide range of civil society activists and representatives from communities, government and oil companies and to travel to some of the oil-producing areas to see for myself what is happening. I have cherry-picked what I found to be the most interesting aspects of each country with the aim of providing a lively, first-hand account of what is actually occurring on the ground. For example, I have focused on citizen power and journalism in Ghana and Niger, women in East Africa (a subject that is not often discussed in the context of oil), legal frameworks in Ghana, the development of Chinese investment and its impact on the environment in Chad, local content in Ghana and Kenya, and the arguments for and against refineries in Uganda.

I encountered a number of difficulties during the research of this book. I was unable to convince the CNPC to allow me to visit their oil project in eastern Niger, nor was I able to travel to the oil-producing areas in Uganda after transparency campaigners advised me against it. I had my laptop, phone and money stolen in Kampala, and on a limited budget it was a struggle to meet all the important characters in every country. In Kenya, the oil industry is so new that there is little to see in the Turkana region and many of the public debates around breaking the resource curse have barely begun. Where I have been unable to provide first-hand reporting, I have provided a summary and analysis of the contemporary discussion among campaign groups and academics.

Africa's new oil producers are coming of age in a world where the global oil price has been exceptionally high for several years, and although it fell dramatically in early 2015, it is likely to increase again. These countries are designing their natural resource extraction programmes with a clear and vivid understanding of how oil has failed other countries. I will not deal in any further detail with Nigeria and Angola – the classic cases of resource-cursed nations – as much excellent material has already been written on this subject. Instead, I will offer a comparative study of five newer African oil-producing countries – Chad, Niger, Ghana, Uganda and Kenya – countries with quite different economies and levels of development. I will ask how the variety of suggested approaches to tackling the resource curse works in different political economies. As Michael L. Ross has argued in his recent book, 'oil does not affect all countries equally' (Ross 2012: 229); perhaps better outcomes can be seen in countries where political institutions and governance are stronger and better developed, where oil does not make up an overwhelming proportion of GDP, or where there are no regional separatist claims or lingering conflicts. I will argue that the fundamental issues in all of the countries profiled are those of governance and the ability of citizens and civil society (by which I mean campaign groups, NGOs and monitoring groups working on natural resources) to influence leaders towards transparent and beneficial ways of using natural resource revenues. I aim to shed light on the interesting and important work being done by a number of campaign groups, such as PWYP and the Extractive Industries Transparency Initiative (EITI), and I will discuss where the global accountability and advocacy debate is today. With such genuine and lively discussions in all the countries profiled, rather than drawing a negative conclusion that Africa's new oil producers are doomed to repeat the failures of other resource-rich predecessors, I will argue that there is some cause for optimism.

of what the World Bank thought it was supposed to do. There was a great deal of pressure from some European countries to establish an entirely new monitoring body – the International Advisory Group (IAG) – to report back on the project's impact and to ensure that Chad's interests and the public voice were being taken into consideration. Observers close to the deal in the early 2000s believe that the project passed the final vote only because of the detailed conditions attached to the loan. 'Some argued that it was naïve as the only guarantee we had that development objectives would be met was that we knew not one penny would have been spent on development without our involvement,' says Robert Calderisi, former World Bank Country Director for Central Africa from 2000 to 2002 and author of *The Trouble with Africa*.[3] 'There was a lot of stress, anxiety and bad blood.'

Nevertheless, the proposed provisions of the CCDP were an important step forward in challenging the notion that the resource curse was inevitable. Rather than simply arguing that poor and underdeveloped countries should not develop their natural resources, the World Bank was involved in a series of discussions that suggested that oil money could be turned from a curse to a blessing. The question was: could good governance really be achieved or expected without first investing in education and expanding civil society capacity? And could those objectives be achieved without rapid economic development, which could easily be delivered through natural resource exploitation?

Revenue management

The cornerstone of the CCDP, designed to reassure the project's detractors, was the passing of a genuinely innovative new law by the Chadian parliament. This law was intended to govern the management and spending of revenues by the government, and to ensure transparency of payments between the IOCs and the state. The revenue management law – or Law 001, as it became known – was passed unanimously by the National Assembly in 1998 after only three hours of debate (Gary and Reisch 2004: 30).

The law required that all direct revenues (i.e. royalties and

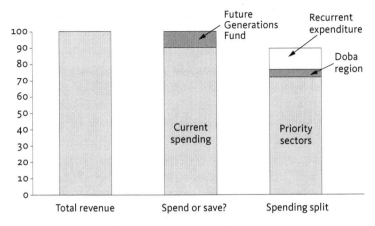

1.1 The division of direct oil revenues according to Law 001 (%)

share dividends) from the sale of oil on the international market for the life of the project should be deposited into an offshore escrow account in London; an escrow account is one where an independent and trusted third party receives and disburses money or documents for the transacting parties. In addition, 10 per cent of the revenues deposited were to be put into an untouchable 'Future Generations Fund'. Of the remaining 90 per cent, 80 per cent were to be invested in five priority sectors; these were defined as education, health and social services, rural development, infrastructure, and environmental and water resources. A further 5 per cent was to go to the Doba producing region, and 15 per cent was allowed for recurrent government expenditure (Figure 1.1).

Finally, the law created the Collège de Contrôle et de Surveillance des Ressources Pétrolières (CCSRP, or the Petroleum Revenue Oversight and Control Committee), a joint government–civil society organisation that was charged with monitoring and authorising the government's spending plans for the money in the escrow account (ibid.: 42).

Environment

The project also established ground-breaking rules on environmental and social standards, with the original loan agreement specifying a collection of texts to cover the norms and standards required; these ran to some nineteen volumes (van Vliet and Magrin 2012: 93). The agreement stated that environmental impact assessments (EIAs) had to be carried out before the project started and a rigorous environmental management plan (EMP) had to be adopted; this was to stipulate measures to avoid adverse impacts on the environment, such as air quality targets and rules on waste management and what to do in the case of a spill or an accident. The project also established a network of environmental monitoring systems, including a Chadian government/civil society body and a group of international experts, the External Compliance Monitoring Group (ECMG). The ECMG continues to visit Esso's production site to verify compliance with the EMP even now that the World Bank is no longer involved and the remaining IFC loans have been repaid. This set of procedures, taken together with the revenue management aspects of the project, has been described as theoretically 'exemplary' (ibid.: 92). The CCDP also ensured that Chad updated its own environmental laws, which included the passing of law 14 in 1998 to establish the principles of 'the polluter pays' – something that has become incredibly important as the relationship with the Chinese oil company CNPC has developed since 2008 – and the 'precautionary method', and of protecting the environment (ibid.: 90).

The political context

Despite these legal frameworks – which in summary established a transparent escrow account for revenue collection, priority sectors for government spending, high environmental standards and a robust system of environmental and spending monitoring – the project still attracted much external criticism. International groups such as Friends of the Earth and Greenpeace argued that Chad's political system and economy were not robust or mature enough to handle such a large influx of oil revenue, particularly as the pressure to get the oil to market quickly seemed to be pushing the scheme forward too quickly. In fact, this conclusion was supported by a report from the Independent Evaluation Group

(IEG), which the World Bank itself commissioned to look into the Chad project in 2008.

In 2000, President Idriss Déby Itno was viewed as a bad choice of African leader to do business with, and many feared that Chad would simply not be able to control the money coming in and going out. Chad was one of the poorest countries in the world, wracked with corruption and with weak and underdeveloped institutions. The country had emerged from decades of civil war only in the mid-1990s and democracy was struggling to take hold. A skilled general and fighter pilot and a Zaghawa from Chad's harsh eastern deserts, Déby had come to power in a coup launched just ten years earlier against his repressive predecessor Hissène Habré. Although he had allowed elections to take place in 1996, the opposition had largely been co-opted with an ineffectual National Assembly, and the country was known for a poor human rights record and a lack of a free press from the dark days of Habré in the 1980s. Chad's political elite was (and still is) tiny, with President Déby surrounding himself with a close cabal and a number of his tribal Zaghawa clansmen; the Zaghawa is a non-Arab, predominantly Muslim group that lives on the border between Chad and Sudan and makes up just 2 per cent to 3 per cent of the population. Even today, the Zaghawa elicit a feeling of frustration in some in N'Djaména who feel that they enjoy a sense of entitlement or dominance in the city. Legal systems are poorly developed in the country and corruption is rife. The rebellions and other internal political crises throughout the years – particularly from members of his own family – have shaken Déby's power base to the core and have shown that it is too simplistic to view him as a case of '*l'État c'est moi*'. For that part of Africa, however, Déby is still a leader with an unusual amount of personal control: 'Déby has a tight grip on power and strives to mute dissenting voices,' says the Economist Intelligence Unit.[4] The challenges against his rule are numerous, with fairly frequent allegations of coup plots being foiled. A number of confident editorials over the years have prematurely predicted his demise, and many believe he suffers from constant bouts of ill-health and even alcoholism. But even after the terrible rebel crises of the mid-2000s, which many thought he would never survive, in 2014 he entered his twenty-third year in power. He is often referred to, even with a touch of respect by some Chadians, as '*Le Grand Survivant*' (The Great Survivor).

The CCDP was devised at a time when global awareness of climate change was increasing and campaign groups were beginning to question the inequities of international trade. The resource curse theory was beginning to gain traction as an explanation for the chaos caused by oil in countries such as Nigeria and Angola. Any projects involving big IOCs wishing to extract natural resources in poor African states would surely run into some vocal opposition. In the early 2000s, oil companies were becoming the favoured targets of environmental protest movements for their apparent refusal to engage on the issue of the role that fossil fuels were playing in climate change. In his book *Private Empire*, journalist Steve Coll reveals fascinating details of the campaigns that were launched by groups such as Greenpeace against Exxon Mobil – the main IOC protagonist in Chad – and the lengths to which the company went to fight back:

> Under [ex-chairman] Lee Raymond, ExxonMobil had persistently funded a public policy campaign in Washington and elsewhere that was transparently designed to raise public scepticism about the science that identified fossil fuels as a cause of global warming (Coll 2013: 184).

As the negotiations over the CCDP heated up, a number of high-profile protest stunts were carried out by campaign groups, such as people dressing up as gorillas to hand out leaflets and releasing a giant helium balloon in the central atrium of the World Bank's headquarters in Washington, to draw attention to the dangers of the proposed Chad project. Robert Calderisi acknowledged that the 'cast of characters' originally involved in the Chad project was 'simply combustible': Shell, which had been responsible for much of the environmental destruction in the Niger Delta; Elf, which had been associated with a number of corruption scandals across French-speaking Africa; ExxonMobil, which had been responsible for the Valdez spill in 1989; and not least Chad's own government and the country's shaky politics (Calderisi 2006: 178).

A law with flaws

Chad's Law 001 was intricately constructed with a view to tackling many of the issues identified by the development of the resource curse theory. However, even in contemporary analyses its inadequacies were identified by civil society and rigorously laid out in a number of reports, including the 2004 report by the NGO Catholic Relief Services entitled *Miracle or Mirage* (Gary and Reisch 2004).

Firstly, the new law that established the escrow account covered only the direct revenues from the oil sales. Direct revenues included royalties of 12.5 per cent on the sale of oil exports – a concessionary deal that Esso had negotiated in 1988 well before there was a realistic proposition of exploiting the oil, complete with a 'stabilisation clause' that prevented the terms of the revenue share ever being altered, even if the global oil price changed significantly (Coll 2013: 159) – as well as dividends on the Chadian government's shares in the two companies set up to run the pipeline: TOTCO and COTCO (the Tchad and Cameroon Oil Transportation Companies). The law would not cover the hefty tax payments or other indirect revenues that would come further down the line once Esso's operations became profitable. Secondly, the law applied only to the initial three wells brought into production by Esso. Even in 2003, with the sector in its infancy, it was clear that there was huge potential for expansion, with several other companies including Taiwan's OPIC and Canada's EnCana already present. Today, the transparency agreement does not cover the payments made by Esso on its four newer well sites, and nor does it cover all the signature bonuses and general taxes paid by IOCs that arrived after the World Bank pulled out, such as Griffiths/Caracal and the China National Petroleum Company in Chad (CNPCIC). Based on figures taken from the 2007–11 Chad

EITI reports, some 75 per cent of everything Chad earns today is missed by the law and passes instead into the annual budget, where it is much more difficult to scrutinise.[5]

Furthermore, Law 001 was vague about the exact definition of a 'priority sector': for example, it did not stipulate whether education spending should be targeted at infrastructure development such as building schools, or invested in new teachers or better training. The temptation for governments to splash cash windfalls on quick-fix building projects that might not make economic sense was already well known in the late 1990s. A final flaw was that the Collège and the committee set up to monitor the spending of the regional funds in Doba (Comité de 5% or 5% Committee) were to be nominated bodies and would include at least three representatives of government. Although provisions were made to eventually create an entirely elected body, that has never happened, and the Collège and the 5% Committee continue to be influenced by political pressures.

The situation was not helped by the fact that the construction of the pipeline was completed a full year ahead of schedule, leaving limited time for institutional capacity building. *Miracle or Mirage* describes how concerns over Chad's weak banking system led to delays of almost eight months between the first revenues being deposited in the London escrow account and any money actually arriving in Chad. The report also details how the ExxonMobil-led Consortium and the government were still debating the modalities of measuring production and sales and calculating revenues a full year after the first oil was sold on the world market (Gary and Reisch 2004: 48). Even today, many of these institutional capacity issues have not been fully resolved. Speaking in 2013, the EITI's national coordinator in Chad lamented the difficulties of tracking payments into the Chadian Treasury, saying that the government still did not have a professionally trained oil economist. He explained that for several years at the beginning of the project the authorities did not monitor the precise breakdown of what each member of the Consortium was paying into the Citibank account, and that he had even had to pay 900 Euros to get bank

24

statements from 2007–10 reissued because no one in the Chadian administration had copies.

It would be wrong to suggest that the World Bank and Esso were unaware of the risks of getting involved in such a complicated pilot project, or that they chose to overlook them. 'The risks were known at the time; this was certainly not something the Bank jumped into,' says Alan Gelb, former Chief Economist for Africa at the World Bank, when I interviewed him about the CCDP. It seems that they expected that the robust structures of the CCDP would be able to withstand the inevitable pressures that would arise and that Chad would gradually change and eventually become an acceptable member of the world oil-producing community. The World Bank would work towards institutional capacity building in the hope that, when the serious money began to arrive, the country would be ready to handle it. Géraud Magrin argues that for 'the World Bank, the project offered the opportunity to improve its image following the backlash it had faced over the disappointing results of the structural adjustment programme' (van Vliet and Magrin 2012: 87). The World Bank evidently believed that the concerns of national and international civil society had been adequately addressed through the CCDP safeguards, and the project was approved in June 2000. In October 2003, amid much pomp and circumstance, the Komé oilfields near the southern Chadian town of Doba were opened by a jubilant President Déby. 'It was a very intimate process,' says Robert Calderisi. 'We were putting our faith in them and they were making sacrifices of pride and sovereignty in order to make sure the project succeeded.'[6]

The military threat

So far so good, but what would happen if those agreements were really tested? When, from 2005 onwards, the harsh and ugly realities of Chadian realpolitik began to impinge upon the carefully constructed details of the agreement, it rapidly became evident that the World Bank's optimism had been somewhat premature.

The issue was the rebels. The first hint that things were deteriorating came in the months following Déby's controversial decision in 2005 to change the national constitution to allow him to stand again for the presidency. Senior figures in his inner circle defected, including his Zaghawa kinsmen and, most significantly, the brothers Tom and Timan Erdimi, who were also President Déby's nephews. While outsiders might have struggled to see the importance of a couple of disgruntled generals heading off into the eastern deserts, Déby was acutely aware of the complexity of loyalties in the border regions.

The defections dovetailed with the crisis that had begun to emerge in Darfur, western Sudan in 2003. Rebel groups including the Justice and Equality Movement (JEM) had been fighting back against scorched-earth policies launched by Sudanese President Omar al-Bashir and his proxy fighters the Janjaweed. Over 200,000 Sudanese refugees had arrived in Chad's parched east from 2004 onwards and the country struggled to care for them. Many JEM leaders (such as Khalil Ibrahim) and members of the other rebel groups such as the Sudan People's Liberation Army (including Minni Minawi) were also from the same Zaghawa clan as President Déby, although of a different sub-branch. Déby, a Bideyat Zaghawa who hails from Amjérass, close to the Sudanese border, became caught in a terrible balancing act, trying to keep his kinsmen happy while at the same time fearful of destroying the good relations he had traditionally enjoyed with al-Bashir.

As the tension heightened between Sudan and Chad, evidence mounted that Déby was giving financial and material support to Sudanese rebel groups such as JEM.[7] Members of the leadership, including Khalil Ibrahim, were often seen staying at one of N'Djaména's plushest hotels. During the later months of 2005, Déby lost control of the balancing act. Unhappy with Chad's apparent support for JEM's operational presence in eastern Chad (including inside a UN-managed refugee camp in Bahai), Sudan pulled its ambassador out and proceeded to launch a proxy war by sponsoring the various new groupings of Chadian rebels. The most prominent members of these groups included the Erdimi brothers and two other former soldiers: Mahamat Nour and Mahamat Nouri.

On 12 December 2005, the SCUD rebel group (the Platform for Change, Unity and Democracy), led by Tom and Timan Erdimi, used the occasion of Déby's fifteenth anniversary in power to issue a statement laying out their programme.[8] Former BBC Chad correspondent Stephanie Hancock recalls leaving her home that morning to attend a routine meeting, only to find a strange atmosphere on the streets:

> The minute I drove out on to the streets in N'Djaména that morning, it was immediately clear something was wrong. I didn't know what at first, but you could read it on people's faces. Normally soldiers guarding ministries and other key sites like the large military barracks would be half asleep; bored, disinterested, dishevelled. But that morning everyone was on alert. There were more soldiers than usual on guard, and everyone seemed edgy. Something big had obviously happened.

As the danger posed by the rebels became increasingly apparent, the rigidity of the spending priorities enshrined in Law 001 soon came to be viewed by many in the Chadian government as external interference in a sovereign state's business. In late 2005, the Chadian army was simply not up to the job of securing such a huge, badly governed space. Although the Ministry of Defence had an estimated 20,000 'soldiers' on its books, only a small proportion of these were loyal, properly trained and ready to risk their necks to protect the President. Déby's bottom line has always been his personal survival – development projects such as schools and hospitals could wait until national security was guaranteed. Now that President Omar al-Bashir had decided to punish him for allowing the JEM to operate inside Chadian territory, Déby appeared to feel that he had no choice. Spending restrictions looked very unfair as the country stared into the abyss. As Steve Coll argues: 'The absurdity, from his perspective, was that at the very moment this threat loomed, he was becoming richer than many of his neighbouring dictators' (Coll 2013: 357).

In late 2005, the lightning bolt came for the World Bank. Chad announced that parliament was rewriting Law 001 to give the government more autonomy over its spending plans; it proposed to scrap the Future Generations Fund and reduce the figure committed to priority spending to 70 per cent of the total (from 80 per cent of the 90 per cent as originally agreed), meaning that 30 per cent of the direct revenues would now pass into the general budget of the state and bypass scrutiny by civil society and international monitoring. Crucially, the proposed new law would amend the definition of development priority spending to include 'domestic security', which most took to mean weapons (ibid.: 360).

The proposed changes were a red line for the leadership of the World Bank. At the helm of the institution was now Paul Wolfowitz, fresh from his position as US Deputy Defense Secretary when the war in Iraq had been launched. In a late-night phone call to Déby in early January 2006, Wolfowitz warned him in no uncertain terms to respect the contractual agreements he had made to spend the oil money on health and education. This cut no ice with Déby, who seemed unaccustomed to being spoken to in this way. 'They talked through French translators for two hours that night. Neither of them budged,' says Coll (ibid.: 360). The next morning Wolfowitz announced that the World Bank would withhold new loans to Chad and a freeze on the Citibank account could follow. Déby refused to back down.

From Déby's point of view, the overturning of the law came not a second too soon, as three months later the rebels (now reincarnated as the FUC or United Front for Change) marched into N'Djaména city centre after a sudden advance from the east. They came within a few hundred metres of the presidential palace. Stephanie Hancock, who found herself reporting live for the BBC from the streets of the capital on the morning of 13 April 2006, wrote:

> By dawn, the first reports of gunfire started trickling in. Soon after, the sound of heavy arms fire burst into life. Nothing can prepare you for how loud the sounds of war are. Windows rattled. The ground shook ... I steeled myself and drove through deserted streets towards the scene of the final battle. The only

other traffic was army pick-ups racing past me in the opposite direction, piled high with the dead and wounded. The following hours were a blur of frantic reporting. But I remember the sorry group of rebels – prisoners now – cowering in a corner. A pile of rebel bodies, dumped unceremoniously on the parliament steps. One fighter, his intestines cradled in his hands, alive but clearly dying. And the crunch of broken glass, scraps of clothing and spent bullet casings underfoot.

Déby survived the attack by the skin of his teeth; by all accounts, he was saved by internal squabbles within the rebellion and a dedicated presidential guard. But he appeared to vow never again to let himself be put in such a vulnerable position. He was going to use the oil money to defend himself. Two days after the rebel attack, on 15 April 2006, Chad's oil minister, Mahamat Nasser Hassan, laid down an ultimatum; he told Reuters that either the Consortium would pay US$100 million up front directly to the government, which the state would use to start paying back the World Bank, or oil production would be shut down. It was a remarkable show of defiance to the seasoned oilmen and the cerebral economists in Washington.

To many people's astonishment, Chad went on to hold a presidential election three weeks later; Déby won with a strong majority, although the main opposition party boycotted the election and there were claims of an abysmal turnout. Few of Chad's opposition leaders have been able to excel – most of the key figures of the last ten years, such as Ngarlejy Yorongar and Saleh Kebzabo, have cooperated with Déby and none of them has been able to mount a serious challenge to his rule. With no credible alternative and with resources and the political sphere dominated by Déby's party (the MPS or Patriotic Salvation Movement), Chadians appeared to choose who they believed could offer some kind of stability.

In the days after the vote, frenetic negotiations began to try to keep the oilfields open. Déby reportedly summoned the US ambassador to Chad to explain his predicament, and pressed home the fact that Chad had been supportive on counterterrorism initiatives. However, he was unequivocal about Esso's need to pay up; according to Steve Coll, he stated: 'This is not a topic for discussion. It's our money' (ibid.: 365). At that precise moment, and somewhat ironically, thanks to the higher than expected world oil price, Esso was on the verge of profitability, which would automatically open a flow of corporation tax revenue into the Chadian treasury. It seemed that Esso believed that if it could convince Déby to keep the fields open, it would soon be paying him a figure not far off the US$300 million he would need to repay the World Bank and terminate the agreement. Esso's Chad manager, Ron Royal, had a series of meetings with Chadian and World Bank figures between April and August 2006. By July 2006 the die was cast and Chad announced that it would end the agreement with the World Bank. The Consortium, however, would stay and continue production.

The Chadian authorities immediately proceeded to shake off the shackles of the World Bank project, redefining the management of the oil industry. In early August 2006, Chad broke off diplomatic relations with Taiwan and began holding secret meetings with the CNPC, which had long expressed an interest in the Ronier oilfields in the Bongor Basin. In late August the government announced that it wanted to set up its own company, the Société des Hydrocarbures du Tchad (SHT); this would effectively be a national oil company (NOC) that would aim to sell and market its own crude and become the 'fourth member' of the Consortium. Days later Déby threatened to expel the junior partners in the Consortium – Chevron and Petronas – over their alleged failure to pay taxes. He also sacked three ministers.[9] From now on, no one would tell Chad what to do with its oil money.

The end of the model project

In September 2008, the World Bank formally announced the end of joint cooperation with Chad after the outstanding loan balance was paid off. The World Bank continued to operate a small office to monitor activities not associated with the oil project, although this too was closed briefly due to security concerns.

The World Bank's dream of creating a comprehensive system of revenue management and transparency was in tatters. 'Chadians can only now cry because the oil money has not contributed to improving their living conditions but rather to fuel armed conflict,' civil society activist Délphine Djiraibe told IRIN news.[10] No one knew what would become of Law 001 and whether Chad would simply rip up what was left of the transparency structures and shut down the escrow account and the Collège monitoring system in the subsequent years. Ian Gary, now working for Oxfam America, feared the worst: 'This unfortunate but predictable outcome shows that the risks are being borne by the people of Chad while the rewards are reaped by the oil companies and government.'[11] The system of environmental safeguards was also seriously in jeopardy, and 'was the first to bear the brunt of the crisis', according to van Vliet and Magrin (2012: 96). Several civil society environmental monitoring bodies were disbanded or had funding cut after the World Bank pulled out, leaving responsibility for environmental regulation adrift between the Ministries of Petroleum and Environment and the newly created SHT.

Many of those who had worked for the World Bank on the project seemed to reluctantly accept the need to pull out in order to protect the Bank's integrity, which could have been seriously compromised through association with a government that was buying arms with development money. Robert Calderisi, who by 2002 had retired from the World Bank, deeply regretted the wasted effort. There was certainly discomfort among staff about the stand-off that had developed between Wolfowitz and Déby, which had razed all potential bridges to compromise to the ground: 'Chadian pride and World Bank doctrine collided at full speed,' says Calderisi of the two men's relationship.[12] One year after Chad told the Bank to leave, Wolfowitz resigned following allegations that he had given a pay rise to his girlfriend, a World Bank employee. Many Chadians could not help commenting. 'I've been waiting for this moment,' a jubilant Rim Nassingar, the country director of the PWYP coalition, told journalists. 'If you're fighting corruption you can't have the head of the institution doing this sort of thing.'

It must be pointed out that, from the Chadian government's point of view, the rupture with the World Bank was far from an ideal solution. Many of the administrators involved in the early days of the project seem to have genuinely wanted the oil money to work for the benefit of the greater population and had bent over backwards to meet the World Bank's conditions. However, by early 2006, the benefits of being seen to cooperate on the world stage were outweighed by the need to restore security. Having lived through war, coups and rebellions for years, many senior figures in the Chadian government understood the dangers only too well and had regretfully given their approval to the increase in military spending. If good relations with the international community had to be sacrificed in the name of the future stability of the country, then it seemed that they felt that this was a reasonable price to pay.

The end of the rebels

In fact, just six months after the World Bank had accepted repayment of the loan and closed the project, the devastating rebel defeat at Am Dam in May 2009 (the aftermath of which we witnessed in the Introduction to this book) signalled the sudden end to the seemingly unstoppable cycle of attack and counter-attack in the proxy war with Sudan.

There were a number of complex reasons why Am Dam proved to be the end for the Chadian rebels, but one of the most important was the fact that by 2009 there had been a dramatic and visible improvement in the equipment capability of the ANT. This was a direct consequence of the increased military spending that became possible once the CCDP with the World Bank had been scrapped and the Future Generations Funds and priority sectors had been milked for cash. In fact, Déby's rearmament with oil money had begun right at the beginning of the CCDP, when at least US$4.5 million of a US$25 million signature bonus paid by Chevron in 2001 was spent on weapons. By 2009, at the height of the rebel threat, Chadian civil society monitoring group GRAMP-TC (Groupe de Recherches Alternatives et de Monitoring du Projet

Pétrole Tchad-Cameroun) estimated that the government had spent at least US$600 million of oil money on arms. But the military spending did not stop there. Using International Monetary Fund (IMF) estimations, by 2014 that figure had reached well over US$4 billion – out of a total of US$10 billion earned in government revenue from oil. The IMF figures show that much of this spending was approved through a process known as *dépense avant ordonnancement* (DAO) or extraordinary budgetary procedure: that is, money that did not pass through the country's normal budget and certainly was well removed from the scrutiny of the Collège. Around US$900 million was spent in this way on the military in 2009 (14 per cent of the total spending budget), US$1.03 billion in 2010 (12 per cent) and US$1.06 billion in 2011 (11 per cent).[13]

The results were dramatic. By 2009 at Am Dam, the ANT was fighting with attack helicopters and armoured personnel carriers, backed up with aerial surveillance from reconditioned Sukhoi jets, bought from Eastern Europe and flown by Mexican and Algerian mercenaries. Déby had also spent large sums on buying the loyalty of the army and purging it of irregular soldiers. In contrast, the UFR rebels were still using lightly armed converted 4 x 4 vehicles with machine guns mounted on the back for hit-and-run attacks. They had little in the way of surface-to-air missiles or effectively armoured vehicles. In the past, using 4 x 4 'technicals' had been a formidable strategy, allowing a large number of highly mobile vehicles to move quickly through the bush, fanning out and blending into villages to avoid Chad's limited aerial surveillance. But at Am Dam these tactics were useless and the rebels were obliterated. Better aerial surveillance and communications at Am Dam meant that the ANT located the rebel columns as soon as they crossed the Sudanese border. The newly purchased planes and helicopters were then used to herd the rebel vehicles from their spread-out formation into a tight grouping on the open plains at Am Dam where the army was waiting. The rebels had barely begun their assault when the helicopters hit them from above, turning escape routes across the dried-out river beds (wadis) into a burning hell.

Simultaneously, the rebel threat was weakened by an astonishing shift in the bilateral relationship between Chad and Sudan. After five years of apparently intractable proxy war, faced with the very real prospect of South Sudan electing to secede in an upcoming referendum scheduled for 2011, and with international pressure mounting on him after he was indicted by the International Criminal Court (ICC) for war crimes in Darfur, President Omar al-Bashir of Sudan seems to have finally conceded that a total victory could not be won in Darfur. As the Chadian rebels bickered and yet again failed to deliver the sweeping strike against Déby he must have wanted at Am Dam, al-Bashir lost interest and began to scale back his support.

In early 2010, Déby and al-Bashir made the stunning announcement that they had agreed to put their differences behind them. Five years of war were over. Those in the international community who had worked thanklessly for several years to bring peace between the two nations must have been confounded by how easily the two presidents kissed and made up. Déby demonstrated his newfound confidence, immediately announcing the cancellation of the mandate of the UN peacekeeping force MINURCAT, which had been struggling to stabilise eastern Chad since 2008. In its place there would be a new joint Sudanese and Chadian army border patrol force. By the end of that year the UN mission closed and its temporary military camps were dismantled. With the rebels in disarray and many of their leaders in exile (Timan Erdimi fled to Qatar and Mahamat Nouri to Europe), many of the lower-ranking foot soldiers publicly apologised for having taken up arms and were reintegrated into the army. Al-Bashir turned his attentions to the south, home to his own problematic oilfields and dissension. Eastern Chad reverted to its desolate, forgotten nature. But the oil never stopped flowing.

Lessons learned for the World Bank?

There is remarkably little literature covering the end of the CCDP and how it was dealt with by the World Bank, but a very interesting evaluation was published in November 2009 by the IEG, a quasi-independent body set up within the World Bank's structures to provide an objective assessment of the results of the World Bank Group's activities. The report, which was accepted by the Bank's board, concluded that the 'pipeline project was a physical, technical and financial success, with the pipeline completed and the oil flowing ahead of time' (WBG 2009: xi); however, it accepted that 'the macroeconomic, development, poverty reduction, governance and institutional development outcomes were disappointing'. In other words, the World Bank financing had contributed positively towards the rapid establishment of Chad's oil industry infrastructure, but it had not met its poverty reduction objectives – the painstakingly created revenue expenditure management system was broadly a failure: 'It had not improved Chad's abysmal poverty indicators' (Coll 2013: 367). Many of the individual aspects of the project were scored by the IEG as having had 'unsatisfactory' or 'highly unsatisfactory' outcomes against their objectives.

Measuring progress against development indicators is difficult in all parts of the world, and for that reason the World Bank had chosen from the start to measure the project's success against the universal Millennium Development Goals (MDGs). The IEG report was frank and critical of the project's lack of impact on development. Ten years after the project started, Chad had still not met any of the MDGs. In particular, the IEG singled out the fact that various governance indicators actually 'deteriorated'. For example, Chad scored fifth from bottom on the respected Mo Ibrahim African leadership index in 2013, ahead of only Eritrea, Democratic Republic of the Congo (DRC), Somalia and Central African Republic – and the latter two can barely even claim to have a government. In the 2013 UN Human Development Index, which measures a range of educational, income and health indicators, Chad failed to budge from the bottom of the table.

Nevertheless, despite all these failings, the report suggests that: 'It should not be concluded from this experience that the [World Bank Group] should not intervene in supporting extractive industries.' It went on to propose that future collaborations could rest on 'combining an insistence on high standards of environmental and social protection with flexible conditionality'. This is a key conclusion, establishing the view that the rules on spending priorities in the Chad project were just too rigid and that future approaches should include a degree of flexibility.

Interestingly, the IEG report defends the World Bank's decision to press ahead, suggesting that with the rising oil price seen in the early 2000s the project to extract Chad's oil would most likely have gone ahead anyway without robust environmental controls and without much of a serious attempt to prioritise spending to certain sectors. As Robert Calderisi claimed, the only guarantee regarding poverty reduction was that not a single penny would have been spent on tackling poverty had the Bank not been involved. It is possible that this conclusion can be supported in light of the speed with which China's CNPC arrived on the scene after the World Bank had pulled out and began a new oil-producing project with next to no explicit poverty reduction objectives (see Chapter 3) – but, of course, this argument can never be tested definitively.

The IEG report also appears to be openly critical of the way in which the project came to an end following that heated late-night phone call between Déby and Wolfowitz.

> Although in high-profile cases strategic guidance and major decisions must come from the top leadership of the [World Bank Group], it is not clear in this case that the top-down direct intervention by the Bank President's Office in 2006 was helpful to formulate a new agreement with a better chance of enforcement (WBG 2009: xiii).

Finally, the IEG report also raises the tantalising question of whether it was just the exactions of the rebel threat that forced the Chadian government to renege on the deal, or whether government buy-in had been unconvincing from the start. Indeed, looking back on ten years of oil production, it is tempting to see a narrative arc emerging – from the first exports of oil, through the changing of the constitution, to the rebel threat and the need to increase military spending just as the oil money began to flow, to the eventual breaking of the deal. One conclusion from that reading of history might be that Chad deliberately agreed to the conditions in bad faith, knowing it would never be able to fulfil them, simply in order to get access to the oil money as quickly as possible in order to strengthen Déby's position. However, that interpretation would miss the significance of quite how unpredictable the rebel threat was in late 2005, and the difficulties all poor and conflict-ridden nations have in any kind of future planning and capacity building.

More helpful perhaps is an interpretation that concludes that the lack of flexibility with which the World Bank insisted on its conditions, even as the worst-case scenario was unfolding rapidly, was diametrically opposed to President Déby's formidable leadership style and his appreciation of how to keep his country from the brink of disaster. Alan Gelb comments: 'In my view, the agreement was too tight in prescribing the use of funds, with only a small part available for discretionary spending by the government.' Robert Calderisi draws a similar conclusion: 'We should have recognised that something which needed so many restrictions and regulations at the beginning was perhaps doomed to failure.'[14]

From the formal end of the World Bank project in 2006, Chadians took full charge of their oil. Discussions over further exploration blocks opened with the CNPC and with other firms such as Canada's Simba Oil, Canada's Griffiths (today renamed Caracal), India's Global Oil and a number of Nigerian companies. With the experience of the World Bank project behind them, the authorities now seemed determined to seize opportunities on their own terms, looking into different contractual arrangements, new relationships and new ways of organising production.

At the same time, the serious money began to roll in. In 2007, once Esso had moved into profitability, the government earned over US$1.17 billion in taxes and royalties on the Doba oilfields' production, a hugely significant sum compared with the US$2.1 billion that had been Chad's GDP pre-oil. Now more than ever, the aspects of the revenue management law that had survived would be put to the test. Despite the fears of civil society, no further serious attempts were made to amend the law in the coming years, meaning that the transparency and accountability systems survived largely intact. The Collège civil society monitoring body would soon be faced with an unprecedented surge in development and construction projects to approve as the money kept flowing in, and the revenues from the Consortium continued to be transferred to and monitored in the London Citibank escrow account.

The question of how to turn this temporary windfall into lasting development is still fundamental to helping Chad on the road to development. However, the results so far in terms of Chad's progress against poverty reduction indicators are far from encouraging. In the next chapter, we look in more detail at how Chad has used its oil revenues and ask how the country could make better use of its windfall.

2 | The aftermath

In the early 2000s, as the CCDP was being conceived, there was simultaneously a growing awareness in civil society and academia about the problems associated with the resource curse, and an increasing effort to find practical solutions. By August 2006, the World Bank project seemed to have ended in failure; however, the project and the debate that surrounded its creation had helped to form an excellent 'living example' of an attempt to put transparency and accountability principles into practice in order to ensure that the resource curse was avoided. Ideas such as a revenue management law, committing the government to spending restrictions, and bank accounts based in other countries where the payments for oil could be traced easily were being tested in Chad's 'laboratory'.

This chapter explores the detail of Chad's oil project, looking at how the key challenges of the resource curse were addressed in practice.

Escaping the resource curse: key themes

Chad's experiences can be broken down into six main areas: the contracting process; transparency with regard to the receipt of money from oil; effective revenue management; civil society engagement; environmental management; and the impact on the local economy. This section explores evolving thinking about defeating the resource curse – this thinking has come from ten years of campaigning by groups such as PWYP, Global Witness and the NRGI, and research by academics such as Karl, Sachs, and Warner and Ross. Finally, the chapter examines how Chad's experiences measure up.

Contract transparency Although I have referred in the Introduction to suggestions made by academics such as Terry Lynn Karl that there is a case to be made for *not* developing natural resources, I assume in this section that most African governments would want to press ahead with development. Therefore, once the decision to exploit is taken, the key next step for a country without significant indigenous technical capabilities is finding an IOC interested in developing the resource. In practice, this means selling the rights to exploitation and negotiating contracts. Contracting is the moment when the crucial terms of the deal are set, enabling the host government to choose the IOC that will give the best value, in terms of both price and, potentially, other aspects of the transaction (technical capabilities, skills transfer, and so on). This highlights the importance of open and transparent tendering or procurement. Many transparency campaigners advocate organising an open auction because secret bids can lead to nepotism and bribery, or companies being offered contracts at an undervalued price. It follows that the contracts should be published and publicly available so that ordinary people and civil society campaign groups can scrutinise whether or not the government negotiators got the best deal. Some transparency campaigners also believe that commitments to publish contracts should be enshrined in law or in national constitutions.

The type of contract used is also important. The most basic and 'old-fashioned' contracts are called concession or licence agreements; essentially, these offer an IOC exclusive rights to explore, develop and sell oil from a specific field. They are sometimes called royalty contracts as the 'government take' (the government's share of the profits) is agreed through a system of royalties (a percentage) paid on every barrel sold, often together with a signature bonus. Also popular are joint ventures; these are often quite open-ended but allow the sharing of responsibility for exploration and production between the IOC and the host government. Finally, the more modern form of contract is known as the production-sharing agreement or PSA; in effect, this allows the state to retain ownership of the natural resources and to negotiate a profit-sharing system whereby the oil company is granted a licence to operate and manage the field.

There are other important contractual questions for governments in addition to simply getting the best price; these revolve around 'ownership' of the hydrocarbons (whether the owner is the country or the IOC), who bears the risk of exploration and extraction, how the profits are shared ('revenue sharing'), what kind of partnering role an NOC might play, whether the companies will pay a signature bonus before exploitation begins, how many local jobs and training opportunities are to be created, and whether local companies can bid for any service and construction-phase contracts (the so-called local content clauses). Governments might also wish to further develop local industry, for example by insisting that an oil refinery for the production of fuel for local consumption is built as part of the deal. Equally important are clauses on the environmental and health aspects of production, including who bears responsibility for clean-ups after an oil spill. Other decisions will need to be made in designing attractive but fair tax regimes, clarifying IOC 'expenses', and agreeing whether profit-sharing arrangements could change if the future oil price rises or falls – this is known as a stabilisation clause.

Clearly, negotiating oil contracts is a complicated business: the multidimensional requirements of such contracts require significant expertise, and IOCs are often better informed than the host government about both industry dynamics and even the country's own resources. Add to this mix the issues of corruption and mismanagement and it is obvious that effective tendering can be highly challenging. How did Chad fare?

Chad's scorecard Effective tendering requires an open political process, but unfortunately Chad has long been plagued by the problem of corruption: the country was ranked near the bottom of Transparency International's 'Perceptions of Corruption' index in 2012. In recent years, a number of senior government officials and civil servants have been investigated for corruption, including the Mayor of N'Djaména, the Education Minister and even the

Minister for Anti-corruption.[1] The US State Department website criticised the government for taking no action following a critical International Crisis Group (ICG) report that highlighted the chronic problem of a lack of open tendering. In early 2013, the Canadian company Griffiths pleaded guilty to bribery charges and agreed to pay a $10 million fine under Canadian law after an investigation revealed secret payments to the wife of the Chadian ambassador to Canada in exchange for oil contracts.[2] Griffiths had bought up a number of old wells near Doba from Esso in 2011, with the intention of reconditioning them.

With this background of corruption, it is perhaps unsurprising that the CCDP did not start off on the best footing. One significant issue was the lack of transparency over the original contracts signed with the Consortium. As was noted in *Escaping the Resource Curse*: 'With the wealth of information on CCDP it can take a considerable search to realise that the key documents, notably the agreements between the government and Esso, are simply not available' (Humphreys et al. 2007: 333). Not once in the discussions between Chad, the World Bank and the Esso Consortium at the beginning of the project does it seem that the prospect of inviting competitive bids for the right to exploit the oil was suggested, nor did they consider publishing those contracts for public scrutiny. How did that happen?

Esso had begun exploration of the Komé fields in the 1970s, and in 1988 the company signed the 'Convention for Exploration, Exploitation and Transportation of Hydrocarbons in Chad' (Coll 2013: 159), guaranteeing them a thirty-five year right to be the lead operator with any future development partner. With Chevron and Petronas finally agreed as partners, the terms of the deal seemed favourable for the oil companies – they had to pay just a 12.5 per cent royalty rate on oil produced and taxes of 50 per cent on the net profits, which could rise to 60 per cent if the world oil price soared. While in the late 1980s the chances of actually cashing in on this investment may have seemed bleak – the country was just emerging from war with Libya and serious civil strife under the reign of Hissène Habré, which was marred by horrendous civil rights abuses – Esso seems to have been playing the long game.

Comparisons with overall government take from oil production in other African oil states suggest that this deal was quite unfavourable to Chad. In Nigeria, government take is close to 90 per cent, and in Gabon and Cameroon it is 75 per cent; in Chad it was estimated at 28 per cent in 2004 (Gary and Reisch 2004: 30), although that figure needs to be treated with caution as it was calculated before full taxes were due. The oil companies insisted that these terms were necessary to compensate for the exceptional risk they would have to take in Chad and the operational difficulties of treating unusually viscous and heavy oil. However, Ian Gary argues that 'Chad's inexperience in negotiating with one of the world's largest companies should not be overlooked as another important factor' (ibid.). Finally, Esso secured a 'stability clause', which placed the terms of the contract beyond any Chadian law that might be passed in the future (Coll 2013: 159).

When the conditions in Chad stabilised during the 1990s and the discussions began with the World Bank to draw up the CCDP, Esso's original agreement was not challenged. However, it would not necessarily be appropriate to lay the blame for this at the World Bank's door: while the terms may not have been the best that Chad could have achieved, there was perhaps a limit to what impact the World Bank's involvement could have had on what was effectively a fait accompli, given that the concession had been awarded long before the World Bank became involved.

Revenue transparency and accountability Once oil production starts and the money begins to roll in, governments have to make decisions about spending priorities; in poorer countries, where almost everything needs to be improved, the clamour for immediate spending on a wide range of areas may be deafening. Governments have to choose whether they want to prioritise health or education; if they want to enact wealth or income redistribution or give a proportion of the revenue to the oil-producing region as a form of compensation for disruption; whether to implement social security policies; or whether infrastructure takes priority over developing human capital. Over the years, academic research has begun to point to the value of transparency in managing natural resource revenues and spending, simply because it would allow civil society and the population as a whole to question what governments were doing with *their* money: 'It has now been recognised that transparency and accountability are the remedies,' argues George Soros confidently in his introduction to the 2007 book *Escaping the Resource Curse* (Humphreys et al. 2007: 1). During the 2000s, these concepts were taken up very seriously by NGOs and campaign groups and enshrined in a number of proposals for 'decision-making chains' – step-by-step plans for setting up natural resource extraction projects.

The two concepts of transparency and accountability have been established in the monitoring of Chad's revenue streams from the Doba oil project, and the innovations of a spending monitoring body (the Collège) and an offshore account receiving all the payments from the Doba Consortium provide us with an excellent opportunity to carefully analyse spending data.

Following the money From 2003 up to the end of 2013, Chad earned about US$10 billion in fiscal oil revenue[3] – this figure includes royalty payments on production, share dividends from the oil transportation companies TOTCO and COTCO, corporation taxes, taxes on profits, exportation taxes, and taxes on company employees and equipment. It covers all the payments made by all the IOCs operating in the country.

In the early days of the project, the only way of understanding what the country had earned was through close monitoring of the royalty payments made by the Esso-led Consortium into the London Citibank account, and by trawling through opaque Chadian government accounts to identify the various tax disbursements made by the companies directly to the Treasury. This was one of the functions envisaged for the Collège, which was given the power to demand figures from the Ministry of Petroleum to assist it in verifying whether sales and production data were correct. Civil society monitoring groups such as GRAMP-TC, PWYP and the Commission Permanente Pétrole N'Djaména (CPPN) also bravely took on the challenge, but all were hampered by Chad's appalling budgetary reporting discipline.

A key organisation that now requires a fuller introduction is the Extractive Industries Transparency Initiative (EITI). Launched in 2003, the initiative drew heavily on the ideas of academics such as Sachs, Karl and Collier about the value of transparency. Crucially, it also recognised the importance of including the views of business. Many IOCs had been influenced by BP's unilateral decision in 2001 to disclose a US$111 million signature bonus it had paid for an offshore licence in Angola; the disclosure had drawn sharp criticism from the Angolan authorities and thinly veiled threats that the company's licence would be terminated (van Oranje and Parham 2009: 33). The thinking behind the establishment of the EITI, which was strongly supported by the UK government, the former Prime Minister Tony Blair and the G8 grouping, was that it would address this question of confidential negotiations and balance it with the need for transparency. It tried to develop 'the notion of equal transparency from the governments and the companies' and the principle of voluntary disclosure.[4] Essentially, this involved countries preparing reports that would detail disaggregated figures for what the companies said they had paid and what the governments said they had received, an idea that clearly had its roots in PWYP. The first country to achieve 'compliant' status was Azerbaijan in 2009, closely followed by Liberia, Nigeria and Ghana. While there has been some criticism of the EITI initiative – mainly that it does not go far enough and that transparency as an objective in itself is not sufficient to deal with the multitudinous problems associated with natural resource extraction – for all the countries profiled in this book, the EITI clearly remains a cherished standard. The N'Djaména team seem to have moved heaven and earth to pull together statistics in a country that came almost bottom in the Index of Open Budgets.[5]

Since Chad applied to join the EITI in 2010, tracing money has become much easier. Although the country made slow progress on meeting the full list of requirements to achieve membership status, after a long delay it managed to produce five annual reports, from 2007 to 2011, that detail all payments declared by the IOCs and everything received by the government. Chad claimed that the rebel attacks of 2005–09 seriously hindered its ability to produce the figures needed for these reports; however, according to the current head of the EITI in N'Djaména Nabia Kana, who resigned his post in the Ministry of Education after he disagreed with a decision to use oil revenues to set up a number of new schools without training staff in advance, equally important was the lack of institutional capacity to identify and make available the kinds of information a full EITI audit required.

> We were very lacking in resources at the beginning. The government didn't know what sort of information we needed and their accounting practices were poor. Chad just accepted the figures they were given by the Consortium for what had gone into the Citibank [escrow] account without tracking it for themselves.

The preparation of the EITI reports has been a Herculean task for the small team in N'Djaména, which operates from a poky office with unreliable power and a noticeable lack of computers in one of the city's fastest growing suburbs. Mr Kana laments what he says is a dearth of dedicated staff in the Chadian Treasury trained in oil revenue economics who would be able to follow the payments made by the Consortium, but he believes that the issue has always been a lack of capacity rather than that the government has been determined to prevent transparency in the oil industry. 'There have been no constraints to our work. It was the head of state himself who said he wanted to join the EITI. We're not getting any pressure from anyone,' he says.

Mr Kana's team is proud of its achievements – the 2007–09 EITI reports have been specially commended by the board for being the first in the world to document dividend payments made to a government from its shares in private transportation companies – in this case TOTCO and COTCO, which handle the movement of crude oil through the Kribi pipeline. And in October 2014 the team finally got what it had dreamed of – Chad was accepted as 'compliant' and a full member of the EITI. Clare Short, the Chair of the EITI Board, said that: 'Reaching compliance with the EITI requirements means that Chad is on the path towards open and accountable governance of its natural resources.'[6]

The 2007–11 EITI reports reveal in fascinating detail the breakdown of Chad's earnings. They include all the payments that fall under the World Bank deal as well as the estimated 75 per cent of further revenues that do not. In those five years, Chad earned a respectable US$7.1 billion in government oil revenues (the IMF figure quoted earlier includes the years 2003–07, before the EITI started reporting), helped in part by enormous increases in the world oil price in 2006, 2008 and 2011. The crash in the oil price after the global financial crisis is reflected in the 2009 accounts, where the annual earnings slump to US$596 million. This situation is likely to be reflected in 2014–15 figures following a similarly dramatic fall in the oil price in late 2014. The EITI report for 2011 shows the addition of a number of taxes and other payments from the beginning of the CNPCIC project, bringing that year's total to US$2.2 billion. A preview copy of the 2012 report suggests that the total for that year is around US$1.9 billion.

The good news is that the five EITI reports show very small levels of discrepancy – in most years just a couple of thousand dollars between what the Esso-led Consortium declared that it had paid and what the Chadian government said it received. This suggests that, overall, the efforts to build transparency into the payments for Chad's oil industry have been broadly successful. By using this system of paying the money into an escrow account and verifying that with company accounts *before* it hits the much less transparent government budget, there seems little latitude for corruption and inaccuracy. Significantly, despite fears after the World Bank pull-out that the Chadian authorities would simply scrap what remained of Law 001, there has been no further attempt to amend it and revenues from the Consortium are still being transferred to and monitored in the London escrow account.

As far as the money *not* covered by the World Bank agreement is concerned, the EITI reports also detail the Consortium's tax payments, as well as revenues from the newer operators including the Taiwanese OPIC and the Chinese CNPCIC. These revenues include corporation tax, tax on profits, land area tax and staff and work permit taxes. Again, the discrepancies seem quite small – in 2008 the Chadian state claimed it had received US$35 million more than all the companies reported paying (about 1.9 per cent of the total), and in 2009 the companies reported US$17 million more in export tax than the Chadian government declared.

Revenue management

As part of the original CCDP, the royalties paid by the Esso-led Consortium were to be deposited into a London Citibank escrow account and earmarked to be spent on 'priority sectors' targeted at poverty reduction. A civil society monitoring system was established to oversee how this money was spent; at its heart was the Collège de Contrôle et de Surveillances des Ressources Pétrolières (the CCSRP or Collège). While this attempt to control government spending was unprecedented, an estimated 75 per cent of Chad's actual income from oil today falls outside this agreement. These monies – mostly taxes on the companies, their profits and their exports – go directly into the government Treasury.

The Collège As noted in the 2004 Catholic Relief Services report, 'in a country lacking effective checks and balances, the joint government–civil society revenue oversight committee [the Collège] created by Law 001 is a unique institution' (Gary and Reisch 2004: 7). It was set up at the beginning of the project with the authority to approve or reject government spending plans for the direct revenues deposited in the Citibank account. The overall objective was to ensure that the oil money was used to tackle poverty and that spending plans were within the law. As we have seen, the body was charged with checking how much went into the special escrow account, overseeing the actual implementation of spending plans (including verifying budgets), evaluating tender bids from prospective contractors for infrastructure and development projects, and approving the release of funds. It was described in the Catholic Relief Services report as 'the most innovative aspect of the revenue management law' (ibid.: 4).

The Collège has nine members: four civil society representatives, one member of parliament (MP), one senator, one magistrate, the national governor of the BEAC (Banque des États de l'Afrique Centrale) and the government treasurer. From the outset, the Collège's effectiveness was circumscribed by its lack of political independence, a situation that has worsened since the World Bank pulled out of Chad in 2006. While most of the members are appointed by their peers rather than selected by the government, there has been a continuing underlying pressure from the government to influence who is chosen. For example, in early 2004 Idriss Ahmed Idriss, the brother-in-law of President Déby, was named head of the central bank, and, by virtue of that position, became a member of the Collège. The Collège suffered from a high turnover of staff at the beginning and was dependent on the government for its budget allocation. In addition, the current Collège vice president, Ahmed Deyeh Christian Matho, points to the fact that all the members are paid only for part-time hours but are being presented with overwhelming amounts of work. 'In 2010–11, for example, the Collège met sixty-nine times to examine 3,097 dossiers of spending plans, 1,443 of which were approved,' he says, adding that often the body has only a few days to examine complex plans.

Any decisions the Collège takes rely on backup from Chad's under-resourced judiciary, and members face the same problem as the EITI team – a lack of timely, audited accounts from both government and the oil companies. They continue to be challenged by the physical difficulties of visiting project sites to ensure that spending plans are being implemented, and they often find 'numerous irregularities, including incomplete projects, waterless wells, and changes to the implementation plans' (ibid.: 58). For example, in the early days of the CCDP, Collège members travelled to Moundou, where money had been approved for the construction of a technical high school, but local authorities reported having no knowledge of the project.

Despite all these difficulties, the Collège has been able to compile some impressive figures relating to what has happened to the earmarked funds. According to the Collège's 2012 annual report, from 2004 to 2011 the Chadian authorities requested a total of US$2.46 billion to be dispersed from the Citibank account to general government accounts; of this, US$1.59 billion has been registered by the Collège as having been spent on 'priority sectors'.[7] This is about 65 per cent – only slightly lower than the government's target of 70 per cent to be spent on priority sectors when the original revenue management Law 001 was amended in 2006. On the face of it, this US$1.59 billion looks like a small figure in the context of the US$10 billion IMF estimates for Chad's total fiscal revenue for oil receipts up to 2013. However, if the portion of Chad's oil revenues that lies outside the revenue management system is taken into account – around 75 per cent – the figures start to make sense.

Credit must be given to the EITI and the Collège for helping to make these figures readily available; they have been very useful for providing a snapshot of what has happened to the money that was set aside for development as part of the original CCDP. However, this section has shown the difficulties faced by the Collège and the EITI in terms of chronic underfunding and a lack of manpower, and quite clearly the limitations of the revenue management law – around US$7.5 billion of what Chad earned can be monitored only if one is able to unpick the government's normal (and highly opaque) budgetary processes. This problem looks set to get worse as more IOCs, oilfields and new revenue streams enter the story and the proportion of revenues lying outside the revenue management system increases.

Ensuring quality spending Tracking revenues, however, is only part of the challenge. Equally crucial are questions for governments about ensuring the quality of spending and how to avoid corruption. Many parts of Africa suffer from a serious lack of

infrastructure – roads, ports and electricity generation, for example – and these things are often at the top of a population's
list of development priorities. However, if institutional control
is weak, new infrastructure projects may be agreed quickly
without proper controls. 'Most countries have a fixation with
infrastructure,' says Alan Gelb, former Africa Chief Economist at
the World Bank, referring to the case of Venezuela in the early
1970s. 'It's partly genuine because it's easy and can be seen, but
it also presents tremendous opportunities for corruption.'[8] Often
there is no competitive tendering or procurement process and
companies with close ties to the ruling class will win contracts,
often with generous benefits. Governments may be reluctant to
spend on 'supply-side' policies such as improving education and
training health workers, which may take years to demonstrate
their benefits. 'It takes at least a generation for the investment
financed by extracting natural resources to bring about social
transformation,' says Paul Collier (2010: 231).

The Doba blues: regional revenue sharing in practice The road
to Doba, a small town in the heart of Chad's oil production
fields, has changed a lot in the last five years. Almost the whole
400 kilometre distance from the capital is now a tarmac road.
Most of the pot-holes have been filled and just a few kilometres
are left unpaved, meaning that the trauma of bouncing up and
down through enormous clouds of idiosyncratic Sahelian dust
is now a distant memory. The road is currently being extended
all the way to the regional centre of Sarh, 500 kilometres from
N'Djaména, and previously a gruelling two-day journey.

About 15 kilometres before the traveller arrives in Doba, they
pass the turn-off for Esso's production site at Komé, a network
of seven major well sites – Komé, Bolobo, Timbre, Maikeri, Nya,
Miandoum and Moundouli – grouped around Komé base camp
where Chadian and expatriate workers are housed for month-long
rotations. One road – variously dirt and tarmac – follows the
trajectory of a series of enormous electricity pylons through a
verdant landscape where hundreds of red 'Christmas tree' well

heads poke out from the undergrowth. Lorries spewing choking fumes rumble past the central processing facility (CPF) where the oil is treated and prepared for the pipeline; smaller 4 × 4s speed along, carrying engineers on their daily check routines. The entrance to the 1,070 kilometre Kribi pipeline, which exports the oil to a tanker terminal on Cameroon's Atlantic coast, is found here. Opposite Komé base camp is the makeshift town '*Quartier Qui S'Attend*' (The Waiting Neighbourhood), a home for hopeful labourers that has sprung up in the ten years since the project began. It is a less than salubrious place, with bars spilling out on to the street, but a testament to its longevity is the arrival of a mobile phone mast. The whole area is somewhat surreal: a vast industrial complex lit up like a shopping centre in the middle of the true African bush. Steve Coll reports that 'some of the Africans who worked behind the tall fences illuminated by safety lights, and who found their lives constrained by ExxonMobil's extensive rule making, facetiously referred to the compound as Guantánamo' (Coll 2013: 350).

The town of Doba looks sad in the rainy season; its red dust forms into clotted pools of mud by the side of the road that are carefully avoided by motorcyclists and pedestrians. Rainwater drips in a melancholy fashion down the worn-out shop fronts and children weave through the traffic carrying begging bowls. Cawing white egrets launch themselves from the tops of magnificent mango trees, flapping their wings indolently against a thunderous sky.

There are new buildings here – most noticeably a pristine general hospital that, on my last visit in July 2013, had yet to admit any patients, and a university on the outskirts of town with a beautiful peach plaster finish that looks like icing on a wedding cake. There is a new covered market and, most famously, Doba's sports stadium, which was completed in 2008. The state's involvement in these changes is conspicuous: a huge hoarding on one of the main roads shows a picture of a beaming President Déby (often known by the sobriquet IDI – Idriss Déby Itno) and the caption '*Mon ambition est de voir tous les Tchadiens réaliser leur rêve*' (My ambition is to see all Chadians realising their dreams).

Doba town and the surrounding administrative region benefit from a special payment of 5 per cent of the oil revenue, a gesture to compensate for the environmental disruption and loss of livelihoods caused by the oil project and an amount that was enshrined in the original World Bank agreement. A special committee (le Comité de 5%) was established to oversee this spending, in much the same mould as the national Collège de Contrôle. The Comité receives its payment from the BEAC, which in turn receives the earmarked 5 per cent of revenues directly from the Citibank account. Proposals for spending plans can come from anyone in the Doba region but mostly originate with committee members themselves, according to Vice President Mbaigoto Inenee.

The Comité has been controversial since it was established in 2005. All of its members, which include local MPs, civil society figures and religious leaders, are nominated and then appointed. What's more, their voting powers are restricted to projects with a value below 50 million Central African Francs (CFA; approximately US$90,000), and even these still have to be authorised by the governor, who is, of course, appointed by the President. Any expenditure between 50 million CFA and 100 million CFA has to be approved by the national Collège and the Minister of Finance, and for everything over that sum, which includes all the major Doba developments such as the stadium, university and hospital, approval needs to come from the President himself. Mr Inenee is defensive: 'We're free to choose the kinds of projects we want to pursue,' he said when I challenged him about the lack of democracy in the way projects are decided. 'We've done a lot of agricultural development, improving access to drinking water, reclaiming farm land and helping to improve animal husbandry. These things really make a difference.'

The project that has attracted the most criticism over the years has been the building of a 2.2 billion CFA (US$3.8 million), 20,000-seat sports stadium in Doba; this has been branded a classic 'white elephant' in a town of fewer than 50,000 people that did

53

not even have a permanent football team. Showing me around the stadium in 2009, local radio journalist Joseph Djikolmbaye (who sadly was killed in a car crash in 2012) said: 'The stadium was built for the young people to show off their talent, but we really don't think this was a priority. Other things should have been done first such as health centres and providing clean water.'[9] Four years later, on my return visit, the stadium was looking even more unloved, with just a handful of friendly matches chalked on the board at its gate and a couple of goats peacefully munching at the grass on the pitch in the hot sun.

The new university and the hospital have not escaped criticism either. Again, the concern is that highly visible new buildings have been flung up in haste without proper research into how they can make any kind of dent in Chad's low development status. Civil society groups in Doba have questioned the need for a new university, given that there are already higher education facilities at the larger regional centres of Moundou and Sarh and that a low number of students pass the baccalaureate – only 6,000 of 70,000 entrants nationally passed in 2013. I met the university's Vice Rector Hamdi Mahamat, sitting in an eerily quiet and mostly bare office in a corridor of empty rooms. He complained that two years after the university opened the library still did not contain a single book. Sitting on a wall in an empty courtyard outside the university, I met a small group of students chatting during their break who were qualified in their enthusiasm: 'When I came from my village to the university I was expecting something amazing,' says twenty-year-old Doum Rafael, who is studying business. 'It's great to have it, but we don't even have spare pens or an internet connection. Oil is good for Chad, you can see a change, but it doesn't go far enough.'

Across the road is a beautifully built new hospital with neatly manicured gardens, still waiting to accept its first patients in July 2013, yet the mayor's office in Doba tells me that there are currently only two qualified doctors to serve the whole of Doba region, an administrative department with a population of over 50,000. Mbaigoto Inenee acknowledges things are not perfect but denies that the Collège is responsible for the lack of planning: 'It's a problem of organisation. We build the schools and hospitals and put them at the state's disposal and then they're not ready to provide doctors and nurses.' From these examples we can clearly see that in the rush to build and make high-impact physical changes, projects are not being properly planned, funded or followed up. In a further indictment, the Collège civil society body charged with monitoring what happens to the money set aside for 'priority sectors' says that in ten years it has had not one request from the government for money to be put towards the training of healthcare or education professionals.

This problem of the *quality* of spending is not restricted to the oil-producing region. In 2006, N'Djaména had barely 20 kilometres of paved roads, and in the rainy season whole sections of the city ground to a halt for days as vehicles struggled through the mud. But an astonishing transformation has taken place, thanks in part to money from the Doba oil project, but also to loans for infrastructure provided by Chinese companies in recent years. Today, most of the city centre and its main axes are paved. When I first returned to Chad in 2012 after a two-year absence I got completely lost on my way to the Hotel Shanghai from the airport. Opposite the presidential palace a vast area housing a military barracks and a number of shacks and shops had been torn down and replaced by 'La Place de la Nation', an open square housing a giant triumphal arch, park benches, open-air TV screens and sculptures of Chadian families and famous wildlife. Chad has borrowed US$5 billion from Exim Bank of China to fund the construction of a railway connection with Cameroon and a new million-passenger airport for N'Djaména. In Abeche, the eastern regional capital, similar improvements have been made in the road network and new buildings.

However, civil society groups in the capital are again critical of the government's decision to spend billions on new buildings and infrastructure without the accompanying investments in human capital, which take much longer to show their success. 'We don't deny there are changes, but it's the quality of the buildings that

55

concerns us and the fact that there are not enough people to work in them,' says Thérèse Mekombe, a Chadian lawyer, Director of the Women's Jurist Association and former Collège member.[10] Projects such as two dual-carriageway flyovers, roundabouts and gleaming new buildings for ministries have been criticised as unnecessary. These projects seem to be classic examples of the problem of 'absorption' – when 'an economy simply cannot absorb the extra cash' and domestic investments become 'the weakest link in the chain' towards development, as economist Paul Collier has pointed out (Collier 2010: 127).

Singled out for particular vitriol by some is Chad's new Mother and Child Hospital (MCH), which has been built on the site of a former market in central N'Djaména. Improving maternal health statistics has been a major campaign issue for Déby's most prominent wife, Hinda Déby, who goes by the somewhat controversial title of First Lady. Her concern is well placed – Chad's maternal and infant mortality rates are among the worst in the world.

Armed with horror stories from local newspapers about how the building had been left with a leaking roof and no sewerage system, I decided to take a look for myself on my last trip to Chad in July 2013. The MCH is an impressive peach-coloured building, with crowds of pregnant women and those with small children arriving at the gates. On first glance I was pleasantly surprised – at least seventy midwives work at the facility. I even got a taste of the quality of healthcare myself – I banged my head on a road sign outside the main gates and was treated to an iodine bath and dressing by five young medics keen to show me that they had washed their hands before cleaning the wound. The hospital is a clean and modern building with running water and a twenty-four-hour electricity supply backed up with generators. Although these might sound like quite basic requirements, they are a distinct improvement on maternity facilities I have seen in other parts of the country; at a hospital in Goz Beïda, I saw a baby born with spina bifida being left to die because no one could pay for a car to take him and his mother to a regional hospital with operating facilities, and at the Chagoua maternity hospital in the capital I saw four babies being born in the space of thirty minutes in a delivery room with no running water and without a single stethoscope for the midwives to check for babies' heartbeats in utero.

However, the new MCH still leaves a lot to be desired. A visit by the British charity Safer Birth in Chad in early 2013 found that the triage room where women are assessed in an emergency and the operating theatre where they would go for caesarean sections are not on the same floor, meaning that women have to be transferred in a lift. The British midwives also found no hand-washing facilities in the triage room, a dirty toilet, only one trolley for newborns in the whole hospital and no food or drinks provided on site. While it is certainly an improvement to offer free healthcare for pregnant women in such a high-profile new hospital, this case again shows how good planning has been overlooked in the impulse to build.

Unfortunately, there is nothing new in this and Chad faces the same pitfalls as many economies before it. As Alan Gelb says:

> Many countries faced with a rapid and unprecedented injection of cash will rush to spend it on high-impact projects and ... often governments actively choose not to spend on education and health because it's more difficult and takes longer to demonstrate success in these areas.

The rush to build also has an impact on the efficiency of public spending. Although the Collège technically has the power to verify how infrastructure contracts for projects funded through Law 001 are tendered, the real power in the infrastructure boom of 2009 rested with the Ministry of Infrastructure. The ministry was headed up by a staunch ally of Déby, Adoum Younousmi, who was favoured for his strong support of the President during the 2008 rebel crisis. An ICG report in 2009 detailed how 'a close ally of the president [Younousmi] monopolises all capital investment credits and the award of public contracts at will' through the second most well-funded ministry after the Ministry of Finance (ICG 2009: 10). The ICG research revealed how 'senior figures from the regime were enriching themselves' by trying to get round rules set up through Law 001 requiring the approval of the Finance Minister for contracts over 10 million CFA ($20,000) by breaking these contracts into smaller units.

Normal budgetary procedures were, and continue to be, discarded. An IMF report on the staff-monitored programme in Chad showed how over 40 per cent of domestically financed spending in 2008 was funded through extraordinary budgetary procedures (or DAOs, as discussed in Chapter 1) – in other words, without normal parliamentary approval (IMF 2014: 7). Chad's official budget is extremely opaque and the Collège is not mandated to evaluate it, which leaves only internal government budgetary checks and balances.

The lack of budgetary discipline and the apparent willingness of certain government departments to ignore their own rules do not apply just to one-off infrastructure spending; they also manifest themselves clearly in Chad's recurrent spending. Shockingly, it was estimated that in 2004 almost 99 per cent of Chad's official health budget disappeared in what is known as 'quiet corruption' (World Bank 2010: 11), where public servants fail to deliver services or inputs that have been paid for by the government. The same report detailed the issue of 'absenteeism': in Chad, some 20 per cent of public sector workers listed on the payroll never show up for work. Independent research through the Open Budget Initiative, which records a number of indicators such as whether the country meets its proposed budgetary timetable or provides easily accessible supporting documents, gave the country a score of only three out of 100 in its 2012 ratings, ranking it sixth from bottom (IBP 2012). While it is clear that the poor situation with regards to public spending was a key part of the background in Chad even before oil, the governance measures taken for oil revenues do not seem to have led to many tangible improvements in guaranteeing the quality of spending.

Spend, save or borrow? We have seen that Chad's record on delivering effective, high-quality public spending has been poor. But thinking back to the shiny new infrastructure in N'Djaména gives rise to another question on revenue management, namely the decision to spend in the first place. What is the appropriate balance between spending and saving?

As the resource curse theory has identified, one of the reasons why oil has such a distorting effect on an economy is because it is non-renewable – once it has been used it cannot be replaced and the benefit it accrues will be over. Therefore, many of the decisions a government faces are essentially about consumption versus investment, and, as part of the same set of questions, whether it should undertake borrowing for public investment projects on the back of a commodities boom, or whether it should save for the future. Furthermore, resource curse theory identifies that global commodity prices are notoriously volatile, making government spending plans difficult to formulate and sustain, and this in turn can have an impact on long-term productivity.

Paul Collier has written about the 'ethics of custody', by which he means that consumption of the natural resource today denies future generations any benefit. 'If we use up a natural asset we must provide those future generations with compensation,' he argues (Collier 2010: 31). The establishment of Chad's Future Generations Fund under the World Bank CCDP was a good example of an attempt to tackle this issue of the non-renewable nature of oil assets, but, of course, we have already seen how that ended in disaster.

Theoreticians have also pointed to the value of stabilisation funds, which can be used by governments to tackle the volatility problem – the funds should accumulate money when the oil price exceeds a target level and dispense funds when the price falls below it, or 'smooth out expenditure'. More simply, governments can also consider setting up a more conventional 'rainy day' savings fund or grant a proportion of total revenue to the producing region as compensation for the disruption of the project.

The volatility problem We will briefly examine what has happened to general government revenues since the beginning of the CCDP – this is the estimated 75 per cent of money *not* covered

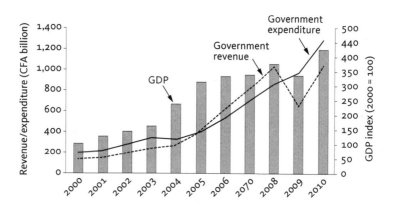

2.1 The impact of oil on Chad's public finances, 2000–10 (source: IMF)

by Law 001 that has gone directly into the national budget. Oil has clearly provided a shot in the arm to Chad's public finances: Chad's overall GDP growth in the last ten years has been strong, with GDP increasing significantly from US$2.1 billion in 2001 to US$13 billion in 2012,[11] and with most of that being attributable to growth in oil GDP after the start of production. Some 90 per cent of Chad's total exports and 70 per cent of its fiscal revenues come from oil. Figure 2.1, based on IMF figures, shows the huge growth in GDP over the period from 2000 to 2010.

As the figure also shows, there has been a huge increase in government revenue over the last ten years; this is to be expected given the enormous sums now being paid in royalties, taxes and other indirect revenues by an increasing number of IOCs. By and large, increases in government spending have followed a similar trend. According to IMF figures, the government's total revenue in 2000 was just over 130 billion CFA and its expenditure was 203 billion CFA. By 2008, revenue had risen to 1.04 trillion CFA – a sevenfold increase – and expenditure was 0.87 trillion CFA.

However, the volatility problem is clear to see in 2008–10, when expenditure shot up to hugely outweigh revenue; the large drop in revenue (from US$1.89 billion in 2008 to US$596 million in 2009, according to the EITI reports) is explained by the dramatic fall in the oil price in 2009, which was precisely the moment when Chad started to become confident about spending its money. As the rebel threat abated and the world oil price hit an all-time high of US$147 a barrel, the government chose to 'splash the cash', announcing a huge programme of infrastructure construction including new hospitals, schools and government ministry buildings, as we saw above. In early 2009, that optimism came crashing down together with the oil price following the global economic crisis. The subsequent collapse in the government's fiscal position and the fact that it was so dependent on oil and had committed an estimated five years of future revenues to infrastructure projects forced it to approach the IMF to ask for help just three years after it had paid off the loan to the World Bank and presumably believed itself free of the strictures of international financial institutions for ever. An IMF staff-monitored programme to help the government balance its books and diversify its economy was signed in 2009 and is still in place.

This dire economic situation looked likely to be repeated in early 2015, when the oil price again fell below US$50 a barrel due to weak global demand and a rise in supply. According to the IMF, this price fall is expected to hit Chad 'very hard', especially as plans for increasing production from the CNPCIC wells has fallen behind schedule. As we have seen, Chad has never had a stabilisation fund and 'has not been able to accumulate savings/buffers to help tackle the volatility of oil revenue'.[12] The hole in the government's budget led to the cancellation of high-profile plans to host the African Union Heads of State summit in 2015,[13] and fears that the country may be unable to finance over US$1 billion in debt incurred when the government bought up Chevron's assets in the Doba oilfields (see Chapter 3). Yet again the government's management of the fiscal position has not been a notable success.

Civil society: the silver lining

Rim Nassingar's office at PWYP is on the first floor of a ragtag building that is home to several NGO headquarters, opposite

N'Djaména's former university building. His door does not close properly and there are never any lights on in the corridor. Rim's journey to work is a daily reminder of the speed of construction and change in Chad: most of the university campus is in the process of being moved to a new, purpose-built site on the outskirts of town. A few years ago this area was buzzing with young, enthusiastic students; today it is starting to feel forgotten, as do many other parts of the old city centre near Avenue Charles de Gaulle, established in the colonial period.

'Sorry for the mess!' says Rim, clumsily making me a cup of instant coffee from a flask of hot water on top of a dusty pile of papers on his desk. He is a broad, smiley man who clearly loves his job and answers any complex query quickly and accurately. Two young men are sitting in the corner of his office, typing frantically on laptops. One of them is a Chadian student doing a PhD on the oil project at a French university. Rim explains with an apologetic laugh that they were hoping to work on PWYP's accounts this morning, but they cannot use the internet because yet again there is no electricity. Dealing with frequent power cuts, bad communications and a lack of funding is something that all NGOs, civil society groups and indeed journalists in Chad have to face on a daily basis.

The PWYP coalition was founded in 2002 by a London-based group of NGO representatives who wanted to campaign on the issues of accountability and transparency and the management of revenues from the oil, gas and mining industries. This aim was sparked by the alleged complicity of the oil and banking industries in the plundering of state assets during Angola's thirty-year civil war and the idea that the then generally accepted principle that IOCs did *not* publish what they had paid to governments 'aided and abetted the mismanagement and embezzlement of oil revenues by the elite in the country'.[14] Since then, the coalition has turned into a global network, with more than twenty-five national civil society groups around the world comprising 350 community organisation members. It has had a number of policy successes, including being heavily involved in the establishment of the EITI and securing a declaration on just natural resource extraction at the UN Security Council.

Chad's PWYP was one of the first networks to be set up when the global initiative began ten years ago. It is a lively grouping of several civil society groups, including GRAMP-TC and the CPPN, which have become steadily more confident in their activism over the last ten years. Rim – who has recently been promoted to Francophone Central Africa Regional Coordinator for PWYP – says the Chadian coalition is particularly busy now as there are so many new companies entering the market, such as the CNPCIC. 'We do a lot of civil society sensitisation campaigns,' explains Rim, 'mostly to get out into the community and explain to people what's being done with their money.' PWYP also took on many responsibilities in the field of environmental monitoring after the World Bank pull-out threatened Chad's high standards, and it runs regular workshops on issues surrounding oil governance for journalists and campaigners. One of the biggest concerns for Rim recently has been the reliability of financial data coming from the government, mostly due to the government's opaque accounting practices; this was one of the reasons why the first EITI reports took so long to put together. Rim says this reduces civil society's ability to follow through on what happens to projects after completion and to conclude whether value for money has been achieved. 'We need to start looking at what the lasting impact of all this money has been. Declaring how much has been earned is one thing but it's useless if we can't see the benefits further along the line,' he says.[15]

The civil society grouping GRAMP-TC works closely with Rim and has also had some notable achievements. The organisation has been run from the beginning by the formidable campaigner Gilbert Maoundonodji, who wrote a doctoral thesis on the geopolitical stakes of oil production at the University of Louvain-la-Neuve in France. The group was involved prominently in the early days of sensitisation at the community level in Chad and continues to run campaigns and awareness-raising sessions in the Doba oil production area. GRAMP-TC is one of the few

they achieved 'compliant' status in 2014. How far this tolerance will go if the government finds itself questioned seriously over its future spending plans remains to be seen.

Environmental protections

The CCDP was once called 'the most scrutinised project in the Bank's history' (Gary and Reisch 2004: 30), and the external monitoring controls that were established were also of the highest order. In addition to civil society monitoring by the Collège and international and national NGOs covering revenue transparency and spending, as outlined above, the World Bank set up the IAG, an independent group of advisers who made regular visits to Chad until 2009 to measure implementation of the project's objectives.

The CCDP also created a set of environmental and social standards for oil production known as the environmental management plan or EMP. One of its lasting achievements was that it required any oil transported through the Chad–Cameroon pipeline in the future to be produced under strict standards governing areas such as the precise chemical composition of the oil, land disturbance and restoration, pollution and the cleaning up of oil spills, waste and sewage disposal and the quality of groundwater, as well as occupational health and the safety of workers. It also set limits for the practice of gas flaring, which is often used when gas associated with an oil find cannot be used and is therefore burned off at the production site. Not only is the practice extremely wasteful – one report estimated that the amounts flared off in the Niger Delta alone could provide one-quarter of Africa's current power consumption – it is also known to be harmful to human health, contributes to climate change and helps produce acid rain (Ajugwo 2013).

At the beginning of the project, the EMP also helped to establish an intricately calculated set of compensation values for land and trees for farmers and communities who would have to move to allow the construction of the pipeline and the associated facilities. It went so far as to work out the economic value of the entire lifespan of a mango tree (which was set at US\$1,635) for example,

66

after local villagers complained that the fixed rate was unfair. This compensation plan was more detailed than anything that had been seen before and has been praised by those working today in other African oil-producing countries that are faced with the difficulties of compulsory purchases of land and paying farmers for any loss of livelihood. What's more, the EMP continues to this day as a system of environmental and social checks and balances and has been taken on institutionally by Esso to govern its continuing activities. Chad's (and the Esso Consortium's) progress against the EMP's standards and rules continues to be monitored every year by a site visit from the Italian engineering consulting company D'Appolonia; the company carries out the research required for the reports of yet another monitoring body, the External Compliance Monitoring Group (ECMG), which was established to verify the spending of the original IFC loan at the beginning of the World Bank project.

Esso continues to stick to the strict rules of the EMP and proudly displays highlights of the year's achievements in its annual report, including 'zero non-compliance situations in the second half of 2012' for the first time ever. The glossy brochure lists in incredible detail each individual case of non-compliance (which can be as simple as a contractor not paying his workers on time) alongside photographs of smiling Chadian employees who speak with pride about their work and communities. The most recent report by the ECMG from November 2012 describes how 'health and safety measures are consistently implemented in agreement with the EMP requirements and industry best practice' (ECMG 2012). There is no doubt that these environmental and monitoring standards can be considered world class; as many insiders in the industry who have worked across the continent's oilfields commented to me privately on my last visit to Chad in July 2013, it is notable that there has been so little death and destruction associated with an African oil project. Some of these people had worked in the Niger Delta and were surprised that there had been only six fatalities in the entire ten-year lifespan of the Doba project. In fact, the Komé field's overall recordable incident rate is below the US petroleum industry average – for Chad it is 0.18 per 200,000 hours worked and in the US it is 0.5 (Esso 2012). Driving around the Komé fields, it is difficult to find any significant evidence of spills, broken wells or pollution damage to flora and fauna. There is nothing like the environmental destruction or social exclusion seen in the Niger Delta.

This matters because it creates standards that are likely to oblige other oil companies operating in Chad to improve their operations. For example, the CNPCIC has long been keen to export oil through the Kribi pipeline as its current production at the Djérmaya refinery for sale on local markets has still not turned a profit. But it is thought that some of the delay the CNPCIC encountered in securing access to the pipeline was because of insistence that its oil is produced to exactly the same grade and high industry standards as the Doba crude (see Chapter 3). It is not only the IOCs that are keen to achieve these standards; the Chadian government is also now growing in confidence about what is in the country's environmental interests. The authorities reacted with lightning speed in August 2013 when reports emerged of oil spills and pollution caused by the exploration arm of the CNPCIC in its Ronier field near Bongor. They immediately closed down the entire operation after it was discovered that the CNPCIC had breached environmental rules and ordered a thorough clean-up (see Chapter 3).

Development of local content and the impact on the wider economy

What did Esso ever do for us? Chad's oilfields have certainly been developed using modern production techniques. It is a fast-developing sector, with deposits that would have seemed unattractive twenty years ago increasingly being viewed as commercially viable, and international investors keen to get access to exploration permits. The boost from the CCDP project has led to increased interest in the country: since 2011, Griffiths/Caracal and the CNPCIC have both started production, thereby increasing Chad's revenues, mining giant Glencore Xstrata has joined the sector, a number of smaller oil companies (including the Nigerian National Petroleum Corporation (NNPC) and Kenya's Simba Oil) are continuing to prospect, and for the first time locally produced fuel is available on the market.

Esso and the Consortium's ongoing commitment to the country is clear; Esso is one of the few international organisations that did not pack up and leave even temporarily during the devastating rebel crises of 2006 and 2008. It is still by far the largest private sector employer in the country, with around 5,100 jobs being filled by Chadians on average throughout 2012 (ibid.) and most of those employed on permanent contracts, which means that they enjoy training opportunities and healthcare benefits. The company's need for good transportation links led to a transformation of the N'Djaména–Doba road and the improvement of an airport landing strip at Komé. Through the corporation's philanthropic arm, the ExxonMobil Foundation, a US$1.5 million three-year project to build the skills and incomes of women in the region has been carried out in partnership with the NGO Africare, and the company has made several donations to the private Guinebor hospital in N'Djaména. Yet it is important to note that these corporate social responsibility (CSR) commitments remain relatively small; author Steve Coll argues that the company's moral compass has always been firmly rooted in the value of simply doing business:

> ExxonMobil's executives generally think that the best thing they can do for a host country is get oil out of the ground efficiently, sell it on fair terms, and then hope the country uses the cash to grow their economy and lift their people out of poverty. I've taken the view that there are some very poor countries like Chad where they really have to interpret their obligations more broadly, but they disagree. They are content with the contributions they can see on their work sites – Chadian employees making good salaries, learning technical skills etc. The rest they leave to the World Bank, the United Nations, Human Rights Watch, and so on.[16]

This attitude was clearly evinced in the words of the Esso Director in Chad, D. Scott Miller, when I chatted to him informally during my last trip to Chad:

> We never set out to concern ourselves with how the money is spent, that's not our job. As I drive around the city I see all these new roads and cars. Look at what's been achieved over the last few years and what's the one thing that's made that possible? It's the oil project. I'm proud of what's been achieved.[17]

However, there has been only a small impact on job creation and the wider economy. This is a key element of the resource curse concept: the extraction of natural resources should be considered differently to other types of economic activity, because there tends to be very little knock-on benefit to the wider economy – investors need only to dig a well or put in a mine to extract the resource. In the producing region around Doba, attempts at improving the manufacturing base and diversifying the economy are unconvincing; for example, a new fruit juice factory in Doba was hailed for its job-creating potential, but was closed when I visited in July 2013. Other sectors, such as gum arabic production, cotton and livestock exportation, have been neglected, and IMF economists believe that Chad's GDP growth has been disappointing in non-oil sectors including transportation, manufacturing and services.

The country's national oil company SHT has played a fairly muted role in the growing sector since it was established in 2006. Although Chad has tried in recent years to increase SHT's participation in projects – for example, declaring it the fourth member of the Doba Consortium after the World Bank pull-out in 2006 and guaranteeing it a 40 per cent stake in the Djérmaya refinery – SHT plays only a marginal role in the running of Djérmaya and is currently more involved in overseeing applications for licences and production permits. However, that situation may be beginning to change: in 2014 there was news that the global commodities giant Glencore had lent Chad over US$1 billion, which it has used to purchase Chevron's 25 per cent stake in the Doba Consortium.[18] This massive deal should allow the SHT to be much more active in the running of the field and may increase the opportunities for local employment.

Furthermore, while the Esso Consortium today employs over 5,000 Chadians, there have been persistent complaints that expats are favoured over locals. The complaints are even louder with respect to the Chinese oil facility in the Bongor Basin. Most of the jobs for locals are low skilled and only in the last few years has a special oil-training college in Mao produced its first graduates with higher standard engineering skills.

In this context, the non-renewable nature of oil assets is a particularly pressing problem for Chad, as all estimates suggest that the biggest oilfields in the Doba region will be exhausted by 2030. Production declined sharply from around 225,000 bpd in 2003 to fewer than 100,000 bpd in 2013, although that figure rose to about 140,000 bpd in 2014 with increased production from the CNPCIC's Ronier field. Although Chad's oil minister confidently asserted in late 2013 that oilfields in the Lake Chad area would double the country's output within two years, the success rate on new finds has been questionable and the rate of increase has been erratic. Furthermore, the CNPCIC is not finding everything plain sailing: despite having thrown vast amounts of money and manpower at old discoveries in the Bongor Basin, the Director of CNPCIC told me in July 2013 that it has been unable to make a profit in three years of production. The Griffiths/Caracal operation remains small-scale, having begun exporting some 14,000 bpd in 2014 from reconditioned old wells that had been abandoned by Esso. If no significant finds are made by 2030, the country's opportunity to convert oil revenue into lasting development may be over.

Bringing it all together: is Chad resource cursed?

Drawing together all the threads of a tumultuous ten years in Chad's history, on the face of it the country seems to fit quite neatly into the category of 'resource cursed'. The country is still exceptionally poor after twelve years of oil production, and has lived through a serious period of civil conflict from 2004 to 2009. But is that the right conclusion to be drawn?

The theme of this book is to establish 'whether these temporary windfalls [of oil revenue] can be converted into a permanent breakthrough in development', as the APP has asked (2013). Of course, there are many complex processes at work in everything I have covered in this chapter, and it is notoriously difficult to make any reliable measure of any country's developmental progress. But there are a few tools at my disposal. The architects of the CCDP chose the MDGs as the yardstick for measuring Chad's progress, so my first attempt at a conclusion is a look at Chad's achievements against these indicators.

The picture is bleak. Chad has achieved none of the MDGs. For example, its progress against infant mortality (MDG 4) is poor. The goal is to reduce the under-five mortality rate by two-thirds or 66 per cent; Chad's rate fell from 208.3 per 1,000 births in 1996 to 169 per 1,000 in 2011, a drop of only 18.9 per cent. MDG 1 was to halve extreme poverty, but Chad achieved a drop only from 54.5 per cent in 2003 to 46.7 per cent in 2011.[19] The picture is similarly depressing if other widely accepted development measurements are used. For example, Chad is still fourth from bottom on the UN's 2013 Human Development Index, ahead of only Mozambique, Niger and DRC (although other African countries such as South Sudan and Somalia were not included in the data set). On the 2013 multidimensional poverty index, Chad scored 0.34 per cent while the average for sub-Saharan Africa was 0.47 per cent. Spending on education is 2.8 per cent of the national budget and on health just 1.1 per cent (UNDP 2013). As a result, literacy levels have barely improved at 34.5 per cent of the adult population, and life expectancy is 49.9 years. Polio, measles and malaria still affect thousands of children unnecessarily every year and persistent food insecurity plagues the country. In 2011, some 3.6 million people were affected by hunger after poor rains (most of them children), and the nationwide malnutrition rate stays stubbornly high at 15 per cent; this level is classed as an emergency by most international aid groups. At the same time, as explained in Chapter 2, the country has spent at least US$4 billion on improving its army and military capability.

And this is perhaps where the biggest questions lie, and where there are no clear answers about how oil wealth can benefit the population. D. Scott Miller's remarks above reflect the complexity of asking whether oil has been good for Chad, and even whether exploitation should have happened at all. During our interview in July 2013, Mr Miller reminded me to think back to where Chad was in 2008 and to where it is today. In February 2008, for the second time in two years, Déby came within hours of being toppled by a ragtag rebellion in which several hundred people died and millions of dollars' worth of damage was caused. This rebel attack was much more serious than the attack of 2006 and many observers at the time concluded that Déby's regime was on the verge of crumbling; he was saved only at the last minute by the incompetence of the rebels and reported assistance from French intelligence. International aid agencies, business and diplomats pulled out in fear, over 100,000 people were internally displaced in the east by fighting, there were 250,000 refugees from Darfur, and the humanitarian agencies looking after them were facing daily attacks as Sudanese and Chadian rebel groups moved through the country's east. Soldiers and heavy weaponry patrolled the streets of the major cities, curfews were in place, a number of foreign journalists were expelled and for months the government enacted emergency measures such as detention without charge and the closing down of mobile phone networks. A multibillion-dollar UN mission arrived with 3,000 peacekeepers and hundreds of logistical and administrative staff to try to stabilise the volatile east, transforming parts of N'Djaména and Abeche into military zones. European soldiers struggled to stop the rebels and bandits attacking humanitarian organisations and stealing cars, money and equipment. Commentators the world over predicted army mutinies or a palace coup against the President and the narrative of a country at war for more than thirty years continued. Neighbouring countries such as Nigeria, Libya and Sudan looked on in horror at the prospect of this vast desert nation being swallowed up in a vortex of chaos.

Five years later, as the Economic Community of West African States (ECOWAS) procrastinated, Chad sent 2,000 of its elite troops to northern Mali without a moment's hesitation. The soldiers stood proud as France's staunchest allies as Operation Serval took on the jihadist rebels who had taken over much of the north of the country after a military coup had deposed Mali's president in 2012. The Chadians' operational capabilities in a harsh desert terrain were highly praised and they killed one of al-Qaeda in the Islamic Maghreb's (AQIM's) top commanders. Weeks later Chadian troops in neighbouring Central African Republic (CAR) helped as the Seleka rebel coalition put paid to the weak rule of François Bozizé, once a Déby protégé (although that success turned sour in 2014 when Chadian soldiers were pulled out after a number of incidents where they fired on and killed civilians). France announced in July 2014 that the headquarters of its new Sahel regional military deployment were to be in N'Djaména – with Chad seemingly the only country in West or Central Africa stable enough to play host to the deployment. In early 2015, Chad sent troops to Cameroon and Nigeria in an effort to curb the devastating attacks in the Lake Chad region by the Nigerian Islamist group Boko Haram. In a remarkable turnaround, Déby has suddenly begun to look like a regional power broker in a dangerous neighbourhood, and a transformed map of Central Africa has emerged – Libya, weak and divided, north-eastern Nigeria on fire with Boko Haram's catastrophic campaign, Darfur once again unruly and President al-Bashir's authority circumscribed by his problems with the newly independent South Sudan. Right in the centre is a strong and apparently stable Chad.

One uncomfortable conclusion that might be drawn from all this is that mutinous soldiers bought off or paid proper salaries and weapons bought with oil money have helped Chad not only to regain its stability but also to play the role of regional power broker. The Chadian rebellion's failure in 2009 can partly be ascribed to a loss of interest on the part of their sponsor President al-Bashir of Sudan, but, as I have already described, crucially Déby seems to have been able to spend somewhere in the region of US$4 billion whipping his army into shape. He was able to put soldiers in armoured personnel carriers instead of 'technical' 4 x 4s and provide them with helicopters and increased firepower. As I have argued, without this investment in the military, there is a very real possibility that the old-fashioned hit-and-run rebel attacks could have succeeded in reaching the capital. Déby could have been toppled. There is nothing to suggest that the rebel leaders Mahamat Nouri or Timan Erdimi had anything approaching a workable plan for improving governance in Chad, nor any broad-based popular support from the population. Watching the disintegration of neighbouring CAR in 2013, as remnants of the old rebel coalitions battled village by village for control of the country, turning with increasing brutality against civilians and sparking an inter-religious war, it is not hard to imagine what may have become of Chad.

As Chad's oil revenues soar over US$10 billion – perhaps beyond the wildest dreams of the architects of the CCDP – the country is at a crossroads. Without serious improvements in democratic space it is difficult to envisage any kind of popular pressure emerging on the authorities to make them change course. If the country continues as it is and no new significant oil finds are made, in less than twenty years this great opportunity for development may be over. With few good domestic investments and almost nothing saved for the future, the country may yet be consigned to the dustbin of resource-cursed nations.

Yet it is not too late for Chad to recalculate its spending priorities, to move away from a narrow focus on infrastructure and construction and on diverting money through emergency procedures to military spending, and to target the money on health, education and development priorities. There is hope that the transparency and accountability measures that have survived will help the country on its path towards a more democratic space. The important question remains as to why the whole raft of measures created by the CCDP was not simply scrapped when the World Bank agreement fell apart, and why initiatives such as the EITI appear to have been encouraged. Why not just bin everything? Could it be that even President Déby realised that a limited (and hopefully, from his perspective, controllable) amount of transparent revenue management can actually be politically desirable?

In conclusion, this chapter has sought to show how many important features of revenue management and transparency have remained, despite the Chadian government discarding some of the strictest provisions of the original CCDP in 2006, such as the Future Generations Fund. It has also illustrated how, over the last ten years, a more composite and 'organic' approach to revenue management has emerged. The measures that have endured and have proved useful have been the EMP; the priority spending sectors enshrined in law; civil society monitoring of the environment and revenues, including the Collège; the use of the Citibank escrow account; and the 5 per cent Doba regional fund. These have been supplemented by newer initiatives such as the EITI, which have led to the production of useful figures that civil society can use to advocate for better management of oil resources, and a system of transparency and accountability is emerging. Arguably this has allowed more oil money to be spent on development than would have been the case had the World Bank not intervened. The IEG's thorough evaluation report on the CCDP (introduced in Chapter 1) concluded that the World Bank's intervention ensured that more revenue was spent on social development than would have been the case if Chad had been left to develop the oilfields alone – although the project had fallen far short of fulfilling its objectives and the 'poverty reduction, governance and institutional development outcomes were disappointing' – and that Chad's oil would have been exploited anyway, with none of the safeguards the World Bank offered. Nevertheless, it is clear that there are many obstacles standing in the way of the free functioning of all these systems: lack of budgetary transparency, extraordinary budgetary practices, pressure to approve badly designed infrastructure projects, intimidation of journalists, under-resourcing of many of the groups advocating for transparency, and so on.

In the next chapters I analyse how these surviving measures from the CCDP are standing up to the test of Chinese investment in African oil. I also ask how those measures and newer initiatives such as the EITI can be used and adapted by the new generation of African oil producers – Ghana, Uganda, Kenya and Niger – to help them avoid the dangers of the resource curse.

3 | Lessons learned for China?

From the air, the Chinese-owned Ronier oilfield in Chad's Bongor Basin is an impressive sight; a neat network of pipelines and geometric car tracks criss-cross the wild bush, a snapshot of the modern industrial world contrasting dramatically with the quiet pastoral scene of Chad's most fertile farming south-western region. The two enormous concrete and metal cylinders of the CPF rise majestically from the dusty ground; a gas flare blazes bright against the bleached horizon. Four years before there was nothing here. In 2009 I tried to follow a stream of 4 × 4s carrying Chinese engineers along the dirt road from Bongor to Koudalwa to see the construction work, but after two hours ploughing through thick red mud and puddles in a lowly Corolla car, our driver started to look suicidal so we turned back.

By July 2013, when I visited, the site was fully operational, pumping about 10,000 to 15,000 bpd of oil twenty-four hours a day from about thirty-five well heads dotted across the twin Ronier and Mimosa fields. Workers at the site tell me that everything here was shipped in from China; it took weeks to reach the port of Douala on giant cargo ships, and even longer to clear customs and then to be transported 1,000 kilometres along Cameroon's appalling roads, on ancient lorries negotiating local corruption, potholes and breakdowns. But the scene at Ronier at first glance looks to be one of absolute efficiency. Much of the oil springs naturally from the ground once a 'Christmas tree' well head is fitted and is pumped to the oil gas manifold (OGM) centre. From here, larger pipes direct it to the noisy CPF, where it receives its first treatment. A row of electricity pylons and a network of pipes connect the main CPF with newer satellite fields and outlying OGMs. Eventually, all the basically processed oil passes to the

Map 3.1 Chad's and Niger's oil infrastructure

head of a 300 kilometre pipeline that leads to a refinery the Chinese built just north of the capital N'Djaména at Djérmaya. There, it is made into petroleum products for sale only on the domestic market. Exploration activities have reached as far as 150 kilometres away in the eastern Salamat Basin, and the CNPCIC says that Ronier's twin field, Mimosa, also has good potential.

Over 1,500 people are employed at Ronier and Djérmaya,[1] many of them Chinese expat workers. Some, like engineer Jack (his 'Western' name), have been here since the very beginning in 2009. He transferred after five years working on the CNPC operation in Sudan. He is a supervisor and spends his days travelling around the site to check that it is running smoothly and to fix technical issues that arise. He is keen to show me how big the site is – he says it has been a remarkable transformation from a malarial swamp when he first arrived. 'The construction of the CPF took less than one year; it was an industry record,' he says, proudly adding that there were no fatalities in the construction phase. Jack's almost ten years in Africa may seem a long time to be away from home, particularly as he works twelve-hour shifts every day of the week, but, like most of the Chinese workers I spoke to, he does not mind because the money is good. He seems genuinely proud of what he does and is rewarded with a one month on/one month off rotation period that allows him to travel home to see his family.

I arrive at base camp on the twice weekly company flight from N'Djaména on a tiny Cessna aircraft. I have travelled from CNPCIC headquarters (HQ) in N'Djaména with Zeng-Jie or 'Jewel' (her 'Western' name), a friendly Chinese lady in her mid-twenties who speaks excellent English – she will be my guide and translator at Ronier. On the plane she asks me all sorts of questions about London and about being a journalist. She is excited to be travelling down south; she has been in N'Djaména working at HQ for a year but this is the first time she has been to Ronier. She tells me how bored she gets at the weekend in the capital; CNPCIC staff are told to stay in the company compound. Jewel says she spends most of the weekend asleep in her darkened room with the air conditioning on, or watching DVDs, and that she can't wait for the company swimming pool to be completed.

We cause quite a stir when we arrive at base camp. The only other woman in the entire camp is twenty-six-year-old Ji Nan, who has been sent to run English language training for the Chadian workers. She is delighted to see another female face. At base camp, the workers live in air-conditioned housing units, with access to a canteen, a clinic and the English and French training centre. The sun is just setting as Ji Nan and Jewel take me on a tour of the vegetable garden and treat me to a proper Chinese tea ceremony with delicate little cakes in a pagoda in the garden. I am given a clean and cosy room in the newly opened block A dormitory. In the evening, a polite Chinese worker knocks on my door to give me a wireless internet dongle. Dinner, a delicious offering of Chinese noodles and tofu, is a quiet affair as most of the workers go to bed at dusk to be ready for the 6am start. The walls outside my room are covered with pictures of workers on the Ronier site as it was being constructed. Each one bears the title 'Outstanding builders' in French and English, and I smile to myself when I spot the one bearing the beaming face of none other than President Déby, wearing a hard hat and carrying a shovel.

I am here at the invitation of the CNPCIC management on the first ever visit by a Western journalist to the Chadian operation. For several weeks it has been touch and go whether Dr Dou Lirong, the general manager of CNPCIC, will let me visit. Many oil production fields around the world are difficult for journalists to visit, and my previous attempts to find out about the CNPCIC operation here in 2008 and 2009 were a resounding failure. Several letters of introduction have flurried between Beijing and N'Djaména, and even on the afternoon before I am supposed to fly I find myself in the Ministry of Communications, waking up the official from his postprandial nap to get one word changed on an authorisation letter. Finally, ten minutes before the offices close and with the ink still wet, I burst into Dr Dou's office in the gleaming new CNPCIC HQ in the Chagoua district of N'Djaména. After another round of anxious questioning, he finally agrees to my visit with the comment that his objective is for the wider world to understand the realities of how the Chinese operate in Africa. This chapter is an attempt to paint a real-life picture of Chinese investment in African oil, and to ask whether the so-called 'no strings' deals between China and African governments are in fact working in the interests of both parties.

'We don't understand why the Western media is so critical'

China's thirst for oil to help it sustain its impressive growth record over the last two decades is enormous. In 1993, the country became a net oil importer, and soon became the world's second largest importer of petroleum products after the US (Taylor 2006:

81

943). It is expected that by 2020 China will need to import between 10 and 15 million bpd to meet its needs – twice Saudi Arabia's current production (Michel and Beuret 2009: 175). Its need to find reliable sources of energy forced the country to reorient itself as an 'outward-looking oil economy', and in 2002 President Hu Jintao launched the 'going out' policy; this was aimed at encouraging Chinese businesses (including the CNPC and the China National Offshore Oil Corporation or CNOOC) to invest abroad. But they were late in seeing the potential of African oil and have tended to find themselves at the back of the queue in Africa: 'China has managed to get hold of only the crumbs from the West's table in places like Gabon and Niger' (ibid.: 178).

However, despite this slow start, Chinese businesses are now profiting from improving trade relations with much of Africa, setting up oil production projects in Chad, Sudan, South Sudan and Niger with astonishing speed. They have obtained the first oil production licence in Uganda and have negotiated good terms on the purchase of oil produced in countries such as Gabon, Nigeria, Congo Brazzaville and Angola. By 2010, the US Energy Information Administration estimated that Africa was the second largest source of crude imports for China after the Middle East, making up 30 per cent of total imports, and trade with the continent was expected to reach US$100 billion by 2010. China has replaced France as Africa's second biggest trading partner after the EU. In places such as Chad, numerous Chinese small businesses have sprung up simultaneously with the oil projects to support the growing Chinese community of expat workers. In N'Djaména there are several Chinese restaurants and two good, simple Chinese-run hotels that are the only cheap alternatives to the three unloved and overpriced international hotels. Chinese entrepreneurs run high-speed internet cafés, car hire and a tea shop (with a 'massage parlour' sign in red neon hanging outside). In contrast to the Westerners who work for Esso and are often seen at the handful of Chadian-run 'expat' restaurants and bars in N'Djaména, by and large it is unusual to see Chinese faces outside the Chinese establishments.

From an outsider's perspective, it can seem that the Chinese are willing to throw almost limitless amounts of manpower and money at their exploration and production activities in order to get the facilities built quickly to the satisfaction of the African governments involved. This is certainly the impression I gained from watching the speed with which Ronier was brought into production in Chad. Academics have argued that the mostly government-owned Chinese companies may be allowed to operate at a loss for an extended period to pursue projects that 'would not be viable under a strictly commercial reading' (Alden 2007: 24). As Ian Taylor writes, they are taking the 'long-term view of energy security, rather than the short-term view of private western companies necessitated by considerations of profits and shareholders' (Taylor 2006: 942). In both Chad and Niger, plans to export oil have been put on the back-burner while refineries to produce fuel for the exceptionally small local markets – a generally much less profitable activity – have been prioritised. Personally, I was astonished at the candid response from Dr Dou Lirong when I asked him in July 2013 how business was going: 'We still haven't made a profit on our operations after four years,' he said with an apologetic smile. 'We will have to make a profit soon or my boss will get tired of waiting.'[2]

Across the African continent, civil society groups continue to complain about China's 'imperialistic' approach, referring to their tendency to draw up opaque contracts and systems of loans and promises of infrastructure with governments. Activists often argue that China is the only real winner in these so-called 'win–win' deals. The Chinese are also accused of not creating enough jobs and opportunities for locals – the 'local content' issue. However, this is only part of the picture. The Chinese way of doing business has clearly offered an attractive alternative to many African governments tired of Western business practices and lectures from the World Bank and the IMF. Paul Collier believes that the Chinese-style deal has a distinct value, arguing that their simple approach of offering loans for infrastructure in return for exploration and production rights may actually increase the value of investment (Collier 2010: 122).

Experience has proved that the Chinese way of doing business certainly yields rapid results. Just five or six years after the initial contracts were signed, both Chad and Niger now have refineries producing oil for domestic consumption – something that is coveted by other African nations, such as Uganda. In Sudan, the CNPC built a 1,500 kilometre export pipeline from the southern oilfields to Port Sudan in just four years (Patey 2014a: 109). Across Africa, new roads, airports, railways and ports are springing up.

The political context: guns, money and oil

Chad's direct relationship with China began in 2006 when the country broke off diplomatic relations with Taiwan, leaving that country with only a handful of African allies. The decision came just weeks after the trauma of the rebel attacks against N'Djaména in April 2006 and President Déby's dramatic falling out with the World Bank over the rewriting of Law 001. As the Esso-led Consortium battled to stop the President closing down oil production at Komé altogether, the Chadian authorities seemed to be embarking on a back-up plan, a robust policy of asserting control over their oil industry. After the humiliating attempt by the World Bank to tell Chad what to do, the prospect of a Chinese 'no strings' business deal must have seemed very attractive.

The CNPCIC bought up the rights to the Ronier and Mimosa fields in the Bongor Basin from the Canadian company EnCana for approximately US$200 million in 2006.[3] EnCana had drilled extensively in the area – situated about 150 kilometres to the north of the Esso Consortium production fields – but had never moved forward with production plans. In exchange for the rights, Chinese businesses promised a far-reaching programme of infrastructure development, including crucially the construction of an oil refinery north of N'Djaména that would finally give ordinary Chadian citizens a taste of the benefits of their country's oil production through the promise of cheaper fuel and an extra 20 megawatts of electricity generation. The deal, with a value of approximately US$1 billion, also involved an enormous programme of road building and promises of loans and expertise to build a new airport, a railway link with Cameroon and Sudan, and a host of government buildings, schools and hospitals. Total Chinese investment in Chad has been huge – Reuters reported that with promises for a new airport and a rail link it had topped US$8 billion.[4]

Chad's enthusiasm for sealing a deal with the Chinese was not only about money. In July 2004 the UN Security Council had imposed an arms embargo on Darfur as the civil war between rebels and the Sudanese government appeared be spiralling out of control. Since the establishment of the embargo there were repeated accusations that China had been involved in arms sales (primarily light weapons) to Sudan and that these weapons had been transferred by the Sudanese government to proxy 'Janjaweed' commanders (UN Panel of Experts 2009); the 'devils on horseback' were largely blamed for the scorched earth policies against the native Fur, Masalit and Zaghawa people. A source from the UN Panel of Experts that investigated violations of the Darfur arms embargo in 2009 told me that this seemed to be despite end-user agreements being signed between the Chinese and the Sudanese governments stating that the weapons would not be transferred to Darfur or to rebel groups. Amnesty International backed up the claims: 'China and Russia are selling arms to the Government of Sudan in the full knowledge that many of them are likely to end up being used to commit human rights violations in Darfur.'[5]

In the vast deserts of eastern Chad in 2006 this was a serious problem. As the Darfur crisis had spilled over into eastern Chad, sending refugees, rebels and arms across the border, President al-Bashir of Sudan had thrown his support behind a motley collection of Chadian rebel groups – including the FUC, UFDD (Union of Forces for Democracy and Development) and UFR, as described in Chapter 1 – in retaliation for President Déby's support of the Darfur rebel groups that were often seen in eastern Chad. Weapons and ammunition seemed to move freely across these zones – items with Chinese markings were found by researchers of the UN Panel of Experts in the hands of the Chadian UFR in 2009 (ibid.). Chad's hands were certainly not clean – the UN Panel of Experts also found evidence suggesting that Chad had been providing weapons to the Darfur rebel movements the JEM and the Sudan Liberation Movement (SLM), both of which contained members of Déby's ethnic Zaghawa group.

It is very likely that part of the reason for hurrying along an oil deal with the CNPCIC in 2006 was that President Déby sensed an opportunity to break the link between weapons transfers and the ongoing cycle of rebel attacks against Chad. Perhaps by creating friendly relations with the Chinese he would be able to persuade them to slow down the supply of arms to Sudan that were slipping into Chadian rebels' hands. With good relations with Beijing, perhaps he could get them to exert pressure on Omar al-Bashir to finally resolve the Darfur conflict. Although, according to the source on the Panel of Experts, at the time there was never any suggestion that the Chinese were directly arming the Chadian rebels, in this complex environment of circulating weapons and shifting allegiances it is easy to see how quickly they had drifted away from their aim of 'non-interference'.

The Chinese contract

With their rocketing thirst for oil, Chinese oil companies – CNOOC, CNPC and Sinopec – appear to prefer a uniform approach to negotiations with governments. Contracts and deals are largely conducted in private and often involve payment for the rights to blocks and oilfields in return for promises to build infrastructure. This is different to the 'Western' model, which involves a payment to the government in exchange for rights over the sale of a share of the oil produced, usually through some form of royalty or PSA. Chinese loans are provided to African governments through Exim Bank (Alden 2007: 24), a government-owned institution whose principal activities are to support the expansion of Chinese business. Some of these loans are low interest while others are to all intents and purposes grants and overseas development assistance. More often than not, the precise terms of the deal – how much the infrastructure is worth, who will build it, the interest rate on the loan, the repayment schedules, and so on – are not made public.

In Chad, often the first confirmation of the contents of one of these deals has been the arrival of Chinese labourers on the street to carry out the work. When I arrived in Chad in 2008, the enormous road-building programme described in Chapter 2 was well under way. Almost every day when I went out in my ramshackle car I had to take a different route – with astonishing speed Chinese bulldozers driven by Chinese workers were ripping up the dirty mud of the city's main axes and laying stone foundations and then tarmac. Within a year I saw the city transformed – in October 2008 there was really only one main paved route, which ran round N'Djaména like an outer ring road; a year later all of the centre of town around Avenue Charles de Gaulle was bitumen. The Chinese works often looked rough and ready and no real alternative routes were provided for drivers, who often had to take their wrecked and ancient cars over huge concrete ramps in the road, throwing up clouds of dust. When it rained, cars and bulldozers got stuck in the mud. On my last visit to N'Djaména in July 2013 I sat for half an hour in traffic trying to pass under a mass of rickety wooden scaffolding holding up the beginnings of a new four-lane flyover beside the smart Hotel Kempinski.

These Chinese deals have been characterised as having 'no political strings' (ibid.: 8), focusing only on business and often without much reference to issues of human rights, labour rights or the environment. This has made them popular with many African countries keen to cut through the red tape that has become associated with 'Western' deals – particularly in light of Chad's experience with the World Bank. 'Energetically pursuing their aims while playing on African leaders' historic suspicion of western intentions is how Beijing generally engages in its oil diplomacy on the continent,' says Ian Taylor (2006: 938). In fact, non-interference in other states' sovereignty has been a consistent theme of Chinese foreign policy since the 1950s, based on a feeling that 'human rights should not stand before sovereignty'. Beijing has sought to position itself as a friend to Africa, something of an unofficial 'leader' in the developing world. The 'no strings' policy means that Chinese companies have focused on the 'mercantile perspective' (van Vliet and Magrin 2012: 134); because of this, they are more likely to 'invest in regions left vacant by the Western majors', areas that may be prone to social unrest, ethnic conflict or civil war.

However, these relationships are facing increasing scrutiny: 'The no-questions-asked policy is coming under greater pressure both outside and within Africa' (Taylor 2006: 945). The most obvious example of oil meeting politics was when the 2008 Beijing Olympics was dubbed the 'Genocide Olympics' by activists working on the Darfur crisis, in reference to the CNPC's continued business dealings in Sudan with President Omar al-Bashir as the conflict raged. A US campaign calling on investors to pull out of holdings in Sudan, arguing that international business dealings were helping al-Bashir, succeeded in persuading a number of asset managers, pension funds and institutional investors in the US and Europe to sell their shares in foreign companies operating in Sudan. The CNPC was even forced to keep its Sudan assets out of its listing on the New York Stock Exchange.

Although the CNPC may have felt that it was simply just doing business, it appears to have been stung by the criticism. The negative attention paid to the Olympics led to the appointment of the first ever Chinese Special Envoy for Africa and to Chinese pressure on the Sudanese government to accept the hybrid UN–African Union peacekeeping force in Darfur. Luke Patey has argued that: 'In the face of activist pressure the Chinese government wanted to make a clear, public demonstration of its commitment to helping the international community solve the Darfur civil war' (Patey 2014a: 109). There are now encouraging signs that China is beginning to engage on issues of conflict, human rights and environment, which they have previously appeared to shy away from. With the outbreak of war in South Sudan in late 2013, when production in their Unity State oilfields was threatened by the rebel takeover of Bentiu, the Chinese were at the forefront of attempts to get the parties to negotiate in Addis Ababa.[6] In addition, a senior Chinese official in 2014 admitted off the record that the 'need to keep oil flowing had made the CNPC break the non-interference principle'; CNPC officials went directly to talk to Riek Machar and other rebel leaders to persuade them not to turn off or attack the export pipeline to Port Sudan.

As a journalist working in Chad in 2008–10, I found it extremely difficult to get any kind of comment from the CNPCIC on the start of their work at Djérmaya. Researching a story about the plans for land acquisition and compensation values at the beginning of the construction work, I tried a visit to the company HQ, a letter, follow-up telephone calls and approaches to contacts I had within the company, but I was unable to get anyone to comment. This seems to be in line with other researchers' experiences: 'Compared with the Western majors, Chinese oil firms are still in the learning phase and their public relations departments are taking more of a backseat' (van Vliet and Magrin 2012: 215). Friends of the Earth also report how NGOs struggled to get information from company HQ in Beijing: 'several groups stated that their letters and emails to CNPC went unanswered; some reported that PetroChina replied with statements that it did not have projects in the area of concern' (Matisoff 2012: 29). Speaking to Chadian journalist colleagues about their experiences in contacting the CNPCIC, many of them said it was virtually unheard of to get CNPCIC comment and that the company had only ever held a handful of press conferences.

However, as my successful attempt to visit the Ronier fields in July 2013 proves, this may be changing. Certainly at that point – before the catastrophic breakdown in relations with the Chadian government had become apparent – the company did not seem to be completely against the idea of an open dialogue. It may have been belatedly realising the importance of communicating with the outside world. From informal chats with workers there, and indeed with Dr Dou Lirong, I found a great deal of frustration about the way in which the CNPCIC's work has been portrayed in Western media. Dr Dou repeatedly appeared perplexed about the way in which China's business in Africa is reported in the international media and seemed to want to correct those stereotypes; 'We don't understand why so much of the Western media is so critical of our work here,' he said. Several Chinese workers at Ronier also expressed to me a sense that the company and the Chinese presence in Africa had been demonised, and that journalists did not want to tell the truth. They also seemed to feel victimised in Chad and that there was a general lack of appreciation for what they had achieved in the country. However, from the perspective of a journalist working to tight deadlines and on a limited budget and used to the idea of getting 'all sides of the story', I did find it frustrating that the Chinese managers in N'Djaména seemed extremely nervous about agreeing to anything without getting the permission of their supervisors in Beijing, even if it meant their side of the story never being told.

Local content and wider economic impact

As is the case with other Chinese natural resource projects in Africa, Ronier has been criticised by Chadian civil society for employing only a small proportion of local labour, and for the issue identified in a 2012 Friends of the Earth report into the worldwide activities of the CNPC: 'obvious disparities in pay between local workers and foreign oil workers' (ibid.: 34). A rough estimate at the Ronier base camp would suggest a bias towards Chinese workers, particularly among those wearing the supervisory blue overalls compared with the red overalls that more junior staff wear. Unlike at Komé, where a small town full of hopeful labourers, *'le Quartier qui s'attend'* (The Waiting Neighbourhood) sprung up outside the gates of the Esso base, there has been little mass migration at Ronier – this may be because of the remote location or because people no longer assume that there will be any jobs created. The official employment figure at Ronier is about 850 Chinese and European expats and 980 Chadians. About 100 informal jobs have also been created, such as guarding well heads (the daily salary for this is about US$4), but a number of young Chadians have been lucky enough to secure contracted jobs in which they can learn a trade.

On my travels around the Ronier oilfields, I met contractor Zhiong Tuo, who was training an apprentice, Ahmad, to carry out a procedure known as 'launching the pig'; this involves sending a large rubber bullet through 1,600 metres of pipeline at speed to test its pressure. Zhiong says that Chadians are now able to carry out many routine maintenance tasks like this, but Ahmad is unscrewing the cap on the pressurised pipeline in front of me with no safety goggles or gloves. Later on that day I meet Mahamat Saleh, an enthusiastic young Chadian who was one of the first generation of graduates from the new 'Oil Exploration and Production' technical college that was set up by the Chadian government in the city of Mao. Sixteen graduates have been taken on at Ronier. Wearing bright red overalls and a hard hat, he is supervising a process that injects waste water from the oil production facility into a 1,000 metre deep well, sequestering it away from the water table. 'I want to be able to contribute to my country,' he says, smiling. 'It's a virgin country. There's so much to do here; I want to help.' Nevertheless, Mahamat says that there have been teething problems, such as problems in communication because most of the Chadians speak French but the Chinese international business language is English, but he has been going to evening classes provided by the CNPCIC to try to improve his English. He also thinks the teams from the two nationalities have not always understood each other, although he is quick to stress that the situation is improving.

The CNPCIC does seem to be making efforts to show that it values the Chadian workforce, with initiatives such as 'Chadian employee of the month' where employees are rewarded for good performance. Their photographs are displayed at the entrance to the dining hall and they each receive a certificate. After dinner, I meet Abakar Omar, a transport coordinator, who starts by grumbling about the fact that Chinese food is on offer night after night. He was taken on in 2008 after working for a private transportation company in the capital. He complains about the low wages, but says that he is pleased with the level of responsibility he is given. 'Some of us are doing really critical work here and that is important,' he says. Despite some difficulties and misunderstandings between the Chadians and Chinese at the beginning of the project, he believes that relations with the bosses are now improving. 'No one spoke the same language and there was some frustration and bad relations in the way we dealt with each other,' he says, 'but today we've got more support from bosses. They have been listening.'

On the issue of community relations and CSR, the Friends of the Earth report argues that the Chinese company is still learning the ropes: 'CNPC generally has not paid much attention to voluntary international standards' (ibid.: 26). Certainly, its efforts in Chad were nothing compared with the slick public relations operation of Esso in neighbouring Komé oilfields. But CNPCIC staff were very keen to show me what they had achieved. The Ronier site lies just a few kilometres from the village of Koudalwa, a sprawling, muddy settlement that is home to several thousand people and has grown since the arrival of the oil project. The company has built a football pitch and a school building for the village, although a quick glimpse inside showed a dark, empty room, graffiti on the walls and broken tables. When a village chief finally arrived to greet me, he told me that all the students and teachers were on holiday. The Chinese have also drilled wells for drinking water in the village, and they have engaged on problems such as the increased level of traffic – they have introduced speed limits on all their vehicles travelling through populated areas after a number of accidents. This reflects an overall impression that the company is more inclined today to take these issues seriously, although its engagement seems 'mostly oriented towards philanthropy and public relations, rather than [being] an integral part of core business operations' (ibid.: 14).

As I wander down to Koudalwa's market, a rabble of women with seeds, vegetables and small baskets laid out on raffia bags on the floor, I notice a group of soldiers sitting lazily in the shade. I had also noticed a container building at the gates of the Ronier site, home to the local contingent of the Chadian 'security forces' deployed to protect the oilfields. My Chinese guides beseech me with a smile not to ask questions – they are just here for my protection. The presence of armed men in the village does not stop the attempts by local people to get their opinions out to the wider world; their views are similar to those I have heard in all the oil-producing countries I have visited. 'We don't understand!' says *Chef de Canton* (head of the township) Abangar Basswa, pushing his way through the crowd towards me. 'We live under the nose of the oil project but fuel has become more expensive since it started. Everything the Chinese produce is sent up to N'Djaména and then brought back here on tankers by unscrupulous traders who mark up the price.' Abangar is joined by others who get more and more vocal as they try to express their points of view – they chime with complaints from elsewhere in Africa about the lack of job opportunities, even for those who have good qualifications. The Chadians in this village clearly seem to think that the CNPCIC should be providing some of the services a government would normally provide, such as water, electricity and paved roads. 'There's nothing to eat and prices have gone up here since the Chinese arrived,' complains twenty-year-old Florence Madjidenein, a mother of two. 'The economic activity is good but it still doesn't create any jobs.'

Djérmaya refinery

The jewel in the crown of the deal with the CNPCIC was the promise to build an oil refinery at a dusty desert site near Lake Chad, about 40 kilometres north of the capital N'Djaména. The first stone of the construction was laid in an elaborate ceremony that was held in the midst of the rebel crisis in October 2008, and that the President chose to use as a very public reminder of who was in charge. Arriving two hours late, flanked by about 100 presidential guard soldiers who stood for hours in high temperatures with their weapons pointing out into the wild bush, he leaned on his trademark cane as he made a long and assertive speech about how oil would be the country's future. Gathered around him were Chinese oil executives and specially chosen representatives from civil society groups, who wore CNPC baseball caps and T-shirts and carried banners reading 'We support the indefatigable leading mason of Chad, IDI [Idriss Déby Itno].'

Although there is nothing unusual in oil-producing countries having to import a percentage of their domestic petroleum needs, many Chadians found it hard to accept that after five years of production by Esso, not a drop had found its way into the Chadian economy. One hundred per cent of what is produced in Komé is exported via the Kribi pipeline. Chad had always been reliant on imports from Nigeria or Cameroon, meaning that any local insecurity or supply chain breakdown could lead to disruption of supply or price hikes. This was particularly frustrating for the population as most of Chad's domestic electricity comes from burning diesel fuel in a dilapidated generating station in N'Djaména. The country has some of the most expensive electricity prices in the world (van Vliet and Magrin 2012: 136) and suffers from frequent prolonged power cuts. Although demand is estimated at some 100 megawatts, installed capacity is lagging far behind at just 31 megawatts.[7]

President Déby, ever mindful of securing his own position, seems to have appreciated that Chadians needed a concrete sign of how the advent of oil production had brought benefits to the population, and that sign was cheap petrol. The Djérmaya refinery began production in 2011. It has a capacity of 20,000 bpd for the production of gasoline, diesel, kerosene, polypropylene, liquefied gas and fuel oil. The government has also announced the creation of a business park around the site of the refinery – seemingly in the hope that a new industry in processing petroleum products can spring up – and that gas can be used as a cleaner way of generating power. The Chinese have also promised to connect their own generating station at Djérmaya to Chad's national grid; this is expected to add a further 20 megawatts to the country's capacity, but at the time of writing it had still not been completed.

China and transparency

The concepts of accountability and transparency have been proposed as the 'cure' for the problems caused by the resource curse. We have seen how the so-called 'no strings' deals between China and Africa may challenge that approach by creating an environment in which deals are signed in secret and the precise terms of what a government receives in return for precious natural resource extraction rights are not made public. But what is the practical experience of the CNPCIC's work in Chad?

Civil society groups certainly feel that the arrival of the CNPCIC on the scene has caused monitoring in Chad to experience a setback. 'We need another mechanism to monitor what China is doing,' said Gilbert Maoundonodji from civil society monitoring group GRAMP-TC when I met him at a transparency conference in Chad in July 2013. 'We have no control over what they do and the structures in place from the CCDP do not apply to their work.' The precise terms of the PSA signed between the CNPCIC and the Chadian government in 2006 have never been made public – this seems typical of Chinese oil investments in Africa. Although we know that the CNPCIC paid around US$200 million for EnCana's concessions, there is no easily accessible information about how much the infrastructure promised to Chad is worth in total, nor about whether Chad took out a loan for this construction work. We also know that the projects the Chinese promised to undertake are not covered by the monitoring work of the civil society body the Collège because most of the contracts were simply granted to Chinese companies apparently without an open tendering process. How much they really cost the Chadian economy and whether they represented value for money seems almost impossible to establish.

What is known is that a 'joint venture' was set up between the parties to run the Djérmaya refinery and the pipeline that connects it to Ronier. The CNPCIC and Chad share profits and losses according to the ratio 60:40. The Chadian 40 per cent participation, through the national oil company SHT, is believed to have been funded through a loan from the Chinese Exim Bank.[8] The CNPCIC has ploughed in most of the capital costs for the field, the connecting pipelines and the refinery, but there are few details about how that affects the share of costs and profits, or how much in recoverable costs they can claim before paying any tax.

On the issue of production payments, however, things are a

bit easier. While none of the payments the CNPCIC makes to the government will ever be covered by the revenue management law or pass through the separate escrow account, the company does declare its payments to the EITI reporting team in country, and they have been included in all of the country reports from 2007 onwards. The EITI confirmed that the CNPCIC has been generally helpful in supplying the information it requires. The company is obliged to pay the same taxes and duties as all oil companies, including 50 or 60 per cent corporation tax, surface area fees, a tax on profits, a statistical tax on exports, taxes on personnel and training and a flat fee. The CNPCIC figures are disaggregated from the rest of the IOCs in the EITI report's annex. In 2011, the company paid a total of US$6.47 million to Chad (EITI 2013a), although it is important to note that this figure covers the period before the Djérmaya refinery became operational. For 2012, the first year the refinery was in full production, the total CNPCIC payment to the state had risen to about US$44 million (ibid.), still a relatively modest figure. This is split between about US$9 million in various taxes and US$35 million in royalties on production, but even the EITI team admits that it does not know exactly how the royalty rate on production from Djérmaya is calculated.

The deal unravels

In 2006, Chad's new oil deal with the CNPCIC looked every bit the classic 'win–win' situation – the CNPCIC gets a block known to contain oil in a country eager to get production started, and promises a raft of infrastructure projects in return. But in 2014, eight years after the CNPCIC agreed to build Ronier and Djérmaya, the rose-tinted spectacles have most emphatically been cast aside. The construction work was completed with astonishing speed, but expectations have not been met. There have been a number of high-profile disputes between the company and the government, particularly over environmental concerns. The long-cherished dream of exporting has been fraught with difficulties. Local demand for petroleum products has been disappointing and both Ronier and Djérmaya are being run below capacity.

Without exportation, the Chadian treasury has been unable to benefit from the full raft of export taxes.

The first disagreements related to the refinery. The sale of refined petroleum products began not long after the facility opened its doors in July 2011, but the Chinese quickly realised that they were being marketed at a price that would not cover their overheads. By January 2012, the CNPCIC said that it had lost over US$4 million, but the Chadian authorities refused to allow a price increase, seemingly because of promises made by President Déby that fuel at the pump would become cheaper. While the details of the sale price agreed in the original contracts have never been made public, the price of petrol did in fact drop quite dramatically at first; from around 650 CFA per litre to about 450 CFA per litre. However, by late 2011 it had begun to creep up again. The refinery was closed repeatedly by the government as the discussions over the price turned sour, leading to shortages and petrol queues on the streets. Eventually, after emergency discussions, the refinery reopened in early 2012, but only after the director of the refinery politely left the country and two prominent ministers lost their jobs.

Environmental concerns

Environmental and safety standards have also been a serious source of dispute. There have been many claims that Chinese oil firms operating in Africa will be inclined to adopt lower environmental standards as a 'bargaining chip' to gain access to markets (van Vliet and Magrin 2012: 229). What is the evidence for this in Chad?

The Chinese operations are covered by all of Chad's environmental legislation (explained in Chapter 1), and the CNPCIC is also bound by its own internal practices. The CNPC is committed in principle to 'zero accidents, zero injuries and zero pollution' (ibid.: 166), and, after some terrible industrial accidents in China, the company has been forced to up its game. However, again due to the opaque nature of Chinese investment in Africa, it is difficult to ascertain exactly what standards are being used in

Chad. Magrin and van Vliet, who wrote a comprehensive report on the CNPC's environmental challenges in Chad, argue that it is necessary to talk of a 'composite' policy because they were unable to find out whether Chadian, Chinese or international environmental laws and standards applied to the CNPC's work. The company completed an environmental impact assessment on the Ronier and Djérmaya projects, but the results were not made public until 2010, a year after construction work had actually started. The exercise in community consultation appears to have left a lot to be desired, having consisted of just one day of public consultation on the compensation and resettlement programme. Although the company has adopted compensation rates previously recommended by EnCana, it has been faced with the difficulty of 'adapting an individual or community compensation programme to a complex land tenure system in which the State is the sole landowner, but where local populations enjoy land use rights under customary law' (ibid.: 177). The company was further challenged by the fact that many in the community around Koudalwa knew about the generous and comprehensive system of compensation pledged to villagers in the Doba oil project area.

However, it is the issue of environmental management that has really emerged as the CNPC's Achilles heel. The company's reputation for clean and spill-free operations has already been tarnished in neighbouring Sudan, where it has been accused of a poor approach to the environment. As Luke Patey has revealed:

> The environmental impact of oil development in Sudan is complex, ranging from oil spills to the ecological imprint of road construction ... to 'produced water', which comes to ground along with extracted crude oil and holds toxic concentrations of chemicals and minerals (Patey 2012: 564).

A number of sources in the CNPCIC have continued to raise concerns about the quality of the initial set-up. These sources claim that corners were cut in health and safety policy and the quality of equipment purchased in order to complete the Ronier operation quickly. They feel that often cheap and substandard equipment has been used, equipment that would be considered obsolete by some of the Western oil majors. One technician believed that maintenance and repairs are not carried out at Ronier to the same high standard as at Komé, and commented that 'IOCs only come to Africa because it's cheap and they know they can bypass environmental and safety rules'. An analysis of satellite imagery of the topography around Ronier taken in August 2013 by the École des Mines de Paris suggests a degree of degradation around oil platforms and waste disposal sites. The research concluded that there were areas where mud and drilling waste were not being treated properly, and that land was not being backfilled or rehabilitated to its pre-oil production state: 'There is a worrying perspective that the number of suspect sites is very high' (MINES ParisTech 2012: 31). Although I did not personally see a great deal of disturbance of the natural environment as I was driven around Ronier in July 2013, it may be that the CNPCIC management team had decided to show me only the best parts of their operation.

The true scale of the CNPCIC's inadequate approach to environmental concerns emerged in August 2013 when Chad's Oil Minister, Djerassem Le Bemadjiel, angrily decried what he called 'flagrant violations of environmental standards'[9] by the company at Ronier. A number of spills had been discovered, along with trenches where crude had been dumped without being covered. On a visit to the site, Le Bemadjiel said that local Chadian workers had been asked to remove the crude without protective gear. The response from the Chadian authorities was swift – they immediately suspended the CNPCIC's exploration activities, which were being carried out by a subcontractor, Great Wall Drilling, and ordered an audit by the firm Alex Stewart International of the exploration activities of all the companies operating in Chad. The CNPCIC appears to have been taken aback by the decision. After six years at the helm, the CNPCIC director Dr Dou Lirong was forced to return to China.

Although operations were allowed to resume in October, six months later Chad fined the CNPC an eye-watering US$1.2 billion for 'environmental violations' and called on the company to take steps to repair all damage and future damage caused through pollution from its activities. The Chinese company stalled and tried to negotiate over the fine, which represented about 60 per cent of Chad's oil income for that year, but the Chadians were clearly not satisfied. In late May 2014, announcing further 'environmental issues', they suspended the CNPCIC's work again. Five exploration permits – Bongor East, Bongor West, Chari West, Lake Chad and Mandiago East, covering 67,000 square kilometres – were revoked. The dispute was so serious and the threat to Chinese interests so grave that the director of the CNPC travelled from Beijing to Chad to talk to the President.

The dispute also caused major delays to the CNPCIC's plans to export from Ronier. In July 2013, a team of safety consultants and managers from the CNPCIC set off from base camp to visit villages that were lying in the way of the proposed route for a 150 kilometre pipeline to connect Ronier to the Kribi pipeline head at Komé. They were keen to agree compensation plans with the community based on systems agreed during the initial construction phase of the Ronier–Djérmaya pipeline. It had been a long time coming, but it finally looked as if the CNPCIC might be on the verge of exportation, using a much more efficient route than connecting up with the company's export pipeline in neighbouring South Sudan to Port Sudan, a route that had been under consideration at one point. By April 2014, sources at the CNPCIC confirmed that the pipeline was complete and ready for testing, but the dramatic suspension of the company's activities announced in May threw the Chinese plans into chaos. After threats by Chad to take the CNPCIC to an arbitration court in Paris, the dispute was finally settled in late 2014, with the CNPCIC agreeing to pay US$400 million of the fine and to clear up any damage caused. In December 2014, the first exports of Chinese-produced crude finally began.

The issue of exportation through the Kribi pipeline is particularly interesting because it has highlighted the confusion over whether guarantees for clean oil production established under the CCDP in 2003 still apply. Section 4.1 of the original loan agreement between the World Bank and Chad stipulates that:

> any oil developed outside the Doba Basin Oil Fields which is proposed to be transported through any part of the Transportation System in Chad is developed in accordance with the principles set forth in the EMP [environmental management plan] (van Vliet and Magrin 2012: 180).

In other words, any crude produced from Ronier (or anywhere else) would, technically speaking, need to meet the same standards as the Esso Consortium Doba crude if it were to pass through the pipeline.

It is far from clear whether this adherence to the EMP has been insisted on, or indeed whether Chad is still obliged to stick to the original agreements. It is known that Esso continues to use the EMP as a basis for its own production at Komé, but, after a number of approaches to the company's press offices in Chad and the UK, I was unable to establish whether Esso had insisted on the EMP being followed before they agreed to the CNPCIC joining up with the Kribi pipeline. Simply because it controls the pipeline, Esso is effectively gatekeeper to these standards. It is unclear whether the CNPC's 'composite' approach described by Magrin and van Vliet is good enough; certainly, from the Chadian government's perspective, the CNPCIC is failing. The question goes to the heart of the issue of the longer-term management of the original provisions of the CCDP that were so heralded at its inception. When the World Bank pulled out in 2006, it was not made clear who would be the guarantor of those original commitments to protect Chad's environment and ultimately to restore sites to their natural state at the end of production. One close observer of the World Bank project asks: 'What is the ongoing responsibility of the World Bank to provisions in the EMP, on which they insisted and which they signed, that outlive their direct involvement?'[10] Approaches to the World Bank press office on the matter only generated the response that 'IFC's involvement in the project ended in December 2012 when our loans were repaid'.[11]

What we do know is that the Chadian authorities have been unequivocal about the importance of environmental standards, and will not hesitate to close down an operator if they believe the law is being broken. The Chadian Minister of the Environment has stated that all oil companies must follow the same rules, and Oil Minister Le Bemadjiel, himself with a background in the sector, has repeatedly asserted his position to the CNPCIC. Chad is showing clear ownership and leadership. This is important. The CNPCIC has seen its cherished dream of exporting the Ronier crude repeatedly delayed because of environmental failings, and it now knows that it will not be able to violate environmental laws with impunity. As Géraud Magrin commented in an email: 'It is interesting to see how the Chadian government is now using the environment as a weapon in its power relations with the oil companies.' While the lack of clarity alluded to in this section over exactly which environmental rules are supposedly being violated raises the somewhat cynical possibility that Chad is merely using the environmental card as an excuse to bully the CNPCIC into paying more, it also gives some cause for optimism about the health, safety and environmental standards of any future expansion in the industry. Indeed, it could have an impact on the CNPC operations in Niger if they are ever able to make progress in linking up with the Kribi pipeline in Chad for exportation.

The story took a further fascinating twist in June 2014 when Chad secured a US$1.3 billion loan from the commodities giant Glencore.[12] Glencore has been increasing its activities in the country over the last two years and recently bought up the assets of the Canadian company Caracal (formerly Griffiths), which began exporting about 14,000 bpd from the Mangara and Badila fields near Doba in 2013. The enormous loan from Glencore has allowed Chad to again flex its muscles, providing the finance to buy up Chevron's 25 per cent share from the Esso Consortium's production in Doba; significantly, this will allow the national oil company SHT to play a major role in that project and shows Chad's desire to get its people directly involved in the sector. This deal took international bodies by surprise; the IMF had been on the verge of agreeing a US$122 million loan to the country which now looks like peanuts.

With such a strong hand, there remains a distinct possibility that the Chadian government will continue its pressure on the CNPCIC ahead of presidential elections scheduled for 2016. While few Chadians overtly criticise the Chinese, dig a little deeper and there is widespread antipathy towards the CNPCIC, as many ordinary people blame the company for expensive fuel prices and for not delivering the kind of economic transformation many had hoped for when the deals were first signed. It is even possible that the authorities may have considered confiscating some of the CNPCIC's assets or exploration permits in order to assign them to other investors offering more money. This hypothesis is strengthened by the fact that Oil Minister Djerassem Le Bemadjiel felt it necessary in June 2014 to point out that this was *not* what the government was doing, without the question even being raised. As the risk analysis company IHS put it:

> CNPC's future role in Chad's oil sector is now shrouded in uncertainty ... Relations between the CNPC and Chad have deteriorated to a level where full resolution and return to the status quo looks increasingly unlikely (IHS 2014a).

As exportation from the CNPCIC's wells at Ronier finally got under way in late 2014, it seemed that the relationship between Chad and the CNPCIC had been restored, but characteristically the Chinese company having been pushed to the brink by the Chadian authorities until they got what they desired. It remains to be seen whether this rapprochement between the two sides will hold in the long run.

As an aside, the CNPCIC may also have underestimated the commitment of the 'Environment Champion' Idriss Déby Itno. The President has long promoted his environmental credentials, fighting for a voice on the international stage for a country that is likely to suffer some of the worst excesses of desertification due to climate change. In 2008, he announced an outright ban on charcoal use and production in order to prevent deforestation and desertification with just a few weeks' notice, torching vans carrying charcoal as they approached the market and leaving many families to burn furniture or fruits and seeds when the supply of firewood could not keep up with demand. In 2009, he announced an increase in armed patrols in the country's superb Zakouma National Park in a bid to tackle ivory poaching (which, ironically, was believed to be driven by Chinese traders in Chad and Sudan), and the results have been impressive – WWF reported that twenty-one new elephant calves were sighted in the park in 2013 and that there had been not a single case of poaching since 2011.[13] Déby also signed the country up for an enormous programme of tree planting as part of continent-wide plans for the 'Great Green Wall', although Chadian environmentalists have criticised the simultaneous decision to cut down some of the most beautiful mature trees in N'Djaména.

4 | Resource nationalism in Niger

Local content and revenue sharing

The Sahelian sun is beating down on the dried patch of dust that makes up the garden of Bakin Birji's only restaurant. It's hot even though it's still only February – officially the Sahel's winter, although many people these days blame the erratic weather on climate change. We have just arrived after a 30 kilometre journey that took almost two hours of jolting along potholed, dusty tarmac. The only protection from the burning sun is a ragged garden umbrella. Opposite me sits Abdisalam Bou, a tall, slightly stooped man in his late forties, wearing a golden *boubou*, the traditional dress for men around here. The ravages of the Saharan sun are clear to see on his lined face. He is talking in a low, quick voice to my translator in Hausa, fiddling with a cigarette packet and glancing around nervously.

I have come to Bakin Birji, a village north of the eastern regional capital of Zinder, to meet people living on the frontier of Niger's new oil project. About 10 kilometres away, on land traditionally belonging to some of the residents of this village, the CNPC has built an enormous oil refinery; a shimmering piece of twenty-first-century technology has landed like a spaceship on the hazy Saharan horizon. The spikes and towers of the Soraz refinery are just visible from higher ground on the outskirts of the village, but not a lot of people here have visited it. Bakin Birji remains a ramshackle sort of place with goats and small repair shops spilling out on to the tarmac. The only sign of the changing world appears to be the row of oil tankers, ready to take the refined fuel to regional markets, lined up on the main street beside a row of camels.

Abdisalam is clearly agitated. He heard that a journalist was here to visit and wanted to come to share his experience of working on the CNPC refinery project. 'I had to work twenty-four hours a day guarding an electric water pump,' says Abdisalam angrily. 'If I even left for a few hours to visit my family I would get a phone call saying I had to come back immediately because something had broken.' Abdisalam believes that the CNPC was expecting too much of its workers and did not treat them fairly. He is part of a group of about 800 other former workers who are trying to engage a lawyer to fight their case for unfair dismissal. However, the story becomes confused when Abdisalam offers to show me the documents he has kept since his employment at the Soraz (Société de Raffinage à Zinder or Zinder Refining Society) refinery. Abdisalam claims that he was sacked without notice, but the contract he shows me states clearly in French (with a Mandarin translation) that he had been employed for a fixed term of eight months. Confused, I dig a little deeper and ask him on which date he was 'sacked'. He gives the precise date on the contract. 'Did you not read this before you signed it?' I ask without thinking, not realising that his signature is marked with a thumbprint in ink at the bottom. Apparently no one was able to translate the contract into Hausa for him, or to make sure that he understood exactly what he was agreeing to.

The kind of confusion experienced by Abdisalam seems symptomatic of the experience of many ordinary Nigeriens when it comes to the country's new oil project, and echoes the findings of the Friends of the Earth reports into the CNPC: 'The company does not have a systematic way of addressing public concerns about its overseas projects and engaging with stakeholders' (Matisoff 2012: 30). Later on that day I meet a family of Peul (Fulani) traders who are also trying to get legal redress from the government for what they say is a failure to pay the right compensation for the land they lost when the refinery was built. Chaibou Mohammed tells me that his family was promised new land by representatives of the government who came to visit the village with the CNPC, but so far they have received nothing. Others in the village say that they lost their compensation money when a lawyer who had been fighting their case was jailed for corruption (he was later released, according to local media reports). Chaibou and others believe that, as in Chad, the CNPC's consultation with the community at the beginning of the oil project was not conducted properly and that consistent standards for evaluating land were not applied – for example, they claim that they were never informed of the system of calculating the exact value of a square metre of land. This would appear to be in marked contrast to the intricate system of land and tree values agreed with the help of the World Bank during the early phases of the CCDP. However, Mahaman Laouan Gaya, a former Secretary General at the Nigerien Ministry of Mines, denies that and says that compensation has been provided in a timely manner and according to the relevant laws: 'The government has taken all necessary measures to compensate everyone who had their lands expropriated.'[1]

The local regional council is positive about the impact of oil. It believes that the arrival of the Soraz refinery has changed the face of Zinder from a typically dusty and remote Sahelian frontier town to a modern business destination. In the council's offices, where pristine whitewashed walls have been dirtied by the latest dust deposited by the seasonal Harmattan wind, I meet Abdoul Karim Mohammadu, secretary general of the regional council. 'The refinery has had a real impact on unemployment here, which is one of the biggest problems we face.' As well as jobs directly connected to the refinery, he argues that there has been an explosion of new businesses in the service industries, such as food and drink and vehicle repairs, and that the Chinese owners of the refinery have helped in the provision of local services. 'Gas for cooking is now available, new roads have been built and we have a new health centre.'

The effect on employment certainly seems to be real. Each morning and evening, company buses collect and drop off the 720 or so local Soraz employees in Zinder, most of them returning to the more far-flung neighbourhoods of the rapidly expanding city after twelve-hour shifts. The workers are easy to spot, wearing sky blue overalls and carrying company-issue black backpacks as they walk down the city's wide, sandy streets. There is also ample anecdotal evidence of a knock-on effect on the service industry, with a selection of cheap new hotels, restaurants, car hire and vehicle repair businesses opening up.

The workers at Soraz are allowed to join a union, the National Union for Water and Energy Workers. Despite an ongoing dispute with the Chinese managers about the level of pay many of the Nigerien workers receive – less than their 400-odd Chinese counterparts, according to union representative Boucar Elimi, whom I interviewed in Zinder – they have been able to negotiate for more training, and relations with the management seem to be improving. Elimi says that he has a monthly meeting at which he has been able to raise the issue of the salary discrepancy. He concedes that the CNPC says that the difference in pay is down to the Nigerien workers' lack of experience, a similar argument to that heard in Ronier in Chad.

However, despite the local economy beginning to feel the effects of the Chinese investment, Mr Mohammadu and his colleagues on the council cannot hide their disappointment at the lack of progress on implementing a promise made in the new constitution, which was passed in 2010. This promise was to give 15 per cent of any revenues from natural resources back to the 'producing region'. While this 15 per cent has been awarded to the Agadem region in the eastern state of Diffa – which is where the actual drilling and extraction of the oil that feeds Soraz takes place – Zinder has not received an allocation. The government has argued that housing a refinery does not constitute being a 'producing region', but it may be significant that Agadem, some 450 kilometres away, is a very sparsely populated desert region, mostly home to nomadic groups. Mr Mohammadu tells me that Zinder also suffers disruption and environmental pollution associated with the refinery, but that he believes the government does not want to take on the responsibility of compensating a more heavily populated area.

Political context

Mention Niger and petrol in the same breath and most people outside the country will probably not even know that it is a producer. It is more likely that they will mix it up with neighbouring Nigeria, where the experience of oil, conflict and environmental destruction is seared on the public consciousness. Yet here in one of Africa's most remote corners, 20,000 bpd are being turned from crude oil to petroleum products for sale on local markets and are creating new markets and supply chains across the Sahel from Mali to Burkina Faso.

Niger's oil project was launched by former President Mamadou Tandja when he signed an agreement with the CNPC to develop the eastern Agadem fields in 2007. By 2007, Tandja was becoming an unpopular leader to certain sections of the population, with autocratic tendencies much in the mould of many of Niger's former presidents who had come to power through military coups in the 1980s and 1990s. In 2005 he attracted international opprobrium by appearing to deny that the country was experiencing a famine while thousands faced crippling food shortages, and in 2008–09 the government pushed through an anti-terror law to help deal with a Tuareg rebellion in the north led by the MNJ (Mouvement des Nigériens pour la Justice) and prevented humanitarian agencies and journalists from accessing people displaced by the conflict. When he signed the oil contracts, he may have felt that presiding over the advent of production could go some way to rescuing his failing presidency, but just two years later he would attempt to overturn Niger's constitution to allow himself to stand again for office. Unlike his luckier neighbour Idriss Déby Itno, who had taken the same step in 2006, this decision would end with Tandja's deposition in 2009.

The exploitable concession in the country's east is actually quite small and seems never to have been viewed as significant enough to turn the extremely poor country into a major producer, or to overwhelm its economy. In fact, it looked likely that uranium would continue to be the country's main export. The oil deposits seemed insignificant enough to have been largely overlooked by other international oil companies when global prices were lower; for the CNPC, however, with its proven determination to succeed in projects that few others would dare to attempt, Agadem seemed to offer a golden opportunity to gain a toehold in African oil production. The original setting up of the project was clouded in typical secrecy, and when Niger began production in 2011 it barely caused a ripple on the world stage.

The sole source of crude oil for the Zinder refinery is the CNPC's block at Agadem in the Térmit-Ténéré Basin, 450 kilometres to the east in the even more remote and dusty Diffa region. Current estimates suggest that up to 650 million barrels of oil may be recoverable from there. The CNPC operates three fields in the north of the basin and has recently been awarded a number of new licences. The shape and design of the CNPC facility in Agadem is similar to that of Ronier in Chad, and some of those who work in Niger have also worked in Chad. One of them quipped that the facilities were produced using a 'cookie cutter', saying: 'The only difference is that the Chad project is in lush green countryside and in Niger it's in the desert.'

The Soraz/Agadem project was conceived and constructed at almost the same speed as the Chad project. The refinery opened its doors for production in late 2011. As with Chad, complete details of those original contracts, in particular what the Chinese promised in terms of infrastructure building, are difficult to come by. Although there is a constitutional requirement to publish all natural resource contracts, the CNPC agreements escape because they were signed before the new constitution was passed in 2010. However, there are more details in the public domain of the precise breakdown of what the Chinese are obliged to pay in terms of taxes and royalties on production than is readily available in Chad, although the calculations are quite complicated and difficult to monitor. For example, it is known that the CNPC paid a US$300 million signature bonus and that during the exploration phase at Agadem they were paying a surface rent of 500 CFA (US$1) per square kilometre per year on a total area of 27,000 square kilometres. This went up to 1 million (approximately US$2,000) CFA per square kilometre per year when a discovery was made and production began in the block. As in Chad, the Soraz refinery is governed by a similar 60:40 joint venture between the CNPC and the Nigerien state. Soraz buys the oil extracted at Agadem back from the CNPC at a price of between US\$67 and US\$70 per barrel,[2] and on each of these sales the government takes a 12.5 per cent ad valorem royalty.[3] However, details of how much of the Nigerien government's participating share in Soraz has been funded by Chinese loans, or how much of the infrastructure building promised has been funded by loans, are not available.

Resource nationalism: the issue of the moment

Resource nationalism is currently a very hot topic in Niger. In late 2013, the government began a protracted stand-off with the French nuclear giant Areva over the renegotiation of contracts to operate the country's two important uranium mines, Cominak and Somair, which are located in the extreme north of the country near Arlit. France began exploiting Niger's uranium in the early 1970s, when opaque deals were signed between the former colonial power and post-independence leader Diori Hamani. Throughout that decade, nuclear power became increasingly important to France as it sought to break its dependence on oil after the OPEC oil blockade in 1973, and today France's nuclear security is highly dependent on Niger as its second-largest supplier after Kazakhstan. An often quoted figure is that one in three light bulbs in France is powered by Nigerien uranium (Oxfam 2013).

However, forty years after production started, Nigerien society seems to have woken up to the fact that while France's lights are kept on by Niger's uranium, the exporting country barely has any electricity-generating capacity of its own. Important work by civil society organisations in Niger such as Oxfam and ROTAB (Réseau des Organisations pour la Transparence et l'Analyse Budgétaire) has helped to raise awareness about the perceived injustice in Areva's terms of operation in Niger. 'Niger has not benefited at all from uranium production for forty years. These contracts need to be win–win for Niger and not just for the benefit of France and Areva,' Ali Idrissa, the executive coordinator of ROTAB told me in his office in a dusty outlying suburb of Niamey in early 2014. In a high-profile campaign on the issue, Oxfam France published figures that claimed that Areva's annual global turnover is about four times the size of Niger's entire state budget – some €9 billion compared with about €2 billion (ibid.: 1). But the real test of the fairness of the relationship came with the debate over whether Areva was willing to respect the terms of a new mining code that was introduced by the government in 2006; this required royalties on mining activities to increase to between 12 per cent and 15 per cent of sales. Areva's previous licence had been granted before this new code was passed, and secured the company a royalty rate of about 5 per cent and a number of tax breaks.[4] Areva's objection to the new code during the renegotiation of its operating licence centred on the claim that, with world uranium prices falling below US$40 per pound in 2014, any increase in royalties would have made the operation unsustainable.

As the contract renegotiations gathered pace, production was halted briefly at the two mines at the end of 2013, although Areva said at the time that this was for maintenance purposes. This led to a 10 per cent drop in production in the first quarter of 2014, but the government held its ground. When the issue was finally resolved in May 2014, a government communiqué claimed that Areva had agreed to the terms of the 2006 code, but did not specify the precise royalty rate; up until the time of writing, the government has failed to make the new contract available for public scrutiny. In addition to apparently agreeing to the code, Areva promised to spend US$123 million improving the road to its Arlit mines and US$17 million on a local development project and to appoint local managers to both its mines. However, it was agreed that plans to open the company's new Imouraren mine – which, when it comes into production, will be the world's second-largest uranium mine – would be put on hold until the world uranium price recovered from its current low. This is a blow to the government, which has been hoping to use progress on Imouraren as a sign of its successful economic development policy.

The story took a depressing twist in July 2014 when the French president François Hollande paid a courtesy call to Niamey to thank the government for supporting the French military policy in the Sahel. After fighting a broadly successful campaign to chase AQIM and Mujao (Movement for Unity and Jihad in West Africa) Islamist militants from northern Mali, France announced in 2014 that it would increase its military presence across the region, opening or expanding bases in Niger, Burkina Faso, Chad, Mali and Mauritania. (The US also announced plans to open a second base for surveillance drones in Niger.) Ali Idrissa from ROTAB and a number of other transparency campaigners, including Solli Ramatou (see below), decided to use the occasion of Mr Hollande's arrival in Niamey to organise a protest march calling for the terms of the new contract with Areva to be disclosed, saying that the failure to publish was in contravention of the country's 2010 constitution (see below). The Nigerien government's response was the disappointing decision, condemned by the world secretariat of PWYP in London, to round up about ten activists and detain them for the duration of the visit.[5] Ali Idrissa was detained for several days and threatened with being charged with organising an illegal protest. Despite this, he remained unrepentant: 'We expect the government to publish emergency new agreements and amendments thereto, specifying the legal, financial, fiscal, economic, administrative and customs requirements, in accordance with the constitution.'

The uranium issue has proved a catalyst for greater public awareness of the importance of getting a good deal for the production and extraction of Niger's natural resources as a way of tackling poverty. Numerous civil society marches calling for Areva to respect the mining code took place in Arlit, Agadez and Niamey in early 2014, and the airwaves and local press were alive with debates on the issue. There was outrage in some sections of the press over the ROTAB arrests. Given how repressive politics were under the regime of former President Tandja and of military rulers before him, this is a remarkable achievement for Nigerien civil society. 'When you think that just ten years ago it was taboo to even discuss uranium, to have citizens publicly demanding and demonstrating for fiscal justice is testament to how much things have changed. The next challenge civil society in Niger has taken on is oil,' says Alice Powell from the PWYP secretariat in London.

In this arena, public consciousness of the resource nationalism question has coalesced around the issue of the price of fuel at the pump. In a very similar deal to the one in Chad, the CNPC agreed to build the Soraz refinery and start local production of fuel before looking at exportation options. Because of this, many Nigeriens expected that there would be a significant reduction in the price of fuel. In Zinder, campaigner Sadat Ilya believes that this is the crucial issue. 'Resource sovereignty for us revolves completely around our security of fuel,' he told me, jabbing his finger at me as we shared a gut-wrenching Tuareg tea in a tent flapping with a blast of hot Harmattan wind on the outskirts of the city. Despite ample evidence from other countries (including Chad) that refining is not a particularly profitable business and that many oil-producing countries are obliged to import a portion of their domestic fuel needs, a small crowd of colleagues from his NGO who had joined us nodded approvingly as he asked: 'Why should we pay more for fuel which belongs to us?'

It was fascinating to see how many local people wondered why the Nigerien government had not been able to stand up to the CNPC and to try to push the price down, as happened in Chad. Some, such as Saidou Arji from the PWYP coalition in Niamey, even commented that the Nigerien government did not appear to have the 'chutzpah' of President Déby; Saidou believed that Déby was justified in calling the CNPC's bluff on fuel prices.

The figures are hotly disputed, especially as the price has changed several times since the refinery opened, but in May 2014 fuel cost 538 CFA (US$1.13) per litre and was slightly cheaper than similarly produced Chinese fuel in Chad. Sadat Ilya tells me that, despite the government's promises, this price is in fact higher than it was pre-CNPC. According to Mahaman Laouan Gaya, however, the current price is lower than it was in 2012, when it was 697 CFA ($1.47) per litre, and that figure included a hefty state subsidy of 30 billion CFA (US$63.3 million) a year that has since been abolished. 'We actually have the cheapest fuel of any country in the UEMOA [West African Economic and Monetary Union],' contends Gaya.

Whatever the price finally settles at, many Nigeriens are clearly unwilling to pay it at official filling stations – and nor do they have to. Remarkably, in the Zinder region, living under the shadow of the Soraz refinery, smuggled fuel is for sale everywhere at about 380 CFA (US$0.80) per litre. This is one of the reasons why projected local demand has been so low – the refinery can produce 20,000 bpd, but, because smuggled fuel is so widely available, only about 7,000 bpd are being sold inside Niger and demand does not appear to be growing. The surplus is being exported to West African neighbours such as Mali and Burkina Faso. Even at Bakin Birji, just 10 kilometres from the refinery, street hawkers sell illegal fuel in old whisky bottles from rickety wooden tables set up literally in the shade of the oil tankers waiting to be filled with the 'official' fuel. Some of the fuel has been smuggled directly from refineries over the border in Nigeria, and, according to local journalists, some of it is Soraz fuel that has been exported tax-free into Nigeria and then reimported and sold at a cheaper price by unscrupulous businessmen. While the purity of this fuel cannot be guaranteed, and some prefer not to put it in their cars, the proliferation of hawkers attests to its popularity.

Niger's experience with the refinery and the project's seeming inability to deliver cheap local fuel are indicative of the reservations some economists, such as Paul Collier, have about oil refineries. Certainly, the case of Soraz provides an interesting point of comparison for Uganda, which is currently pushing for a refinery to be built as the first step of its plans to develop the oil industry (see Chapter 5). For Mahaman Laouan Gaya, the former Secretary General at the Ministry of Mines, Soraz was a mistake. 'The error we made was to insist on the refinery first,' he says. 'We still can't even pay off the loan [for the facility], and exportation is where the real money lies.' Mr Gaya believes that the refinery was more a matter of pride for former President Tandja, who he believes viewed it as a symbol of nationalism: 'It was political; we wanted our independence first.' I couldn't help asking Mr Gaya why he thought the Chinese – and, in fact, the Nigerien government – tolerated such a blatant act of rebellion as illegal fuel being sold literally outside the refinery gates. 'Niger is in debt to the Chinese for the building of this refinery. So as long as Niger continues to repay the debt, the Chinese don't actually care whether the fuel is being sold locally,' he replied laconically.

Civil society and journalism

The evening call to prayer is sounding in the dusty courtyard of the ORTN (Office of Radio and Television of Niger), the state broadcasting company, which has a regional office in Zinder. Lawail Babalé, a journalist working for the station whom I have come to meet, is washing his face and hands from a green plastic kettle, carefully moving his long white *boubou* out of the dirt. The first sliver of a crescent moon has appeared on the deep blue horizon, and I watch it quietly rising across the night sky as I wait for Lawail to return from the mosque.

In his office, a single 40 watt light bulb swings on an exposed cable; on his desk is a dusty PC and a pile of papers that looks as if it hasn't been moved since the invention of the printing press. A small generator gurgles outside the window and I wonder absently how they manage to get a radio programme on air with that racket constantly going on. Lawail knows the script: 'You see how we haven't even got any electricity when Areva is taking all our uranium to benefit France?' He complains like many before him about the cost of fuel, but becomes animated when I ask him what he thinks oil can do for his city. 'Zinder is really moving today. People who had the initiative to set up new businesses before it started have really benefited,' he says enthusiastically. Lawail has heard about the battles over the petrol price in neighbouring Chad and he thinks the Nigerien government could be tougher. He tells me he would like to do a special feature report on the economic development of the town since the arrival of Soraz.

Niger's journalists are a courageous bunch and they have been enjoying an unprecedented period of freedom since the new constitution of 2010, brought in by the transitional military junta, decriminalised abuses of journalism such as defamation and publishing erroneous information, making these civil offences punishable by fines. Before then, Niger was known for its repressive attitude to journalists – and to wider civil society – symbolised in cases such as that of RFI's Moussa Kaka, who was jailed under the Tandja regime for making contact with the former Tuareg rebel group the MNJ. Today, journalists are beginning to feel confident enough to take on the issue of natural resources, interviewing civil society groups such as ROTAB and organising debates on the issues. While the country's low literacy levels mean that newspapers have extremely low circulations (sometimes fewer than 2,000 copies a day), most ordinary people listen to the radio and the country has over twenty private radio stations and more than 100 community radio stations.

However, the years of repression and a lack of reliable funding and professional training have taken their toll. As in Chad, Niger's journalists have been slow to develop their own sense of what their job should be about; very few journalists are able to make a proper living from their wages and are therefore open to bribes or want to cover only those stories for which they are paid. 'It's a really great story, but I haven't seen any reports by local journalists on the issue of the price of fuel or the fuel smuggling over the border,' says Lawail. He thinks the problem is a lack of initiative. 'Civil society have tried to interest them in the story about Zinder not receiving the 15 per cent of its supposed share of the national revenue; they've offered research and interview opportunities but so far no one is biting.' I gently push him on the issue of why he himself has not reported on the story, and he just smiles apologetically and gestures vaguely towards the broken equipment on his desk.

Reuters correspondent Abdoulaye Massalatchi says the job of a journalist in Niger is hard but blames the government and the CNPC for not being more transparent:

> In the whole time that I've been reporting on oil I can only remember one occasion when the CNPC called a press

conference. It was after there had been rioting in the Diffa region when young people were protesting about lack of jobs.

He believes that the lack of professionalism and training among Nigerien journalists means that either they are scared to challenge big companies such as the CNPC, or they simply do not have the knowledge or education to understand the issues. 'Even if we are able to get a minister or official on the phone, they never tell us anything useful. Or they don't know themselves!' he laughs.

One of the biggest challenges for journalists in places such as Niger and Chad is an average salary that is sometimes no more than US$100 a month. Journalists regularly expect to be paid to turn up to press conferences and would rarely consider paying US$100 a day to hire a vehicle to travel to oil-producing areas for on-the-ground reporting when often they do not have the contacts or access to get anything useful for a report. The financial constraints also apply to international journalists, but it unfortunately seems easier for them to approach companies such as the CNPC for interviews, or to gain access to government officials. Like anywhere else in the world, Nigerien newspapers and radio stations can be influenced by owners, and editors seem unlikely to want to take the risk of letting a journalist work on a big investigation for several days if nothing comes of it. This is in contrast to Ghana (see Chapter 5), where journalists such as the award-winning Kwaku Owusu Peprah from Joy FM are paid a proper salary, and have access to a car and an expenses system for their work. In addition, Kwaku told me that his editor positively encourages him to go out and find the oil stories. Another issue for many journalists in Niger is training. Although there is a good journalism training school in Niamey, IFTIC, which attracts students from across West Africa, many of those working for Nigerien radio and newspapers have not studied journalism. So far, there has not been the same focus on giving journalists specific training on resource extraction and gas and oil as seen in Ghana. None of the journalists I spoke to said that they have been invited on an 'extractives' training course, but both Abdoulaye and Lawail agreed that they would be personally very interested in taking part in such a course. While the profession remains so chronically underfunded and training at such low levels, it seems it will be some time before Niger's journalists develop the skills to produce ground-breaking reports on the country's new oil industry.

In a similar fashion, civil society in Niger is also still finding its feet after years of military rule from independence until the 2000s. 'Civil society in Niger has operated under very difficult circumstances and for many years was subjected to intimidations and harassment for their work on natural resource transparency,' says Alice Powell from PWYP. The arrest of transparency activists in July 2014 shows quite clearly how fragile new-found freedoms to campaign on natural resources are. Although the government of Mahamadou Issoufou, elected after the military junta the Supreme Council for the Restoration of Democracy stepped aside in 2011, began its term by promising more open and democratic government, dramatic moves against prominent opposition figures[6] have shown that the country still has a way to go to put dictatorship behind it. Compared with the explosion in civil society and campaign groups working on extractives in countries such as Ghana and Uganda, Niger has only a handful of active local groups – ROTAB, PWYP and GREN (Deliberative Group on Extractives in Niger), led by the formidable trade union activist Solli Ramatou, who was one of the activists briefly detained during President Hollande's visit. These groups are all small, underfunded and in many cases run by volunteers. Civil society activism in Niger has not attracted the same kind of international spotlight or support as groups in nearby Ghana.

Contracts and revenue transparency

Tapping into the trends of resource nationalism that have been slowly sweeping across Africa in the last ten years, promoted by academics and campaign groups, Niger has made some impressive commitments towards transparency, at least on paper.

When Colonel Salou Djibou and his Supreme Council for the

Restoration of Democracy led a military coup in 2009 against former President Mamadou Tandja because of his unpopular attempt
to change the constitution, many Nigeriens openly cheered them.
International players found themselves obliged to condemn the
soldiers, but many ordinary Nigeriens' faith in the Supreme Council was repaid when free and fair elections took place just a year
later. But the Supreme Council's actions did not end there. One
of the many important steps it took during its brief tenure was to
oversee a referendum on a new constitution, which was approved
by a 90 per cent majority in October 2010. Among many important
provisions, article 150 of the constitution stated that natural resource contracts must be published, as well as national resource
revenues on a disaggregated, company-by-company basis. The new
constitution also outlined the setting up of a Future Generations
Fund and other measures to promote the transparent management
of natural resource revenues. Much of the focus on transparency
was encouraged by the interim President Marou Amadou, who had
served as a long-term member of Niger's PWYP coalition (and is
now the government's official spokesperson). Taken together, the
NRGI described these new measures as 'extraordinary', and there
was much optimism that Niger was beginning its journey on the
path towards natural resource extraction on the right footing.

Niger is also in the EITI and has been compliant since 2011.
The most recent report for 2011 was published in early 2014 and
gives a clear breakdown of what the country earned that year
from all natural resource extractions – about 53 billion CFA or
US$112 million. Most of this comprised royalties on mining, as
the report does not cover production from the Soraz refinery,
which opened only in November 2011. Unofficial figures for the
first oil-producing year of 2012 (which have yet to be verified by
the EITI) suggest that Niger has earned about US$39 million in
royalties from the CNPC through the sale of about 4 million
barrels of oil produced at Agadem for the Soraz refinery under
the terms of the agreement outlined above.[7] Commenting on the
2011 figures, EITI communications manager in Niamey, Boubacar
Soumaré, told me in an interview that the discrepancies between

the government and company declarations are quite small at around US$2 million (or 2 per cent of the total). The 2011 EITI figures also reveal that, although natural resource extraction in Niger (principally gold and uranium) makes up over 70 per cent of the country's exports, the entire sector contributed only 5.8 per cent of total GDP. The rest of the country's GDP is made up mostly of international aid money and agriculture. This low figure for extractive industry earnings clearly shows that, while the sums earned are significant, they are far from being transformative. As Boubacar Soumaré puts it: 'We need to develop our extractive industries so that there is a bigger cake to divide up, and the cake needs to be better shared.'

So Niger has made some reasonable steps towards making constitutional commitments to transparency over what it is earning, but how does it fare when it comes to ensuring that these revenues are used transparently for development? The constitution makes the important point that Nigerien natural resources belong to the Nigerien people, and articles 152 and 153 outline priority sectors for spending: agriculture, livestock rearing, health and education. However, the document stipulates only that natural resource revenues should go directly into the government's general budget and makes no provision for a special separate holding fund (as seen in Ghana and Chad). There is nothing in the constitution to suggest the setting up of an official civil society monitoring group similar to the Collège in Chad or the Public Interest and Accountability Committee in Ghana to ensure that the government does what it says it is going to do, nor is there mention of a 'stabilisation fund' to weather the country against future volatility in the world oil price. Further commitments are made, however, to insisting that Nigerien nationals are chosen for employment opportunities.

Slow progress

Despite these good commitments, implementation has been disappointing so far. Yet again we are faced with the question of how far legislation can go in delivering development goals and promoting transparency without the political will to back it up. Civil society has already noted a number of violations of the law. Through analysis of the 2012 budget proposal, ROTAB noticed that the government was planning to allocate only about 14 per cent of the national budget to education as a 'priority sector', while they had previously pledged to allocate 25 per cent.[8] At the time of writing, there has been no movement on the proposal to set up a Future Generations Fund, and the contracts agreeing the terms for the second round of exploration licences for the future development of Agadem – awarded to the CNPC in late 2013 and therefore clearly covered by the transparency clause in article 150 – have yet to be published in the government's official journal. Much to the disappointment of civil society campaigners, the details of the new contract signed with Areva in May 2014 governing the Arlit uranium mines have still not been published, and the decision to arrest transparency activists planning a protest on the issue to coincide with François Hollande's visit sent a chill through civil society in Niger. Of particular concern for members of PWYP was the fact that former star transparency campaigner Marou Amadou – now the government's official spokesman – made no public comment on the arrests. Groups such as ROTAB currently only have the government's word that the terms of the 2006 mining code have been respected by Areva, and very little leverage to scrutinise new contracts signed in the oil industry.

Perhaps more worryingly, there is evidence that instead of rebalancing the national budget in favour of the four priorities identified in the constitution, the country has in fact diverted money to military spending. Niger has faced a growing threat from Islamic extremism in recent years because of its proximity to Mali, which was torn apart by Islamist and Tuareg rebels following a coup in March 2012. Niger has made its opposition to terror clear and has allowed the US and France to set up new military bases on its territory, but that appears to have inflamed some of the Islamist groups. In May 2013, the country was hit by a twin suicide bombing at the uranium mine in Arlit and at a military barracks in Agadez, in which over twenty people died; the attack was claimed by the AQIM renegade Mokhtar Belmokhtar, who specifically cited Niger's support for the French Operation Serval in Mali as the reason for the attacks. A number of workers from Arlit have been kidnapped and held hostage by AQIM-linked groups in recent years. In response, Niger's President Issoufou has made an international name for himself by denouncing terror and promising the country's support in Mali and against Boko Haram in Nigeria. Some have argued that this has been at the expense of other national priorities. In this context, the country's military budget quadrupled between 2009 and 2013; although it is still relatively small at US$200 million,[9] there is much concern, even from one source at the heart of government, that this means money is not being spent on schools and hospitals. 'Terrorism is only one problem among many,' says counterterrorism expert Sergei Boeke. 'Niger seems to be militarising the state and we know from counterterrorist approaches in other places that it doesn't always work.' Saidou Arji from PWYP agrees that it is hard to get development on the agenda: 'It seems that there is a lack of political will. The government seems to be focusing on other priorities and natural resource transparency and sector allocation is not one of them.'

Future success

Niger has taken important strides in recent years to assert sovereignty over its natural resources, and the dispute with Areva over the uranium royalties goes to show how resource nationalism is becoming a crucial topic for many ordinary people. Nevertheless, if the country is really to see dramatic benefits from oil, it needs to find a workable means to export that oil. Production from the Soraz refinery is unlikely to increase much in the short term as long as cheaper smuggled fuel is meeting domestic demand. The government and the CNPC believe that an estimated 1 billion barrels of oil exist in the new Agadem 2 block; if this is exported, the country's daily production could increase from 20,000 bpd to between 60,000 and 80,000 bpd, possibly bringing a windfall in revenues for the country. Exploration continues, with the CNPC also looking for oil in the northern Bilma block in partnership with Canadian TVI Pacific's TG World, and the Algerian company Sonatrach prospecting in the nearby Kaffra block.

Being a landlocked country almost in the centre of West Africa's landmass makes any plans for exportation complicated and inevitably costly for Niger, but the country is hopeful that it can benefit from the CNPC'S existing oil infrastructure in neighbouring Chad. In July 2012, Niger's Oil Minister Foumakoye Gado signed a memorandum of understanding with his Chadian counterpart to build an extension to the Chad–Cameroon pipeline to allow exportation from the Agadem field. In late 2013, a confident President Issoufou announced that exports of oil could begin as soon as 2016 and Cameroon agreed to allow exportation through its section of the Kribi pipeline and offshore terminal. The proposed route would run from Agadem over the border into Chad and would then link up with the existing CNPCIC infrastructure at Djérmaya, a distance of about 400 kilometres (see Map 3.1). Nigerien oil can then travel south through the pipeline from Djérmaya to the oilfields at Ronier, and hopefully through the new pipeline that connects Ronier to the Esso Komé fields and the Kribi exportation pipeline. This route has the added advantage of avoiding Nigeria, where the potential for attacks and bunkering on a pipeline running through Boko Haram's heartland could be high. However, as explained in Chapter 3, this project has been delayed because of the dispute between the CNPCIC and the Chadian government.

Mahaman Laouan Gaya also wonders whether this really is the best option. 'The Kribi pipeline has a top capacity of 250,000 bpd,' he says. 'Esso are already sending 100,000 bpd along this route, and if the CNPC in Chad add another 60,000 bpd that only allows us a maximum export capacity of 90,000 bpd.' Knowing the difficulties between Chad and the CNPCIC, he and other analysts wonder whether the Nigerien government should also revive plans drawn up under the Tandja regime to build another export pipeline that would run the breadth of Niger's territory, across the border to Benin, and out to sea at Cotonou. There are currently no plans to develop this route.

It is still very early days for Niger's oil production – it is only just three years old. In 2012, the first year that Soraz was operational, the country earned just US$39 million in royalty payments on Agadem production, and it is still paying the CNPC back for the initial infrastructure loan. Even with future additional tax payments added, this is clearly a sum not yet sufficient to make serious dents in poverty and development indicators and is certainly not going to be a decisive factor in any economic boom for the time being. Niger remains almost at the bottom of the UN's Human Development Index, ranked alongside the Democratic Republic of Congo. Life expectancy is just fifty-five years, the mean years of schooling for adults is 1.4 years, and 43 per cent of the population live on less than a dollar a day. The country encounters severe food crises every few years, the most recent being in 2012 when some 5 million people were judged to be at risk of hunger.

Nevertheless, important steps have been taken in the country's prospective approach to transparency and accountability, with clear commitments to publishing contracts, following the EITI and investing in the future. The experience of the protracted battle with Areva over the royalty paid for uranium extraction shows that the country's civil society and population at large are beginning to engage seriously on the issue. 'It is in these early stages that crucial decisions are made which can set extraction on a certain path,' says Alice Powell from PWYP. While some of the anti-democratic moves of the current government signal that the country may still have a way to go to put its history of repression behind it, the kernel of transparency and accountability has been sown. The constitution clearly states that natural resource revenues should be used for development, and there is some hope that expansion of the Chinese project in the east will have a knock-on effect on the alleviation of poverty.

Assessing China's success

When the CNPC landed two significant oil deals in the Sahel in 2006, it may have seemed that the company was on an unstoppable trajectory to success. The CNPC had significant production

experience behind it in Sudan and now had the prospect of ac-
quiring more licences in Chad and Niger and joining up the
two projects to allow for exportation. The 'no strings' contracts
discussed earlier promised infrastructure development with no
political interference, but only if Chinese companies were allowed
to do the work. No equivalent monetary value was assigned to
the promises. The absolute secrecy that surrounded the signing
of the contracts suggested that the Chinese companies may have
been getting a very good deal. Much of the narrative on China
and Africa in academia and the media over the last ten years has
portrayed the relationship between African countries and Chinese
businesses as one of 'exploitation' or 'neo-colonialism', suggesting
that China was really the only winner in the so-called 'win–win'
deals. For example, Ian Taylor argues: 'By closely engaging with
oppressive regimes and turning a blind eye to abuses, China is
in danger of being associated in the local population's eyes with
subjugation and exploitation' (Taylor 2006: 955). Back in 2006 it
may have seemed that Chad and Niger would fit neatly into that
reading, being desperately poor countries with little power to fight
back against China's growing appetite for oil and the seemingly
unfair deals with which they were being presented.

However, eight years after contracts were first signed, that
analysis may look simplistic. China's oil industry in the Sahel
has sprung up with astonishing speed, but, as I have noted in
the last two chapters, the results have been disappointing, particularly for the CNPC, which has struggled to start exportation
from either Chad or Niger. In the short term, the promises to
build refineries may have looked relatively easy to deliver, while
the CNPC kept its eye on the greater prize of exportation. But
if this is all the CNPC has to show after ten years, the financial
sense of the projects must surely be questioned at some point.
The CNPC seems to have met its match in Idriss Déby Itno,
whose insistence on high environmental standards appears to
have confounded the company's Beijing bosses and has led to
a highly damaging disruption in production. Although Niger's
government has been much less pugnacious in its approach to

the Chinese, the oil project there is still far too small to make any kind of dent in China's overall need for energy security. If the CNPC thought that oil production in Africa was going to be an easy 'no strings' affair, the Sahelian experience has surely taught the company a painful lesson.

5 | Civil society power in Ghana

'I always remember the first time I did a report on oil,' laughs Kwaku Owusu Peprah, a young journalist in Sekondi-Takoradi, Ghana's 'oil city'. 'It was just after they announced the find. My editor wanted me to go and see what was happening. Honestly, we thought I'd be able to see the oil rigs. I had no idea how far offshore the site was.' We are sitting in one of Sekondi-Takoradi's plushest new venues; a nod to the increasing number of expatriates who are coming here to work in the oil industry, CoffeeCorner is run by a young Dutch couple who wanted to offer the perfect Sunday brunch experience. Kwaku and I stare at the long menu of different coffees and breakfast deli muffins. 'What's the difference between a cappuccino and a latte?' he asks me, grinning. 'You know, Ghanaians generally just drink Nescafé with powdered milk!'

Kwaku is a radio and video journalist for Joy FM, one of Ghana's biggest and most popular private radio stations. He is one of the station's rising stars, winning the Ghana Journalists Association 'Journalist of the Year' award in 2010 for his reporting from Sekondi-Takoradi. He tells me more about his experience writing on oil. 'It was the first big story I'd been asked to do back in 2007. The road to south-west of Takoradi was blocked so my editor told me to hire a canoe and sail out on to the sea to get a look at the oil production facility. We went for about four miles on rough waters before we decided it was too dangerous,' he says. 'Honestly, we just thought the oil platform was there – no one realised it hadn't been built yet. Even the chief in the village closest to the site didn't know what was going on. He said he wanted to meet the President! Looking back on it, it was very funny. None of us had a clue about the oil industry!'

The picture is very different today. Pick up a copy of any major

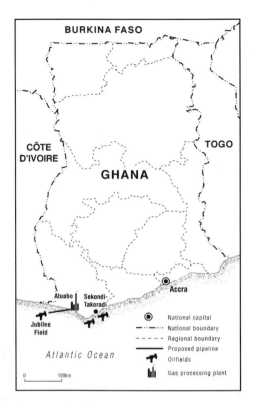

Map 5.1 Ghana's oil and gas production

newspaper in Ghana or turn on the radio and you're likely to hear some kind of discussion on oil – whether it's a reported new find, a debate on the economic impact or a pressure group calling for greater transparency. Citizen power is alive and well in Ghana and young journalists such as Kwaku are at the heart of public education on the issue. While Kwaku does not play down the difficulties he faced in the early days – from grasping the complexities of oil production to establishing reliable contacts at Tullow Oil (the UK company that is the main operator at Ghana's Jubilee oilfields) and the Ghana National Petroleum Corporation (GNPC) who would be willing to answer questions rather than just broadcast at stage-managed press conferences – it is still very refreshing to compare Ghana to Chad, where journalists are harassed by the authorities and face enormous obstacles

Civil society in Ghana

to their ability to travel to the oil-producing areas to carry out investigative reporting.

There has been a determined effort to organise special training courses on oil for journalists, with a view to increasing the quantity and quality of nuanced reporting on the issue. An introductory book for journalists, *Covering Oil*, has been published by the Open Society. This is a helpful resource, looking at aspects of the industry such as contractual arrangements, the nature of IOCs, environmental problems and the various systems for ensuring transparent revenue management and social development and is used on the courses. 'The challenge we have today is to keep the interest up even when the issue seems less important to the general public,' says Kwami Ahiabenu II, from PenPlusBytes, the International Institute for Information and Communication Technologies Journalism, one of the organisations that works with the Open Society West Africa and Revenue Watch to run the training courses for journalists:

> Now people realise that oil is only a small part of our economy the excitement is starting to fade, but that doesn't mean they should stop caring. The issue now is making sure that the law is followed to the letter. We can't rest on our laurels about transparency in new contracts and deals.

His team is most proud of a report by Joy FM's Israel Laryea, one of their trainees, which broke the story that civil society oil-monitoring groups believed that the flow meters on the offshore floating production storage and off-loading (FPSO) facility at the Jubilee field were not working properly – which had the potential to affect the measurements of how much oil Ghana was receiving. While some of the training courses have been criticised for focusing too much on the technical and engineering side of oil production, by and large journalists such as Kwaku think that they have helped Ghana's media enormously. 'I've seen a change in the way editors at base commission stories,' he says:

> They encourage us to go back to stories months later to see if

there has been a change. The number one priority is to make the news, to always think about how oil would affect ordinary people's lives. My editor gets it – he's always asking me: 'How do I get my mother in Kumasi to understand that this story affects her?'

Any journalistic visitor to Ghana cannot help but be impressed by the sheer number of civil society and pressure groups working on oil. NRGI has its regional Africa office in Accra, and PWYP is a strong and dedicated network of NGOs. Independent think tanks such as the IMANI Institute and the Africa Centre for Energy Policy (ACEP) carry out original research and publish reports on the topics associated with transparency and accountability, and hundreds of Ghanaians are on GOXI, the Facebook of the extractive industries world. Oxfam America has been instrumental in setting up the Civil Society Platform on Oil and Gas, which holds debates and conferences and provides training and information in order for local groups to hire an 'extractives person'. Oxfam has also worked towards setting up monitoring mechanisms to encourage civil society to follow up on environmental impact assessments and the efficiency of government spending. 'Civil society has become key in shaping things,' says Richard Hato-Kuevor, Oxfam's local Extractive Industries Advocacy Officer. In some ways it may even be that Ghanaians are finding that, as the darlings of the transparency world, the demands on their time are becoming burdensome; I found it harder to meet activists and campaign groups there than in any of the other countries I visited.

Ghana's black gold

Great excitement and optimism surrounded the discovery in June 2007 of about 600 million barrels of oil reserves in the Jubilee field. The oilfield straddles the boundary between two blocks, Deepwater Tano and West Cape Three Points, about 60 kilometres offshore in Ghana's south-westerly coastal region. This amount was significantly more than initial predictions that the field might contain only around 250 million barrels. The day after

131

the discovery, then President John Kufour told the BBC: 'We're going to really zoom, accelerate, and if everything works, which I pray will happen positively, you come back in five years, and you'll see that Ghana truly is the African tiger, in economic terms for development.'[1] Champagne corks were popped at Osu Castle, the seat of government, and the President dismissed the dangers posed by the so-called resource curse that seemed to have plagued its West African neighbour Nigeria and other African countries. 'Some are doing it well and I assure you if others failed, Ghana will succeed because this is our destiny to set the good pace for where we are. So we're going to use it well,' he said.

Progress on developing the field was relatively fast, and Ghana's oil production came on stream in 2010 when President John Atta Mills turned on the taps in a ceremony that was a little more toned down than the euphoria of the first discovery. Today, all of Ghana's production is offshore, with the Jubilee field served by an FPSO that has a capacity of 120,000 bpd. The UK's Tullow Oil is the operating partner in a consortium that includes the US companies Kosmos and Anadarko, and, as stipulated by law, the GNPC has a 10 per cent stake. The field began by producing about 55,000 bpd, which increased to around 105,000 bpd by the end of 2013. A development plan for later discoveries in the nearby Tweneboa, Enyenra and Ntomme (TEN) offshore field has been approved by the government, and it is hoped that the new stream of production will begin in 2015–16, yielding another 80,000 bpd according to Tullow Oil.

Ghana is no stranger to grappling with the paradox that natural mineral endowments may not produce the kind of wealth and development that might be expected. The country is a long-established gold producer, second only to South Africa on the African continent, exporting about 89 tonnes a year.[2] This makes up a large part of Ghana's natural resource exports, earning the country about US$4 billion in revenues each year. It also produces bauxite, manganese and diamonds. Gold mining is mostly concentrated in the Western region and the Wassa West district around the town of Tarkwa, where thousands of artisanal miners eke out a living by working tiny plots of land with their hands. There are also several large commercial pits such as the Iduapriem pit near Tarkwa, which is owned and operated by AngloGold Ashanti and employs about 1,500 Ghanaians.

Gold has been known about in the Western region for hundreds of years, but, since production was ramped up in the 1980s, some of the phenomena of what might today be identified as the resource curse have occurred. In particular, a number of reports have described environmental damage, expropriation of land and industrial conflicts between the artisanal miners (or 'galamsey') and the larger companies. One 2010 Oxfam report details how the official gold industry offers low wages and few opportunities for employment for unskilled labour (Yankson 2010). Of particular concern – as is the case across West Africa's small-scale gold-mining operations – is the impact on health. Often the unofficial pits are open and 'galamsey' workers are sent in with little protective gear. Accidents involving collapsing pit shafts are common. The artisanal miners, who often sift the gold in hand-held pans, use mercury and their bare hands to refine the gold dust, which has to be burned off, producing poisonous fumes. These workers often have little or no job security and generally work for pitifully low wages.

Much of the activity surrounding transparency in the oil industry today started life in campaigns to improve working conditions and government accountability in the lucrative gold-mining industry. Groups such as WACAM (Wassa Association of Communities Affected by Mining) and ISODEC (Integrated Social Development Centre) have been at the forefront of attempts to publicise the realities of the mining industry in Ghana and to push the government to begin implementing the EITI process within Ghana's mining industry in 2004. WACAM works to promote the rights of communities affected by mining, addressing issues such as livelihood protection and environmental damage. There has been some progress: government has responded by implementing a compensation programme that allows for 10 per cent of revenues to be deposited in a mineral development fund for distribution to mining communities – this is a significant amount for areas such as Tarkwa Nsuaem Municipal Authority, which generates about 50 per cent of its revenue from mineral royalties. Many of these provisions have been discussed at the community level and have helped to inform public opinion about the necessity of setting out clear standards and rules for the governance of natural resource extraction projects before the industries are established.

Transparency and revenue management

The regulatory framework for oil production was developed concurrently with the Jubilee field – it was fast-tracked at the time of the 2007 discovery – and involved the drafting of a number of new bills and a review and update of several existing laws. This section outlines some of the most significant of the new bills that have been passed since oil was discovered.

The Ghana Petroleum Regulatory Authority (GPRA) Bill of 2008 established the GPRA and was designed to regulate, oversee and monitor upstream, midstream and downstream activities. It sought to clarify the status of the national oil company GNPC, which had previously had a somewhat ambiguous role as both the industry's main player in Ghana and its regulator, as well as granting the right for the state to have a 10 per cent stake in any oil production deal; this right is exercised through the GNPC. The fiscal terms for companies were laid out, including a royalty of 5 per cent, carried and participating interest of 10 per cent (to support the GNPC's involvement) and corporation tax of 35 per cent. This law was backed up by the passing of the 2011 Petroleum Commission Act, which provided the legal basis for a commission to 'regulate and manage the utilisation of petroleum resources' by promoting the sector, issuing permits and monitoring compliance with the law.[3]

The country then moved to put in place a law on the management of revenues, the 2011 Petroleum Revenue Management Act (PRMA), which has been praised as 'innovative' by civil society groups. This bill established a strong disclosure regime covering sales and production data and net receipts from oil, and ensured

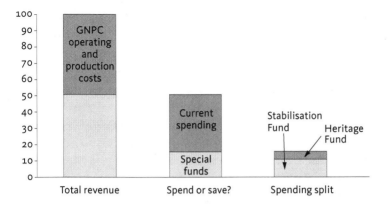

5.1 Breakdown of revenues from the sale of oil in Ghana (%) (*source*: NRGI)

that these sums were all paid into the Petroleum Holding Fund (PHF), a separate account where all money from the sale of oil was deposited; this is similar to the offshore Citibank escrow account established in Chad, except that this account is held in Ghana. From this fund, the GNPC's operating and production costs are subtracted; the costs currently hover at around 50 per cent of the fund's value. Of the remainder, 70 per cent goes into the national budget. Of the remaining 30 per cent, 70 per cent goes into a stabilisation fund, which is designed to help the country ride out any major fluctuations from the calculated benchmark price of oil on the international markets, and 30 per cent is invested abroad in a 'heritage fund' for future generations (Figure 5.1); again, this is similar to Chad's now defunct Future Generations Fund.

For the money directly entering the general budget, the law stipulates clear controls over priorities for spending – the Minister of Finance is responsible for choosing four areas, which currently are road infrastructure, agriculture, capacity building and paying off debts used to create the country's oil and gas infrastructure. Perhaps most importantly, the law allowed the creation of the Public Interest and Accountability Committee (PIAC), a civil society body charged with monitoring the government's progress in implementing the laws; this is a similar concept to the Collège de Contrôle in Chad. The PIAC is composed of thirteen members of non-governmental actors such as the Ghana Bar Association and the Civil Society Platform on Oil and Gas, and is charged with producing biannual oversight reports on what Ghana has earned and spent. Chad's experience in setting up the Collège seems to have had an impact on the discussions over how to get transparency and accountability enshrined in law. 'Trying to learn from what happened in Chad has been quite explicit,' says NRGI's Africa Regional Coordinator Emmanuel Kuyole. 'The Collège in Chad had no power to sanction anyone, had government members among its ranks and its independence was challenged by being dependent on government funding. We tried to avoid those mistakes but so far the PIAC's influence has been somewhat limited.'[4]

Contracts

A law governing the upstream issues of contracting (i.e. the level of royalties as well as choosing between the PSA and joint venture forms), procurement, environmental protection and hiring – the Petroleum Exploration and Production Bill – has yet to be passed at the time of writing. Encouragingly, civil society has been vocal in the debate on the bill and the government has seemed willing to allow criticism and alternative ideas to be put forward. One major criticism has been that a number of contracts for the TEN fields development are being discussed before the law has been formally approved. Mohammed Amin, from civil society campaign group ACEP, says: 'Right now it is not the best law it can be. Other countries such as Angola and South Sudan have better similar laws. But it's being done back to front. This should be the first step we took with establishing legislation but in fact it's the last!'

While this issue of approving contracts before the final law is in place is certainly not ideal, given the principles of contract transparency outlined in earlier chapters, Ghana has taken some encouraging steps compared with the other countries profiled in this book. Although there is as yet no legal provision in the above bills for contracts to be published, in 2011 Ghana became one of only a handful of countries in the world to make such contracts publicly available when it put seven of the original Jubilee field contracts on its ministerial website – a move ordered by a ministerial directive. Although the disclosure came a full six months after the first oil had been pumped, and after the contracts had already been published on the US Securities and Exchange Commission website following Kosmos's company listing process, it is still significant and has been praised by organisations such as the World Bank Institute and the NRGI. After the disclosure, Tullow Oil's George Cazenove said that the company's decision to follow the ministerial directive was a 'no-brainer'. Tullow Oil's decision in early 2014 to disclose all its payments to foreign governments, including Ghana, in its annual report is another step forward. Yet despite the popularity of these moves, Mohammed Amin still argues that the voluntary principle is not enough and is calling for the establishment of mandatory legal protection and a registry to be established for all future contracts.

Local content

At the time of the announcement of the oil find in 2007, expectations were high about what it could deliver in terms of developing the local economy and human capital. As with other expectations, these dreams seem to have faded a little in the face of a reality in which the industry is not expanding as fast as many had hoped – in mid-2014, production was still at 105,000 bpd instead of the initial 120,000 bpd predictions. While many Ghanaians have found indirect employment with onshore service companies based around Sekondi-Takoradi and in the fast-expanding hotel and restaurant sector, direct employment figures for the Jubilee field are still low. In total, in 2014, Tullow Oil employed 281 people in its entire Ghana operation, although, encouragingly, 86 per cent of these were local Ghanaians.[5]

Many of the calls to increase local employment and Ghanaian buy-in to the oil project have been recognised in the Petroleum (Local Content and Local Participation) Bill, which was finally passed in late 2013 after a lengthy delay. The regulation is designed to promote job creation and local expertise throughout the petroleum industry, as well as in associated service companies, and it requires companies to submit local content plans to ensure that they comply with the law. It also calls for skills and technology to be transferred to the GNPC with a view to it one day being able to enter into ventures on its own. The bill further allows for indigenous Ghanaian companies to be given preference in the granting of petroleum agreements and licences, while there should be at least 5 per cent equity participation by an indigenous Ghanaian company other than the GNPC before an IOC is deemed qualified to enter into a petroleum agreement.

The legal requirement for participation and the 10 per cent stake for the GNPC raise interesting questions about capacity and to what extent the IOCs may be expected to support a national oil company's participation. The GNPC was founded in 1985 as a state-owned oil company under former President Jerry Rawlings when Ghana's oil industry was tiny. While the organisation has certainly been on a rapid trajectory of development since the Jubilee discovery, many analysts still question the extent to which it could realistically lead its own operations or partner up with larger IOCs. Civil society campaigners say that the company lacks equipment and skilled personnel. A stall at an oil and gas conference held in the Accra International Conference Centre in January 2014 clearly highlighted the difficulties the GNPC faces. The only joint venture the company has been able to engage in so far is a 20 per cent stake in a project led by Technip's engineering arm to provide underground drilling services. A project to partner with AGM Petroleum in seismic testing on a 25:75 basis still necessitates AGM having to carry the costs of the operation.

On paper, this collection of laws and provisions for contract transparency looks impressive, and follows many of the recommendations for breaking the resource curse outlined in Chapter 2 – particularly in areas such as transparency of revenue flows, managing oil price volatility and investing for sustainable development. These achievements in establishing robust legislative frameworks for natural resource extraction were recognised in the

2013 Resource Governance Index published by the NRGI. Ghana scored 63 out of 100, the highest rating of any African country, with its performance being described as 'partially successful'. Countries such as South Sudan, Zimbabwe and Equatorial Guinea were close to the bottom of the index and classified as 'failing'.[6] While this report covered only the mining sector, it nevertheless showed the power of Ghana's legal frameworks. However, according to NRGI, the country's score could have been improved by greater efforts in the 'enabling and implementation environment' domain – effectively, the lower score here picked up on the issue that these impressive laws are not always respected, an issue that will be discussed in more detail later in this chapter.

Pathway out of poverty? The impact on the economy of the oil-producing region

It's a humid, sticky evening near Sekondi-Takoradi's main market. All around me I can hear the muezzin call; motorbikes, taxis and pedestrians hoot and push past, hurrying home for the evening prayers. Dark descends quickly in this ageing part of town where street lights are few and far between.

The irony of being lost does not escape me. I have come to meet a group of residents who have been involved in a new project to name each and every one of the roads in the city's tangled networks – their motivation being to help people find their houses more easily. I stand in the rapidly descending twilight, with my guide Mohamed from the NGO Global Communities, which has helped to implement the street-naming project together with the Sekondi-Takoradi Metropolitan Planning Authority. We're on the phone to the local deputy, who is trying to explain where we are to meet the community. He tells us to walk between two rickety roadside shacks and down an uninviting alleyway between the mosque and another road. Mohammed shines the torch on his mobile phone to indicate to me the pools of stagnant water and refuse, while continuing to shout into his phone to ask the deputy whether we should be turning left or right after the mosque.

It's a typical scene for any seasoned African traveller. Any journey in a big city will take a completely unpredictable amount of time due to traffic jams and the inevitable getting lost. In Sekondi-Takoradi, Ghana's 'oil city', the problem seems to be compounded because the city is growing at such a breakneck speed. Oil companies and the service and construction companies that work with them – for example Schlumberger, which provides drilling and seismic services – have arrived in the city because of its port, airport and good communication links, despite the fact that the offshore Jubilee field lies about 150 kilometres further west along the Ghanaian coast in territorial waters close to the Ivorian border.

The city is being seen as something of a Ghanaian Eldorado, with thousands flocking here looking for work and opportunities. Officials from the Metropolitan Planning Authority (MPA) estimate that the city's population has doubled since the announcement of the oil discovery, from about 300,000 in 2007 to 600,000 in 2014. Jacob Ntiamoah, Deputy Development Planning Officer at the MPA, whom I met at a hotel in the city, believes the dream is a reality for many: 'Those who saw the opportunities and got in early here, in offering decent hotels and restaurants, they've really made it.' My own hotel on the city's rapidly expanding outskirts is gleaming and new (and expensive!), with a huge flat-screen television in my room. The owners clearly have an idea of the needs of the UK expat worker clientele – in the restaurant I found HP Sauce, Heinz Salad Cream and Kellogg's Rice Krispies. The MPA itself has bold plans to improve the city's infrastructure and boasts about how the city is booming – Ntiamoah tells me that there are plans for several multi-lane roads, flyovers, offices and warehouses, as well as expansion plans for the port and airport.

However, the first-time visitor to the city may be surprised by how rural it still feels some eight years after the oil discovery. There is little in the way of a new city centre, the roads are in a poor condition, and the signs of 'development' seem to be most evident in the mass of new houses, urban sprawl and ubiquitous traffic jams. A recent report by Global Communities revealed how local people have not seen an improvement in services – only 60 per cent are connected to running water, public sanitary facilities and sewers are few and far between, and large areas of the city have little or no access to health clinics or hospitals (Global Communities 2013). Interestingly, it is also quite hard to see any evidence of the oil industry – on the outskirts of town there are a number of large warehouses and areas of cleared land belonging to the oil and service companies, and the 'Oil Village' – an optimistically built development of new luxury apartments for oil workers – lies at least 15 kilometres from the services of the town centre. As the Jubilee oilfield is so far west and completely based offshore, opportunities for business development have been limited: many of the expatriates who work there simply pass through Sekondi-Takoradi airport on their way back to Accra and on to international flights home, experiencing little of what Ghanaian entrepreneurs are offering in the city.

Nevertheless, many feel that the city's character has already changed; as we walk around the market, my guide Mohammed from Global Communities explains how rents for shops and accommodation have more than tripled since oil was discovered. He complains bitterly about traffic jams and the deteriorating quality of the road network, particularly when it comes to transporting heavy equipment for the oil industry along dilapidated coastal roads. The lack of decent road infrastructure is recognised as a serious problem by the MPA, but there is some confusion about who should ultimately take responsibility for tackling it; although the government has made it a national 'development priority', not much progress has been made in this area so far. While new hotels and restaurants are easy to build, civil society complains – in a similar manner to campaigners in Chad – that little of significance has been done for the benefit of the local population. The MPA's Jacob Ntiamoah agrees with this view: 'We have to wake up and realise that oil should be a good thing for the development of our town – we don't want it to end up like the Niger Delta.'

Regional compensation and the environment

The issue of a form of regional compensation for the Sekondi-Takoradi region as the 'producing area' – similar to the concept of the 5% Committee employed in Doba (Chad) and the 15 per cent allocation to Agadem in Niger – has been a thorny one. As things stand, the local population, in particular a number of influential chiefs along the coast, claim that they should receive between 5 per cent and 10 per cent of the revenues from oil to compensate them for the damage and disruption to their areas. However, as the Jubilee fields are some 60 kilometres offshore, it is difficult to prove this impact on coastal communities. In addition, analysts argue that central government has been keen to avoid giving special treatment to the issue of regional claims lest this lead to a federalist sentiment in other regions that have been negatively impacted by the gold-mining industry.

While the mining areas do get a special dispensation, so far it looks unlikely that Sekondi-Takoradi's claim for a revenue share will be successful, simply because the oil is under the sea. Communities that are reliant on the rich fishing grounds off Ghana's coast are angry, saying that oil has disrupted their livelihoods. Abuesi, 10 kilometres east of Sekondi-Takoradi, is typical of such communities. Of its 9,000 people, two-thirds depend on fishing; spilling out along the shore, its brightly painted wooden canoes nestle on the sand in a natural harbour. The hot air is ripe with the smell of fish; local women lay out hundreds of tiny herring to smoke on large metal racks and local children nip over to steal them while the women's backs are turned. Nana Kojo Kondua IV, a small man in his seventies wearing a bright 'kente' cloth shirt and an even brighter smile, is the president of the Western region branch of the Canoe Fishermen's Council. When I visit his home in Abuesi on a sticky Sunday afternoon, he explains that fishermen have begun to worry about the prospect of confrontations with the oil companies on the high seas: 'There is an exclusion zone of 500 metres radius around the Jubilee platform which means that fishermen cannot access that area, but many of them feel that the lights of the platform attract the fish and this is the best fishing ground.' Proudly showing me a number of special commendations he has been given by international organisations such as Oxfam America for his work advocating on behalf of fishing communities, Chief Kondua says that fishermen on their small canoes have clashed with national security agency vessels trying to enforce the exclusion zone, and that there is a constant fear of collision with the recent increased maritime traffic.

There have already been a number of minor cases of environmental problems in the ocean, including a spillage of 706 barrels of contaminated mud for which the US firm Kosmos was fined US$26 million in 2010.[7] Friends of the Nation (FON) is a local grass-roots NGO that has around forty-five volunteers who go out regularly to carry out community monitoring of the impact of the oil project all along the southern coast. The team has discovered over twenty dead whale carcasses beached on Ghana's beaches since 2009. Kyei Kwadwo Yamoah from FON says that he believes there may be a link with Tullow Oil's offshore production facility (FPSO). This claim has been firmly denied by Tullow Oil and the Ghanaian government, which said that no clear link could be established between the dead whales and oil.[8] Another of Kyei's concerns is that oil production began before environmental frameworks and ways to protect livelihoods were properly established:

> That was our mistake – we focused too much on revenue sharing. People here did not think about environmental damage. They just wanted schools and access to revenue. Little thought was given to protecting livelihoods which already exist and our ecosystems.

Kyei believes that the existing pre-2008 legislation covering environmental damage is inadequate and should be updated because it was written before the full implications of oil production were known. In fact, he was eager to draw a parallel with the EMP from the Chad World Bank oil project, wishing that a similarly rigorous document was in place in Ghana: 'We should have had donors coming in to force us to accept these conditions like they did in Chad, but instead they thought Ghana was able to manage these issues by itself.'

In response to these complaints, Tullow Oil, the lead operator in the Jubilee field consortium, says that it has gone to great

143

lengths to address the fishermen's concerns in places such as Abuesi. Chief Kondua confirms that the company's representatives came to the village to consult with them on issues such as the exclusion zone. Tullow Oil says that the restrictions are there for safety reasons and Chief Kondua acknowledges that the problem of depleted fishing stocks off Ghana's coast pre-dated the arrival of oil production and may be linked to overfishing in breeding grounds and harmful local practices that include using drag nets, cyanide and dynamite. Tullow Oil was also keen to point out the environmental and social achievements noted in its 2012 CSR report and that environmental and social impact assessment studies were carried out on the field. According to the CSR report, there have been successes; these include the 62 per cent decrease in carbon dioxide emissions that was achieved in 2012 after flaring was reduced at the Jubilee field, and a reduction in oil spills across all their global operations from fourteen to five (three of these were in Ghana). However, the report also showed a 12 per cent increase in the company's water usage (98 per cent of this is sea water in Ghana) and also an increase in waste generation (Tullow Oil 2013). With little visible impact onshore and vast distances of ocean water to be monitored by small voluntary groups such as FON, the difficulties of assessing the true environmental impact of an offshore project such as Jubilee cannot be overstated.

Eldorado missed?

While Ghana has taken commendable steps towards putting in place legislation to promote transparency and accountability in its oil industry, and up until now environmental damage seems limited and certainly does not echo the problems seen in areas such as the Niger Delta, the country is still learning to deal with a problem that many civil society activists are calling 'expectation management'. President Kufuor's jubilant comments to the BBC in 2007 show to what extent some politicians seemed to believe that oil could prove to be a panacea for all the country's economic ills. In the 2008 presidential election, both parties – the National Democratic Congress of John Atta Mills and the New

Patriotic Party of Nana Akufo-Addo – made elaborate claims about how they would spend the oil money that was due to come into government coffers during the next presidential term, including Akufo-Addo pledging to provide universal free secondary school education. As in Niger and Chad, politicians made ill-informed claims that the advent of oil production in the country would lead to a fall in domestic fuel prices and an end to a problematic reliance on imports. But today there is a palpable sense that many ordinary people's hopes have been disappointed. 'We warned from the start that the projections about the quantities of early production and the implications for revenue were unrealistic,' says Franklin Cudjoe, president of the Ghanaian think tank the IMANI Institute. 'All parties were making fantastic claims, that we would be earning US$1 billion a year within five years of the start of production.' Significantly, by the 2012 general election campaign, the number of proclamations concerning oil's magical powers had dwindled conspicuously.

Ghana has experienced a number of serious economic woes in recent years. The cutting of fuel subsidies and the associated increase in transportation costs, higher food costs and a hike in energy bills led to inflationary pressures of up to 11.9 per cent in the third quarter of 2013,[9] meaning that the cost of living has rocketed in recent years for many ordinary people. Government debt rose to US$24 billion in early 2014 – more than half of GDP. There has also been a significant fall in the value of the Cedi – it lost 23 per cent of its value between 2013 and 2014 – with analysts believing that the main culprit is the 'tapering' of US quantitative easing. The fall of the Cedi has put further pressure on the price of imports. In a dramatic gesture, in February 2014 the Central Bank was forced to limit foreign exchange withdrawals, which effectively meant US dollars, as this has become the currency of choice for many businesspeople connected with the international oil industry.[10]

So what role has oil played in the overall economic picture? Thanks to Ghana's membership of the EITI and the hard work of the PIAC, which is charged with compiling biannual reports of income and outgoings, it is relatively easy to see what the country has earned. The country became EITI compliant in 2010 and in 2011 it committed to expanding its reporting to cover oil revenues. At first glance, the figures are surprising – although the entire extractives sector accounts for 56 per cent of the country's exports, it makes up only about 6 per cent of GDP (Ministry of Finance and Economic Planning 2013). In the most recently available EITI report – which is for 2011 (ibid.) and covers the early days of the Jubilee project – oil was still only the third largest export behind gold and cocoa. The Ghanaian government's share of oil produced in Jubilee adds up to about 18 per cent of total production (this includes a 5 per cent royalty and carried and participating interest paid by the companies) and is paid in oil. The excited claims that the country is sitting on a 'black gold mine' are somewhat tempered by the PIAC's figures, which suggest that this 18 per cent earned the country only US$444 million in 2011 and US$414 million in 2012. Up until 2013, the PIAC reported that none of the IOCs in Ghana had paid any corporation tax, which, according to the terms of the 2008 act, should be levied at 35 per cent. The PIAC says that the delay in the commencement of corporation tax is due to capital expenditure allowances that the companies incurred in setting up the oil industry, and that from 2013 the companies have begun to pay (PIAC 2012).

With a GDP of US$42 billion,[11] Ghana has a much bigger and more complex economy than Niger or Chad – in 2011 the World Bank reclassified it as a 'lower middle-income' country. This is significant because it means that the moderate sums earned in oil revenues will not dominate GDP in the way they do in Chad. Although revenues look set to increase in the coming years, an additional US$858 million from 2011–12 is a welcome addition but seems unlikely to go very far towards resolving the country's wider macroeconomic problems.

Accountability and quality of spending

General economic woes aside, the question remains whether the provisions in Ghana's laws covering the 'priority sectors'

146

for expenditure of oil revenues offer the chance to successfully promote development and poverty reduction. As we have seen in Chad, a potential solution for making oil money work for development is to establish legal protections for using natural resource revenues to meet social development goals. Encouragingly, Ghana's PRMA of 2011 allows four priority sectors for development to be chosen for spending, 70 per cent of which must be in the area of public investment. This gives hope that oil money can be specifically targeted towards development, but at least one of the current priorities – paying back foreign infrastructure loans – has been controversial. Moreover, as the PIAC's 2012 report noted, the early signs are not encouraging. The 2012 national budget allocated oil money to thirteen different sectors, instead of the mandated four, with the new sectors including public safety, social services and environmental protection. The PIAC concluded that this 'defeats the objective of priority setting, meant to achieve optimum impact' (ibid.: 19) and 'creates the danger that consumption spending would be promoted over investment spending'. ACEP and others criticise the fact that ministerial discretion applies to these priority choices, thus making them somewhat arbitrary, and call for a better national development plan to ensure that revenues from petroleum are guided by transparent procurement procedures and that projects are completed on time and to a high standard. These fears are reminiscent of those in Chad; there, as we have seen, the fact that a development project looked impressive on paper was no guarantee that it would be able to contribute anything to the country's development in the future – or indeed whether it would even happen.

In recent years, Ghana has made important strides in poverty reduction, being the first sub-Saharan country to meet MDG 1 of halving extreme poverty before 2015.[12] The number of people living in extreme poverty fell from 51.7 per cent in 1991–92 to 28.5 per cent in 2005–06 and continues to fall, but this all happened *before* the advent of oil. The country comes 135th on the UN Human Development Index, but while this puts it in a strong position compared with other West African countries, life expectancy is still just sixty-four years, literacy has reached only 71 per cent and more than 10 per cent of the population still does not have access to clean water.[13]

Again in an echo of Chad, a number of important national infrastructure developments have been promised but progress has been slow. One of the most talked about is a plan to supply the country with natural gas from the Jubilee fields through the construction of a gas processing plant at Atuabo in south-west Ghana; this in turn will feed the Aboadze electricity generating plant. The government is keen to switch to gas as a cleaner and more reliable fuel for electricity generation, since current problems with electricity generation continue to hamper development and demand is expected to increase by 12 per cent year on year.[14] The government recently announced that it wants to increase the country's generating capacity to 5,000 megawatts by 2016 (this would be a doubling of current capacity).

The US$1 billion Atuabo project involves laying a pipeline from the Jubilee field to shore and building a 150 million standard cubic feet capacity plant. The construction of the plant and the pipeline is being carried out by the Chinese firm Sinopec. However, the plan has fallen well behind schedule because of a combination of technical problems and a delay in releasing funds. The project is 85 per cent financed by the Chinese Development Bank (CDB) and 15 per cent by the Ghanaian government, but the CDB loans have been delayed repeatedly. According to analysts at the IMANI Institute, this appears to be partly due to the CDB's insistence on a higher number of barrels of crude oil per day to be paid by Ghana as collateral for the debt.[15] The delays have become a major headache for Tullow Oil, which had planned in its original construction of the Jubilee field that excess gas produced would be sent to Atuabo. While the company waits for the plant to be completed, the excess gas has to be re-injected into the Jubilee field, which is the main reason for the lower than expected yield of 105,000 bpd as opposed to 120,000 bpd. According to local news reports, the Jubilee Consortium is even reportedly seeking permission to flare off some of the excess gas,[16] which could have implications for the health of the local population. At the end of 2014, the plant was still not fully operational. Once again, questions about the quality and efficiency of government spending of perceived 'windfall' cash are pertinent. 'My worry is about Ghana getting value for money for these projects it seems determined to surge ahead with,' says NRGI's Emmanuel Kuyole. 'The smartest thing to do is reinvest and this gas plant is a good example of that, but look how much time and money we're wasting with delays and lack of planning.'

The limitations of transparency

When the EITI was first proposed by British Prime Minister Tony Blair, many hailed it as an ideal way of positively encouraging governments and companies to move towards voluntary transparency. However, although the initiative has seen much success, there has been an increasing awareness that transparency on its own is not sufficient to counter the dangers of natural resource extraction revenues going to waste or being put to nefarious purposes. As the case of Chad so clearly demonstrates, a log of what the country has earned does little to influence questions about how the money is spent. In Ghana, the EITI's representative, Franklin Ashiadey, concedes that the process is vulnerable to corruption and says: 'It is not a magic bullet.' Similarly, the country's transparency and accountability laws look excellent on paper, yet civil society has already identified a number of issues with the implementation of the laws regarding spending. In fact, 'a lack of respect for the law' was one of the most common complaints I heard during my research trip to Ghana. How well are the country's mandated transparency institutions working? And is money really being put towards development?

One of the greatest difficulties currently affecting implementation of the much hailed PRMA is that the PIAC is not receiving its full funding allocation from government. This appears to be because of delays in getting parliament to pass into law a funding mechanism for the body and then getting those funds released from the Ministry of Finance, but none of the transparency campaigners I spoke to could fully explain why this was the case. The delay is clearly hampering the body's ability to carry out its work of monitoring spending revenues and preparing biannual reports, and without a permanent home, the organisation has been forced to temporarily operate from the offices of NRGI. It suffered significant delays in publishing its 2013 report: 'It's very frustrating having to carry on without even knowing if we have enough money to finish this year's report,' laments Major George Ablorh-Quarcoo (retired), Chairman of the PIAC. 'I carry on and think sometimes I'm completely alone in this work. But someone has to do it!' The PIAC is already limited by its lack of legal sanction to compel institutions to provide information or to enforce its findings.

Despite these difficulties, the PIAC has still been able to produce some excellent reports covering the period to the end of 2012. The reports are incredibly detailed and show that civil society monitoring in Ghana is still working, despite being hobbled by a lack of funding and associated delays. The reports include information on precise lifting tallies for crude oil production, breakdowns of what Ghana has earned through the sale of oil, surface rental and taxes, as well as information about what the government has spent the money on. As ACEP pointed out, this immense level of detail actually takes the PIAC reports 'ahead of the requirements set out by the EITI' (ACEP 2013: 5).

The PIAC was able to identify a number of issues for the year 2012 that are still to be resolved. Firstly, it was noticed that overall revenues for 2012 were below expectations – receipts for 2012 were US$61 million, 14.8 per cent lower than the amount the government had budgeted for. This had an impact on transfers into the petroleum funds (the PHF, the heritage fund and the stabilisation fund), which were 82 per cent below target, but this was also partly due to the fact that some surface rentals and corporate income taxes were not being paid. The PIAC also noted a general disappointment that the investment performance of the petroleum funds 'has not yet yielded high returns'. On the issue of revenue spending, the report highlighted that the Ministry of Finance 'does not seem to have implemented the plan of expenditure from Petroleum Revenue approved by Parliament in 2012', adding that no details had been provided for expenditure on the four priority areas identified by the Ministry. The PIAC also identified that the GNPC received US$18.2 million (15.2 per cent) more than the amount approved in the annual budget, which 'had the effect of drastically reducing the amount that should have been lodged in the Ghana Petroleum Funds' (PIAC 2012: 16).

Other civil society groups have carried out similar monitoring activities and have noticed irregularities in the application of the law. ACEP complains that the country performs badly in terms of budget transparency, making it difficult for civil society to clearly trace the oil revenues and what they are spent on – the organisation points to the fact that Ghana fell in its ranking on the Open Budget Index from 54 per cent in 2010 to 49 per cent in 2012. ACEP is also critical of the apparent inability of parliament to carry out its full range of oversight activities; for example, the organisation noticed by looking through a copy of the budget that some 65 million Cedis had been allocated to the Office of the President – a figure higher than the amount allotted to agriculture – although this had not been identified in law as a priority spending area. 'Either the parliament didn't realise or didn't notice that allocation,' says Benjamin Boakye from ACEP with a wry smile. 'There is a problem with compliance with the law.' However, it is worth noting that civil society was able to uncover this 'oversight' simply by taking the time to read through government documents that are freely and widely available – something that would still be virtually unthinkable in countries such as Chad and Niger.

From the discussion in Chapter 2, one recalls that academics and civil society organisations have recommended the creation of future savings funds to compensate for the non-renewable nature of oil – but in this respect Ghana's 'heritage fund' has been quite divisive. The IMANI Institute, for example, thinks that it is a bad idea. 'Saving for a rainy day is not useful,' says IMANI's Franklin Cudjoe. 'Estimates suggest that the oil is only going to last twenty years and there are very real challenges which need addressing today, such as roads, electricity and water.' He argues that the money earned by the heritage fund's performance since it launched is 'peanuts'. In 2012, for example, the net return for the heritage fund was just US$57,000, bringing its total value to US$21,694,000 (ibid.: 24). Cudjoe blames the government's 'lazy' decision to choose only ultra-safe assets and suggests a number of alternative ways in which it could be managed. In fact, this chimes with a new report launched in 2014 by NRGI into the performance of sovereign wealth funds around the world, which found that they often fail to meet their objectives and 'are poorly managed and off limits from the oversight of civil society and the media'.[17] This also echoes Chad's desire to scrap its Future Generations Fund, with President Déby determined to use the oil money at his disposal to deal with the country's most immediate needs.

Civil society campaigners are also disappointed by the clause in the PRMA that allows the GNPC's production and administration costs to be deducted before oil revenues are allocated to the national budget or the petroleum funds. This figure has hovered around 50 per cent of the total, but last year was close to 60 per cent. 'There's no public scrutiny of how the GNPC comes up with its figures of how much it has spent; we believe it doesn't have the capacity to carry out everything it says it is planning to do. Financial decisions are made alone and they only have to report to the Minister. The GNPC should be more upfront about the details of their spending,' says NRGI's Emmanuel Kuyole, suggesting that the decision to use some of that public money to sponsor the Ghanaian football team the Black Stars' visit to Brazil in 2014 was undemocratic. In addition, the PIAC report from 2012 identified that some 26 per cent of the GNPC's total funds of US$61 million for that financial year were unspent (ibid.: 16). As Kuyole notes, it has been hard for transparency campaigners to discover what happens to that unspent money.

Finally, on the issue of whether a government should borrow on the back of a commodities boom, further controversy has surrounded clause 5 of the PRMA, which allows for debt to be collateralised against future oil production. This clause specifies that debt can be issued against up to 70 per cent of future revenues from oil. However, the clause became particularly unpopular when the government successfully negotiated a loan to cover the costs of road construction with a Chinese bank; the loan was collateralised for fifteen years, contravening the law that stated that the maximum period should be seven years. While these proposals for debt collateralisation, if managed sensibly, may ease the immediate debt burden of the country, with the problem of volatile world oil prices (seen quite clearly in the price crash of early 2015), there is an inherent danger that loans backed by oil in the good times will become increasingly difficult for a government to service in the bad times. Civil society is right to point out that at the very least the government should follow its own rules on the level of permissible collateralisation.

Ghana's transparency scorecard

There is no doubt that Ghana already has an impressive record in oil governance in terms of setting up legal frameworks to ensure that the industry is developed in a transparent and accountable manner. The sheer number of laws is testament to this, as is the number of knowledgeable and committed organisations dedicated to following what happens to Ghana's oil wealth. Tullow Oil's decision to publish its contracts in Ghana was an important step towards transparency, and has since been followed by an announcement that the company will disclose all its payments to national governments.

The future seems bright, with the promise of another 80,000 bpd from the TEN fields coming into production in 2015–16. Ghana's Oil Minister, Emmanuel Armah Kofi Buah, has said that at least US$20 billion in investment capital will be ploughed into the industry in the coming years, with the expectation that the country's viable reserves could be increased to 5 billion barrels. Exploration continues in the offshore fields south-west of Sekondi-Takoradi, but also in the Volta Basin and in other areas along the Gulf of Guinea coast. As potential reserves increase, associated infrastructure improvements, such as the large road-building project and the long-awaited Atuabo gas plant, will contribute to the country's development. Increasing revenues will continue to play a role in the government's budget. In fact, with oil exports already estimated at over US$4 billion per year and deep structural changes taking place in the gold industry that may adversely affect its profitability, the IMANI Institute's Bright Simons told me in a telephone interview that he believes that oil could even overtake gold in the near future as Ghana's number one export.

With just two complete years of oil revenue figures to work from, it is still difficult to draw meaningful conclusions about Ghana's attempts to manage its oil revenues. It is early days to decide whether the earnings from oil are genuinely having an impact on social development. The country's political and economic context is quite different to that of some of the other countries profiled in this book – for example, the economy is much larger and more diversified than Chad's, where the budget and GDP have been dominated by oil. As Michael Ross argues in his 2012 book on the resource curse, the scale of oil resources is important in evaluating how damaging oil might be to an economy; 'the greater the oil wealth, the more secretive the budget' (Ross 2012). In the case of Ghana – unlike Chad – it can be argued that the government is forced to be more democratic than it might have been if the Jubilee finds had been bigger.

Encouragingly, there does seem to be potential for some of the openings that have been created in politics and civil society in recent years to contribute to an overall improvement in governance of the oil industry. Ghana's democracy is still largely intact after twenty years – and the country has negotiated its way peacefully out of two electoral crises in 2008 and 2012. This strength may go some way to helping the country push for full implementation of legal frameworks without this opening the door to the kind of civil strife and repression seen in less mature democracies such as Niger or Chad. Simply because oil does not currently seem to have the potential to overwhelm the economy, it may be easier for Ghana to set itself on a more level-headed pathway than, say, in neighbouring Nigeria.

Nevertheless, there are still serious concerns about Ghana's progress. The successes achieved by creating robust legal frameworks are somewhat marred by the delay in passing the Petroleum Exploration and Production Bill, which has held back progress on getting contracts published. As discussed in this chapter, civil society groups such as Oxfam complain that the contracts for the expansion of the industry in the TEN fields have already been negotiated without any public monitoring or oversight, running ahead of the finalisation of this legislation. 'Those discussions are finalised, officially, at Cabinet and, unofficially, in closed-door sessions by the President and his advisers. Ministers actually take a Cabinet oath to keep these matters confidential,' complains the IMANI Institute's Bright Simons. Furthermore, there is still a vital need for civil society and parliamentary opposition to push for full implementation of the intricately designed laws, as the numerous failings picked up by the PIAC report demonstrate. The failure to provide a budget for the PIAC, the lack of transparency over the way in which the GNPC utilises its sizeable budget allocation, the lack of complete clarity over how decisions about spending priorities are made, and, of course, the issue of expectation management are all serious flaws in the country's otherwise good record.

6 | The East African miracle?

There is little doubt that East Africa is being seen by some as the next big thing in African oil and gas. With significant finds of oil in Uganda and Kenya, and natural gas in Tanzania and Mozambique, IOCs the world over are watching keenly to see where the best profits might be found. Tullow Oil, the young British company keen to capitalise on its high drilling success rates and a reputation for moving fast in Ghana, has described East Africa as being 'at the heart of an emerging powerhouse in future global oil supply markets' (Tullow Oil 2014: 12). In Uganda, Tullow reports reserves of up to 1.7 billion barrels and is currently appraising a discovery in the Waraga EA2 field. Oil giant Total has also made six discoveries further north in the Albertine Basin on the shore of Lake Albert, and the Chinese firm CNOOC has just been granted a production licence for the Kingfisher site to the south. In Kenya, where Tullow operates five onshore blocks, it has drilled a number of successful wells in the South Lokichar Basin in the Turkana region, and current estimates are that there may be some 600 million barrels of recoverable reserves. A picture is beginning to emerge of a region rich in oil, the exploitation of which could help transform the economic prospects of the regional grouping the East African Community (the EAC, which comprises Burundi, Kenya, Rwanda, Tanzania and Uganda). Production could start soon – a memorandum of understanding for a commercialisation plan for the Albertine Rift Basin was agreed between the three companies and the Ugandan government in early 2014 – and industry insiders suggest that investment in the sector could top US$50 billion in the next twenty years. In Kenya, the government has signalled that it wants to move fast on implementing new legislation in order to bring the Turkana fields into operation by 2016.

However, despite the rosy outlook being portrayed by the IOCs and the two governments, there are already a number of brakes on the rapid commercialisation of the oil deposits. First is the crucial question of export capability. Both the Turkana and Albertine deposits are onshore and require substantial investment in an export pipeline. Although a number of routes from Uganda and Turkana to the Kenyan coast have been proposed, including as part of the giant LAPSETT (Lamu Port–South Sudan–Ethiopia Transport) regional infrastructure project, and it has been reported that contracts for the work in Kenya have been signed,[1] so far no feasibility study has been carried out nor is it clear who will pay the estimated bill of between US$2.5 billion and US$5 billion. It has been suggested that the work would be easier and more cost effective if it were envisaged as a regional project involving collaboration between Uganda and Kenya, but Uganda's focus on exportation has been side-tracked by the country's desire to get a refinery built for the production of petroleum products for local sale. Hopes that South Sudan could be involved – South Sudan has long expressed a desire to free itself from reliance on the export pipeline running north through its neighbour Sudan to Port Sudan – have been dashed by the outbreak of deadly violence there since late 2013.

The development plans have been further delayed while national parliaments debate the necessary oil legislation. Cognisant of the difficulties faced by other African countries that have pressed ahead with oil exploitation before laws were agreed upon, Uganda has examined its own legislation in fine detail. It took over two years to pass two bills covering upstream (exploration and produc-tion) and mid- and downstream (transportation, storage, sales, and so on) activities. Conversely, civil society in Kenya is working hard to *slow down* the speed at which oil laws are being debated there with a view to achieving community consultation, a good-quality law and a more inclusive national dialogue.

So who will be the first to produce oil? Kenya and Uganda pub-licly remain on friendly terms, and, as George Boden from Global Witness says, they 'will benefit from each other's participation', but there is a sense that Kenya's apparent determination to press ahead quickly could lead to rivalry between the two nations. Certainly, in the two years since I began the research for this book, not a great deal has moved forward in Uganda, but Kenya's oil sector has gone from being an afterthought to an essential ingredient in this book. If Kenya does achieve its ambition of producing by 2016, Uganda may not enjoy seeing the prize for being the first nation in East Africa to produce oil swiped from under its nose.

The stakes are also high for the oil companies involved. Tullow Oil, seemingly frustrated by delays in Uganda, has been playing a tough game. The company's Chief Operating Officer told *The Wall Street Journal* in February 2014 that it is considering selling part of its stake in the Ugandan fields to concentrate on production in Kenya,[2] although Ugandan officials at the Ministry of Energy and Mineral Development said that they had received no official notification of that from Tullow. Whatever the outcome of what looks like a gamble by Tullow to try to push the Ugandan government forward, there are plenty of observers who feel that, with Africa's accumulated knowledge of the dangers inherent in oil production, Uganda's cautious approach is perhaps preferable to Kenya's desire to race ahead.

Towards a regulatory framework: Uganda

The importance of setting up clear regulatory frameworks ahead of production cannot be overstated, and in this regard Uganda has made some important progress. However, the process has been slow, causing some frustration among IOCs such as Tullow Oil who are keen to push forward with production. What follows is an analysis of the political context in Uganda and a round-up of the current debates on oil laws, which can help explain why things have not moved as fast as some would have liked.

Oil and politics As with all the countries profiled in this book, Uganda has its own unique political context into which oil production is being inserted. Uganda, like Ghana, has a larger economy than Chad or Niger, and the current size of oil deposits does not look likely to overwhelm the country's GDP. More importantly, oil is playing into a complex political dynamic in which an ageing president who has been in power longer than even Idriss Déby Itno in Chad is attempting to continue to assert his control and ensure the country's future stability. Many observers have criticised what they say is Uganda's descent into increased political repression in recent years as Yoweri Museveni has sought to hang on to power. 'At the centre of Uganda's oil policy and the future of the sector is the figure of President Yoweri Museveni,'[3] argued Tony Otoa, the Executive Director of Great Lakes Public Affairs. As an example of the President's attempts to centralise control over the development of the oil project, he cites the choosing of security firms linked to Museveni's own family to operate in the oil-producing zone and questioned 'whether Museveni will try to ensure he stays in office to enjoy the fruits of Uganda's natural wealth'. The conclusions of these local media reports are backed up by analysis from think tanks, such as the Washington-based Center for Strategic and International Studies, which makes an explicit link between oil and what has been described as President Museveni's system of buying loyalty: 'The discovery of large quantities of oil in Lake Albert ... has provided a potential lifeline. Museveni is counting on oil revenues to buttress his patronage network' (Barkan 2011: 2).

Uganda is losing its reputation as an African democratic success story. 'Over the last 16 year period there has been a shift from a consensus-based leadership style of the early years of Museveni's rule, to one that is characterised by top-down executive control,' argues another report (ILPI 2013: 19). Politics has become more polarised; for example, in May 2013 a number of vocal National Resistance Movement (Museveni's party) MPs were finally expelled from the ruling party after a long battle with the President, having been found guilty of contravening the constitution. As seen from a speech made about oil by the President in late 2012,[4] which accused some civil society groups of being foreign agents, civil society and NGOs have also found it increasingly difficult to operate. In early 2014, the government passed two seemingly socially repressive laws: the Anti-Homosexuality Act, which laid down life imprisonment as a penalty for homosexual acts, and the Anti-Pornography Law (the 'Anti-Miniskirts Bill'), which, among other things, prohibited women from wearing short skirts. The outrage from European donors led to a number of programme suspensions.[5] Coupled with a 2012 UK decision to freeze aid following the discovery of a corruption scandal in the Prime Minister's office, there has been conjecture that Museveni may be facing acute budgetary shortages. Many have speculated that the President may be eyeing oil as the solution to this situation: 'This is a high stakes gamble to plug the budgetary hole,' argues Dickens Kamishiga from NGO AFIEGO (the Africa Institute for Energy Governance).

I met Gloria Sebikari, Senior Communications Officer at the Ministry of Energy and Mineral Development, at the ministry offices on the shores of Lake Victoria one dreary Friday morning. Offering me a selection of pastries and fresh coffee, she explained the government's oil strategy and the progress of its various petroleum legislation, using a slick PowerPoint presentation. 'We need a comprehensive plan and that takes time,' she said. Pushed on the issue as to whether Kenya might overtake Uganda and become the first East African nation to produce oil, she replied: 'They might be perceived as moving fast but this requires long-term commitments as we try to maximise the value of everything in this project for Ugandans.'

The country's National Oil and Gas Policy, which was adopted in 2008, is the key document governing the objectives and strategies for the industry. Its policy goal is identified as: 'To use the country's oil and gas resources to contribute to an early achievement of poverty eradication and create lasting value to society' (Republic of Uganda 2008). Using the policy as a baseline, Uganda began to debate two laws governing upstream and midstream activities in 2011. After a slow start, things began to hot up when a group of five MPs requested the recall of parliament over the issue in

October 2011. 'This was crucial in getting the whole nation to engage on the issue,' says Isaac Imaka, Oil Correspondent for the *Daily Monitor* newspaper in Kampala, who has followed the story since the very beginning. 'People suddenly realised it was in the national interest to get this right.' As the parliamentarians took a greater interest in the draft laws, a number of international donors supported the parliamentary discussions, such as the Democratic Governance Facility and International Alert, which organised meetings and training for MPs. Eventually a Parliamentary Forum on Oil and Gas (PFOG) was formed to examine the draft laws; a number of its members even travelled to Ghana in order to learn from the West African experience.

The parliamentarians eventually proposed a number of recommendations, which included splitting the upstream and midstream sectors into two separate bills, the advice that the NOC should be a 100 per cent state-owned company, and the establishment of a civil society monitoring body for the industry in a similar vein to the PIAC in Ghana and the Collège in Chad. Isaac Imaka says that the strength of the challenge to the original bill took a lot of people by surprise: 'President Museveni was taken aback by the clamour for debate.' However, after a promising start things soon ran into difficulties. Some of the legislators' ninety-three recommendations were adopted by parliament, including that the NOC be state-owned, but a number of them attracted the disapproval of the President, most notably the suggestion of removing clause 9. This clause gave what a number of MPs believed was excessive powers to the Minister of Energy to negotiate, grant and revoke oil licences. President Museveni made it clear that he wanted the clause reinserted into the draft bill and showed his anger in a December 2012 speech in which he railed: 'Those who were illogically and desperately opposing this are being financed by foreign interests.' He went on to criticise per diems paid to participants on the oil training courses and suggested that the PFOG was unnecessary given that the constitution already mandated a similar oversight committee. Many observers have come to see the burgeoning row over oil as part of a wider, ongoing face-off between a number of parliamentarians and the President. According to one European diplomatic observer in Kampala: 'When it really matters, Museveni knows how to put his foot down; the mask of democratic accountability dropped.'

Two laws were eventually passed to govern upstream and midstream activities – the Petroleum Exploration, Development and Production Act 2013 (PEDPA) and the Petroleum Refining, Commission, Transport and Storage Act 2013 – but there were a number of flaws. In the new PEDPA, clause 9 was back, and crucially there was no clear provision for the publication of contracts – one of the most important first steps recommended by transparency campaigners. The idea of a civil society monitoring body similar to the PIAC was also rejected. Although Museveni claimed in his December 2012 speech that Uganda would receive at least a 70 per cent revenue share from the IOCs, there is no legislative provision for Ugandans to be able to verify that. The Ministry of Energy and Mineral Development seems to suggest that the principle of protecting commercially sensitive information is more important than transparency. 'We don't want it [transparency] to be part of the law as it reduces our bargaining power,' explains Gloria Sebikari. There are still some attempts to push for better transparency on contracts, and citizens are allowed to submit a freedom of information request to look at the contracts – but for only 15 minutes at a time and without being able to bring a pencil and paper. 'We might never know how much Uganda really earned from oil,' laments journalist Isaac Imaka.

Revenue management The issue of revenue management is no less complex. Provisions for accountability over government spending are currently up for debate in the draft Public Finance Bill (2012), which was stuck in the parliamentary process for most of 2014. The bill governs all aspects of government fiscal and macroeconomic management, with a subsection on oil. It proposes the establishment of a separate account for petroleum revenues that will be audited by parliament, the Auditor General and the Accountant General, with the funds to be split between an allocation to the annual budget and investments (i.e. a 'futures generations fund') to be managed by the Bank of Uganda. According to the theoretical approaches to breaking the resource curse discussed in Chapter 2, this is a good start, but some of the provisions are already being met with opposition. For example, the provision for a 'future generations fund' is politically unpopular. In October 2013, Finance Minister Maria Kiwanuka argued:

> The split [between the national budget and investment] effectively prohibits the government from ever accessing the principal of the Petroleum Investment Reserve for budget financing. This is likely to prove incredible in a country with relatively limited oil reserves and large long-term development needs.[6]

Furthermore, the details in the law are scant. Percentages for how much should go into each fund are not given – in contrast to the case in Ghana – nor are specific development 'priorities' for recurrent spending stipulated. The President did, however, outline his priorities in the December 2012 speech; these were electrification, developing the railways, scientific education and training, roads, agriculture (irrigation) and investing in real estate abroad. No stabilisation fund to guard against price volatility is proposed in the draft law, but the act does recommend that 7 per cent of the revenues from royalties should be shared with the producing districts.

The proposed bill has the advantage of seeming to set up a transparent system whereby oil revenues can be traced, but it relies on the power of largely existing institutions such as parliament and the Bank of Uganda to carry out the function of budgetary scrutiny. The idea of a civil society monitoring body has not been resurrected after its defeat during the debate on the PEDPA, although the bill does suggest the establishment of an advisory committee to examine investment plans. Transparency campaigners remain unconvinced. 'The results will depend on how autonomous and free from political interference parliament and institutions such as the advisory committee can be in their oversight responsibilities,' says Paul Bagabo from NRGI Uganda.

One of the biggest concerns today of Uganda's very active civil society community (and indeed some donors) is that the Ugandan government appears to have pulled back from a reassuring pledge made in the 2008 Oil and Gas Policy to sign up to the EITI. PWYP, which held a conference on how to implement the EITI in Kampala in 2013, has been disappointed that in recent years there has not been a firm commitment or timetable suggested by the Ministry of Finance. 'We've learned from other countries that the EITI is a major way to be able to achieve contract transparency and it would encourage goodwill from the international community if our country shows it is trying to do the right thing,' says Winnie Ngarbiiwe, PWYP's Uganda Coordinator. Recognising the authorities' reluctance, civil society groups have suggested getting some of the principles of EITI included in the Public Finance Bill currently being discussed. As for the Ministry of Energy, the issue again appears to be that the EITI may hamper the government's room for manoeuvre in secretive contract negotiations. 'Our fear is that if we commit to this ... our freedom will be curtailed,' said Gloria Sebikari when I pushed her on the point.

It is an interesting point, but I was left feeling that perhaps the Ugandan government is out of step with the tide of transparency and accountability that is flooding the oil industry after the ten years of campaigning by academics and groups such as PWYP and NRGI. Things may be moving faster than the Ugandan authorities can control. In early 2014, Tullow Oil committed to disclose the details of all its payments to foreign governments,[7] which included figures on VAT and PAYE in Uganda from 2012 that have already been published in the company's annual report. The company says it would be willing to publish a limited set of contracts; it has not yet done this because of Uganda's reluctance. 'There can't be any smoking guns,' says George Cazenove from Tullow Oil. 'This would be a great opportunity for us to show we've nothing to hide.'

Tullow Oil made its disclosure commitment ahead of implementation of the new transparency and accountancy directives that were signed into law by the European Parliament in June 2013 and will become law in 2015. The new rules mean that any EU-based oil company will have to disclose its payments. This EU directive follows on from the important Dodd–Frank Wall Street Reform and Consumer Protection Act, which was passed by the US Congress in 2010 and requires 'full disclosure of any payment made'. The law obliges US companies to report on payments in excess of US$100,000 on a project-by-project basis in annual reports that have to be filed with the Securities and Exchange Commission (SEC). Although the American Petroleum Institute, which represents companies such as Chevron and ExxonMobil, has brought a legal case against the SEC, the new law was welcomed by transparency campaigners. The APP commented:

> Over half of the world's total value of extractive industry market capitalization is found on U.S. exchanges alone … Once the new laws are in operation, global companies will be held to account for a far higher standard of disclosure than currently required under the EITI (APP 2013: 76).

It marked a significant shift in recognising that voluntary disclosure alone was often not sufficient. 'The strength [of voluntary reporting] lies in moral persuasion and an appeal to enlightened self-interest: governments and companies that fail to comply run the risk of reputational damage. An underlying weakness of the EITI is that it has no recourse to mandatory reporting standards, or to sanctions,' argues the APP (ibid.: 75).

To refine or not to refine? The advent of production in Uganda has been delayed by the debate over whether to establish a local oil refinery. This is a now familiar story. Uganda has been traditionally dependent on imports for its domestic fuel consumption, which is currently about 27,000 bpd. Some of that is imported from Kenya, where just one oil refinery with a capacity of 70,000 bpd at Mombasa serves the whole East African region. Uganda is understandably perplexed by the soaring costs of importation, which currently stand at US$1 billion annually, and the country has lobbied hard at meetings of the EAC for support for building a new regional refinery in Uganda. The issue was mentioned in the President's landmark speech on oil in December 2012,[8] and the proposal is clearly laid out in the government's plans for commercialisation, which detail the establishment of a 30,000 bpd refinery (which can be increased to 60,000 bpd) at a site known as Hoima in the Albertine Basin as the 'first phase' of development.

As we have seen from the experiences of Chad and Niger, refineries have made only meagre dents in the cost of fuel and have not fully guaranteed domestic fuel independence. Demand in both countries has been weak, which has reduced government benefits from tax revenues on the sale of refined products. Despite the optimism of many local communities when the construction phase begins, we have seen that only small numbers of permanent jobs have been created at the refineries (just over 700 in Niger and 600 in Chad), and that these are generally reserved for more educated workers from the capital cities. Local employment opportunities are often only in insecure, low-skilled jobs such as driving, guarding facilities and cleaning.

Perhaps more importantly, committing resources and time to building refineries restricts the opportunities for the development of the much more profitable export capability. In Chad, work began on the construction of the Djérmaya refinery in 2008, and it was only in late 2014 that the CNPC was able to begin the first limited exports through the Esso-controlled Kribi pipeline. In Niger, too, the company's production capacity is being held at 15,000 bpd when it is thought the Agadem fields could easily yield over 60,000 bpd, partly because the smuggling of cheaper fuel from Nigeria has lowered demand for the 'official' fuel. While the IOCs in Uganda have said that they are not unequivocally against the idea of a refinery, and the proposal was included in the memorandum of understanding that was signed between the government and the three oil companies in February 2014, there are still concerns about the scale of the project and whether it might result in overproduction for the regional market. Tullow Oil has explicitly said that it will not invest in a refinery, instead calling for an export pipeline to be developed in tandem: 'We must have a route to market,' says George Cazenove.

Despite the IOCs' reticence, the idea of a refinery as a symbol of national independence is popular with the Ugandan press, civil society and the public at large. The government is pressing ahead with plans and has already opened a competitive tender process for the estimated US$2.5 billion construction contract. Six companies, including Chinese and Japanese firms and the Jersey-based Petrofac, have been shortlisted for what will be a public–private partnership, and are submitting detailed bids ahead of a final announcement.[9] The government hopes to get the refinery into production by 2017–18.

The land expropriation and compensation process has begun in Hoima district,[10] but there has been hostility at the community level, which has made the process slower than the government would have hoped. At issue is the resettlement action plan (RAP), which is being used to acquire some 29 square kilometres of land at Kabaale in Buseruka Subcounty. The Ugandan constitution states that compensation for land must be 'fair and adequate' and that the land and buildings on it need to be valued and fairly compensated (International Alert 2011). Around 7,000 people are affected by the compulsory land acquisition, most of them having been given a choice between a cash payment and resettlement on new lands (Global Rights Alert 2013a: 5). Responsibility for determining the relevant values lies with local district land boards, but Paul Bagabo, from NRGI Uganda, claims that in practice there has been little clarity. 'How do you determine fair?' he says. 'Many people argue they should get more just because the land is being used for oil but we have no provisions or best practice to follow.' The process has been further complicated by the fact that there is no real legal system of land tenure. In some cases families had settled on lands that had been granted according to customary law, meaning that they do not have documents demonstrating their ownership and therefore their right to compensation. There are tales of seemingly unfairly low values being placed on land, such as one man who was offered US$350 for his house, and rumours that a 'land rush' is going on as investors seek to buy up land that could prove more valuable in the future. Questions have also been raised by the PFOG about the effectiveness of the Ugandan consultancy charged with implementing the expropriations, Strategic Friends International.

The NGO Global Rights Alert (GRA) is run by a charismatic Ugandan woman, Winnie Ngarbiiwe, well-known to activists working on natural resources across East Africa. After several pestering texts and emails, I managed to get an appointment with this busy lady, and on a sultry Friday afternoon dragged myself up two flights of stairs to her downtown Kampala office, determined to find time in my complicated schedule of meetings with civil society activists to see one of the few prominent women working on the sector (more on that later). As well as her NGO work, Winnie runs a useful and up-to-date website called Oil in Uganda, which is an aggregate site for all kinds of valuable articles and information on the oil industry, and she is also the National Coordinator of PWYP.

Winnie's NGO, which was founded in 2007 to campaign on the extractives industry, has worked hard to bring the voices of the community in Hoima to the outside world. Through a number of reports including *Our Land is Our Bank* and *Sleepless Nights*, which were written in November 2013, GRA has brought the stories of these communities, and especially the women, to light. These excellent reports look at how well communities understand the RAP and whether it has been implemented fairly and consistently across all the families affected. Although Uganda has signed a number of international human rights conventions, GRA found that in some cases people had been 'told under duress to sign [valuation] documents', 'told under duress to acknowledge payment of compensation when no information ... had been given' or had been 'ordered not to plant perennial food crops' (Global Rights Alert 2013b: 8). The NGO found cases where people had signed documents they could not read and did not understand – these were similar to stories I heard in Niger and Chad. It concludes that the 'government needs to do better to provide adequate and accurate information', and calls for the establishment of legal aid or work with NGOs to provide help to individuals who have grievances.

In practice, most people have opted for compensation over resettlement, and GRA went on to investigate what had happened to people who had actually been told they would receive money. In some cases payments had been delayed for up to a year. Where payments had been made, they were often given to male 'heads of households', which further eroded gender relations in the communities as women were very rarely consulted about what to do with the money. Although training sessions had been held in the communities to help them plan for the impact of one-off payments that might be more than a family could earn in a year (3,500,000 Uganda Shillings or US$1,370 per acre was typical), they sometimes found that people had made bad investment decisions such as purchasing a motorcycle to offer 'boda boda' taxi services when the local market was already saturated. In other cases, women had been unable to stop their men wasting the money on alcohol and one-off luxury purchases.

These issues go to the heart of what has been experienced in all of the communities I have visited, from Bakin Birji on the doorstep of the Soraz refinery in Niger to the Sekondi-Takoradi fishermen, where the focus seems to have been on assigning monetary value to land and compensation, and therefore missing the point that existing livelihoods need to be protected. Time and again, people's expectations that the arrival of oil will create jobs and new opportunities that will change the local economy have been dashed, and those who find themselves living 'on top' of the oil see their ways of life permanently disrupted. Once people who traditionally practised mostly subsistence agriculture have signed away their rights to the land and have spent the cash compensation, they are left with nothing. For example, the *Sleepless Nights* report notes that one-off compensation for trees and crops might never reflect their true value: 'fruit trees like mangoes and jack fruit provide an immediate source of income ... yet if they are cut down take several years to bear fruit if they are replanted from seedlings' (ibid.: 14). Once again, the stringent rules of the CCDP in Chad in terms of agreeing set rules for compensation and land values were mentioned with respect in my interviews with civil society. Peter Magalah from ACODE (Advocates Coalition for Development and Environment), another think tank and campaign group on the extractives industry, was disappointed that Uganda's compensation process has not been as consistent. 'Chad was a good example; they had a value for everything and they anticipated the problems that would follow when the communities received the cash. We have not done as well at that.'

While Uganda has yet to see any genuine threats to peace and security in the communities that will be most affected by the commencement of oil production, if left untended, some of these frustrations could easily become a spark that lights wider discontent. The Lake Albert region is close to the border with troubled eastern DRC, where the Ugandan army has been accused of involvement in attempts to chase out various rebel groups including the M23. It is a region far from the capital, where small arms have been known to circulate. Prospection data suggest that there may be more finds in the border region with DRC, particularly under the waters of Lake Albert, which is claimed jointly by the two countries. In recent years there have been fears that despite bilateral agreements between the two countries, disagreements about who owns the oil could increase.[11] Others fear that Uganda's military intervention in neighbouring South Sudan – again close to the oil-producing region – in favour of embattled President Salva Kiir in early 2014 could have consequences. 'There could be blowback from these foreign adventures,' says one diplomat. 'Uganda's oil is located in a notorious trouble spot and any future infrastructure could become a target.'

Local content, environmental and social impacts The experience of all the other African oil producers profiled in this book has shown that Uganda needs to demonstrate clearly to its people that oil benefits the population. How does it do that? The issue of 'national participation' still looms large in many ordinary

Ugandans' grasp of what oil can do to 'contribute to the early eradication of poverty' (Republic of Uganda 2008). However, as we have seen in places such as Ghana, oil rarely has a significant knock-on benefit for the local economy. Economist Paul Collier clearly warned Uganda of those dangers in a speech in Kampala in 2013, when he said that: 'Oil is an overly capital-intensive sector. There are no jobs.'[12]

Uganda has nevertheless taken some important steps towards ensuring that Ugandans are ready to take part in production. The 2013 PEDPA defines the legal basis for the establishment of an NOC that will be state-owned and have the right to participate with a stake of 15 per cent to 20 per cent in future development projects with IOCs. The law also obliges the IOCs to employ Ugandans if a suitably qualified candidate exists and to 'show that they have tried to hire locally', according to Gloria Sebikari. The government has established a number of training institutes and university courses, including a postgraduate course in petroleum geoscience at Makerere University, and several groups of students have carried out internships abroad. Sebikari's PowerPoint presentation when I visited the ministry offices optimistically suggested that 'national participation' would even lead to increased foreign direct investment, infrastructure development and technology transfer.

So far, the results are quite encouraging – CNOOC has committed to 70 per cent of its staff being Ugandan and Total to 60 per cent, and of the 203 staff employed by Tullow Oil, 88 per cent are locals. Tullow Oil says that it has carried out a baseline study to establish how much of its local supply chain can be provided by Ugandan companies and what can be done to scale up that supply; the company estimates that during the construction phase up to 13,000 jobs could be created, many of them in services (with 25 per cent of those being unskilled). However, in the long term only about 3,000 direct, permanent jobs will be created in operations. Civil society again remains unconvinced. 'It's good that this has been mentioned, but how can inexperienced Ugandan companies compete with multinationals [service companies] such as Weatherford and Schlumberger?' said Peter Magalah. 'What constitutes a Ugandan-owned company is very vague. We could end up with local branches of the international companies, which is not creating any value for us.'

Environment Protection of the environment also needs to become more of a priority. Uganda's tourism industry contributes nearly US$400 million to the economy every year.[13] Uganda's flag is emblazoned with the national bird, the crested crane, and the country is endowed with a number of beautiful national parks that can rival any in neighbouring Kenya. These include the Bwindi National Park in the remote south-west, where populations of highly endangered mountain gorillas hang on, protected by soldiers from the Uganda People's Defence Force, and the Rwenzori Mountains National Park, where the fabled 'mountains of the moon' can be found. Some scientists have estimated that the region is home to 30 per cent of Africa's mammal species and 51 per cent of its bird species (International Alert 2011: 40).

One of the jewels in the crown is Murchison Falls, a stunning national park located on the shores of Lake Albert, which is home to hundreds of bird species, giraffes, hippos, elephants and crocodiles and was visited by the famously insatiable hunter Ernest Hemingway. However, this national park also happens to sit squarely on top of the EA1 block, joint owned by Tullow Oil and Total, where six discoveries in the Ngiri field are currently being appraised. While concerns for the future of the national park did not feature prominently in any of the interviews I carried out with civil society activists in Kampala, there are already reports from a number of tourists and tourism companies about patches of forest being destroyed to make way for Total's drilling platforms, and access roads being cut across the official routes inside the park. There are also concerns about the protection of Lake Albert itself, should any spills or chemical seepages get into the water table. George Boden, Uganda researcher from Global Witness, is worried:

It is an incredibly valuable ecosystem. There are many concerns. The worst of which would be a major spill which would cause huge damage not only in Uganda but also potentially in adjacent countries too. Other concerns are poor waste management, flaring or illegal bunkering, which would give rise to lower levels of pollution and contamination affecting animals and humans alike. Secondary activities such as road building, population increase and poaching are likely to affect flora and fauna, particularly in the national parks.

There is some protection available for the park and Lake Albert, principally under the constitution, which states that 'the government holds in trust for the people and protects natural lakes, rivers ... forest reserves and national parks' and asserts the right of Ugandans to a clean and healthy environment. The National Oil and Gas Policy, the National Environment Act and the PEDPA make provisions for the restriction of flaring and pollution, as well as laying guidelines for decommissioning. According to the Oil in Uganda website, individual EIAs supervised by the National Environment Management Agency (NEMA) have to be carried out for each separate activity, including, for example, the drilling of a new well. However, the website claims that these are often of poor quality and are not publicly available.[14] Tullow Oil says that it is signed up to a set of voluntary best practice policies endorsed by the IFC known as the 'Equator Principles' for determining, assessing and managing social and environmental risk. But it may already be too late. Global Witness and the NRGI both say that they are concerned that the Ugandan institutions charged with protecting the environment are ill equipped. 'Bodies like the NEMA and UWA [Uganda Wildlife Authority] are at the back of the queue when it comes to influencing decisions and policy. They lack enforcement capacity,' says Paul Bagabo from NRGI Uganda. 'I'm sad to say it but we're seeing a trade-off between tourism and oil.'

Future success? Ultimately, the realisation of Uganda's oil potential for the benefit of all comes down to the government's ability to strike a balance between protecting Ugandans and creating a business environment in which IOCs are keen to invest. Uganda's evidently cautious regulatory approach is a good start, but it is fair to say that in recent years the relationship between Tullow Oil, one of the main investors, and the Ugandan government has deteriorated. The high point came with confirmation of the discovery of a 1.1 billion barrel field in 2006, but by February 2014 the group's Chief Operating Officer Paul McDade was telling the *Wall Street Journal* that Tullow would consider selling part of its stake in the prized Ugandan field in order to concentrate on its operations in Kenya, where things appear to be moving faster. For Tullow spokesperson George Cazenove it is an obvious enough point. 'It was just an answer to a question,' he says, 'but we can't continue spending all this money without any clear outcome.'

So what happened? The problems started in 2010 when the US firm Heritage Oil sold US$1.3 billion in assets in the Albertine Graben to Tullow Oil, but left without paying the full amount in capital gains tax (CGT) demanded by the Uganda Revenue Authority. The Ugandan government then passed on a US$313 million tax liability to Tullow Oil, refusing to allow it to develop its fields until the money was paid. Tullow successfully sued Heritage for the full amount in 2013 at a tribunal in London and won a subsequent appeal,[15] but the case became a repeated source of headaches for the company. In March 2013, allegations were made in the case that Tullow officials had tried to bribe Uganda in order to help meet the President's 'short-term demands', although these claims were dismissed by the High Court. There are also a further two outstanding court cases. Tullow has been assessed by the Uganda Revenue Authority for a further CGT liability of US$473 million for selling part of its operations to CNOOC and Total; an appeal against this is still ongoing at the time of writing. And finally there is a dispute over Uganda's requirement that VAT of 18 per cent must be paid up front on the importation of goods and services, which the oil companies dispute; this is currently being heard at the International Centre for Settlement of Investment Disputes (ICSID).

Just a month after the Heritage case, Tullow's lucrative deal with the British football team Sunderland FC to sponsor the team shirt fell apart. When the US$20 million deal had been signed just a year earlier, Aidan Heavey, Tullow's Chief Executive Officer (CEO) said: 'Everybody will be wearing the Sunderland shirt; every kid in every school will want a Sunderland shirt which says "Invest in Africa", believe me.'[16] The shirt was actually sponsored by an organisation called 'Invest in Africa', a not-for-profit body that had Tullow Oil as its founding and only partner. This ambiguity was picked up by British newspapers and a BBC North investigation, and a number of groups including the London-based campaign group Platform criticised what it called Tullow's 'unfavourable' contracts for oil production in Africa. In the end, it seems that Sunderland FC was unhappy about the negative press coverage and the sponsorship deal was scrapped one year early. Despite these stories, it is important to stress that during the process of research for this book, my contact with Tullow Oil has indicated that the company is keen to be open and do the right thing in all the African countries in which it is operating. It has been easier to approach Tullow than any of the other IOCs covered in this book, and the company was present at a number of civil society events concerning the oil industry I attended.

While a memorandum of understanding was signed between Total, Tullow, CNOOC and the Ugandan government in February 2014 to provide a 'framework' for commercialisation of the fields, to date, after eight years, the only company to actually gain a production licence is the Chinese CNOOC, which had its field development plan for the Kingfisher field approved in late 2013. So far, no significant production has begun in the Albertine Basin and it remains unclear whether Tullow Oil will ever get to recoup its significant investment or whether it will choose to focus on Kenya, where things seem to be moving more quickly.

Kenya

If Uganda has gained a reputation for moving cautiously as it prepares for the impact of oil on the economy, its neighbour Kenya seems to be trying to achieve the opposite. Just a few years ago, although the country had a well-developed midstream transportation and distribution sector, few believed the rumours initiated by exploration in the 1950s that the country's northern Turkana region could hold significant oil potential. All that changed in March 2012 when Tullow Oil announced that it had found oil in the South Lokichar Basin. 'It is ... the beginning of a long journey to make our country an oil producer,' said then President Mwai Kibaki.[17] In 2013, Tullow reported that it had successfully flow-tested the two initial discoveries at Ngamia-1 and Twiga South-1 in Blocks 13T and 10BB. The company currently estimates that the finds contain 600 million barrels of recoverable oil. The country has forty-six exploration blocks available, and forty-four of them have been licensed for exploration (Republic of Kenya 2014: 19).

The government has indicated that it is keen for production to start by 2016, but there are a number of important practical constraints on establishing production. Kenya is in a similar position to Uganda in that the oil finds are deep inland and in a remote and underdeveloped region, but rather than talking of a refinery, Kenya seems determined to plough on with plans for an export pipeline. Tullow's annual report for 2014 shows a proposed route for an underground, heated pipeline (Tullow Oil 2014: 31) that would run some 850 kilometres from Lokichar to Lamu on the eastern coast. Yet the challenges of starting what would be the longest heated pipeline in the world are immense and require the passing of Kenya's oil legislation, likely regional agreement on the route of the pipeline (if it is also to pass through Uganda and South Sudan, as shown in Map 6.1), land acquisition and not least the securing of finance and investors. Tullow has already confirmed that it does not intend to invest in the pipeline, although Kenyan civil society sources believe that initial contracts have been signed with an unknown investor.

Kenya is also struggling to cope with the threat of terrorism on its territory and the damage that this threat is doing to its ability to sell itself as a safe place for investors. Two of the proposed routes for the pipeline end at new export terminals at either

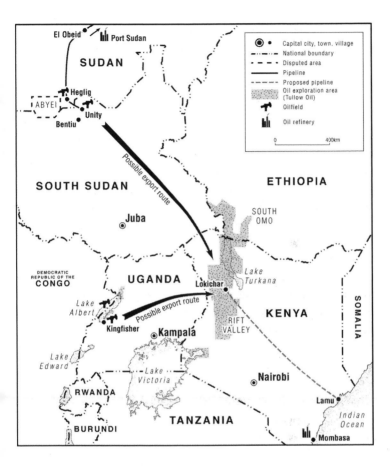

Map 6.1 Export pipelines in East Africa

Mombasa or Lamu on the Kenyan coast, but Kenya's prominent role in sending troops into Somalia to fight the Islamist group al-Shabab has made it a target. There have been a number of attacks against businesses and communities in the coastal region, whose large Muslim communities already bear a sense of grievance against heavily centralised power in Nairobi. The country suffered a terrible blow with the Westgate attacks of September 2013 when a group of suspected al-Shabab attacked the shopping mall, which was popular with Westerners, over several days, taking a number of hostages and killing at least sixty-seven people. There is a real danger that establishing a multibillion dollar export facility so close to the Somali border would be an irresistible target.

In addition to the practical constraints, many civil society groups in Kenya are actively trying to slow down development, concerned that things are moving forward too quickly and that business development is running ahead of legal frameworks and guarantees on protecting livelihoods and the environment. 'Civil society is having to play catch-up and we haven't yet got a full appreciation of what it all means,' says John Ochola, Chairman of the Kenya Civil Society Platform on Oil and Gas (KCSPOG), which itself was only established in 2013. As with the other countries profiled in this book, Kenya faces a range of important questions around local job creation, revenue sharing and livelihood protection, revenue management and regional sharing. This section will look at the concerns surrounding the pace of change and the impact on local people's lives, and how the country proposes to deal with these issues in a complex and evolving political environment.

Policy and legal framework One of the important things to realise when analysing Kenya's approach is that the country's entire policy and law-making environment is going through an enormous period of change at present. 'Kenya is at a crucial turning point in its history. The country has engaged in a deep institutional transformation,' argues Patricia Vasquez (2013: 1), author of *Oil Sparks in the Amazon*, who has completed research for the World Bank in Kenya. The debates on the proposed new oil legislation are taking place after the passing of a new constitution in 2010; this followed devastating post-election violence in 2007–08 in which some 1,300 people died and tens of thousands were displaced. Although many of the grievances surrounding the violence are yet to be addressed – particularly in the area of justice, as the fraught attempts by the International Criminal Court to prosecute current President Uhuru Kenyatta and his deputy William Ruto demonstrate – encouragingly there still appears to be a general mood in the country that there must be no repeat of those dark days. Elections in late 2012 passed off reasonably peacefully; as Kenyan journalist Wairimu Gitahi told me when I visited Nairobi in April 2014: 'People were so shocked by that violence. When it comes to oil, they know their history. They know it can cause conflict. They're asking themselves, how do we prevent it happening again?'

The new constitution was approved by 67 per cent of voters and there is hope that it will make progress towards 'redressing grievances against centralised governance and uneven economic development' (ICG 2013: 2). One of its most important provisions is a long-awaited process of devolution, involving the creation of a new set of forty-seven counties that will enjoy a much greater degree of autonomy and an allocation from central government to their own budgets. This is particularly of interest to Turkana County, where the oil deposits have been found, as it is one of the most marginalised regions in the country. 'Deep-rooted inequalities, especially in the areas where oil and gas reserves are located, are one of the main challenges to Kenya's socioeconomic and political transformation. Kenya remains one of the world's most unequal countries,' says Patricia Vasquez (2013: 30).

It is in this context of huge institutional change that debates on a legal framework for the oil industry are being introduced. Like Uganda, Kenya has expressed a commitment to update legislation before the advent of production, but despite a pledge by the Energy and Petroleum Principal Secretary to present the first draft of new oil laws by 2014, everything is being held up while the legislative process associated with the new constitution is completed. 'In an ideal world, the constitutional changes would have been completed before the advent of oil,' says Charles Wanguhu, Coordinator of KCSPOG.

The provisions for the governance of petroleum have been included in a section on fossil fuels (coal, petroleum and gas) in a wide-ranging draft Energy Bill that covers the country's entire energy needs from electricity generation to renewables to nuclear power. The fifth draft of the bill dedicates just thirty-one pages to oil. It starts well with a declaration that oil resources are held in trust by the national government for the people of Kenya, and that the proceeds raised from their exploitation shall be shared between the national and county governments and the local community. In practice, the proposal is that a 20 per cent share of oil revenues will be sent to the producing county, Turkana, with 15 per cent of that going to local government and 5 per cent to local communities. It proposes the establishment of a 'sovereign wealth fund' to save for future generations; this will receive not less than 5 per cent of the government's share of proceeds. The bill also recommends the creation of a National Fossil Fuels Advisory Board, which is charged with negotiating with international companies to get the best deal for the government on petroleum exploration and production licences, and a National Upstream Petroleum Authority to regulate the industry.

Besides the commitment to grant 20 per cent to the producing community, there is nothing in the Energy Bill on priority spending or revenue management, nor are there any guarantees that payments from IOCs will enter a separate, easily trackable account. There is no mention of creating a civil society monitoring body to check what happens to the money earned from the industry, although KCSPOG has identified the PIAC in Ghana as a good example. There is no proposed legal requirement for contracts or earnings figures to be published. There are only a couple of references to the need for IOCs to employ 'local content' but little detail about what that means or how it might be developed.

The good news is that significant amounts of information about energy policy in Kenya are available on government websites. It is also worth noting that many of the areas that the Energy Bill does not mention seem to be covered by the constitution and by other laws that are currently being developed, such as the draft National Energy Policy 2014 and the updated Petroleum Exploration, Development and Production Bill (the Upstream Bill). The draft Energy Policy makes some good recommendations, for example fleshing out details on how to increase local content participation, and making a commitment that Kenya's oil industry will be developed 'in line with' the EITI. While there is as yet no direct commitment to publish oil contracts, article 35 of the 2010 constitution does give the right of access to information for all Kenyans, and a proposed new bill in this area should allow individuals to access contracts. Furthermore, President Kenyatta told journalists on the sidelines of the US–Africa summit in 2014 that he would back full contract disclosure.[18]

The current review of the Upstream Bill is taking place with technical assistance from the Kenya Petroleum Technical Assistance Project (KEPTAP), a US$50 million World Bank project designed to support capacity building in Kenya's institutional approach to developing the oil sector. The review proposals include drawing up a 'model' PSA that will have clear fiscal and contractual terms, proposing updated environmental provisions, more detail on local content and the principle of open and competitive tendering for oil concessions. However, to the annoyance of civil society, while these laws are being debated, the old Petroleum Act is still in use; the act was written in 1986, well before Kenya had any realistic chance of production. 'We believe there should be a moratorium on granting new licences until this is all sorted out,' says Ndanga Kamau, Oil and Gas Policy Adviser for Oxfam Kenya.

Although these proposals go a long way towards matching the suggestions for avoiding the resource curse from academics, campaigners and NGO groups profiled in this book, civil society groups in Kenya are disappointed that they are still in large part only proposals. Even though there is still so much to be agreed, the government appears determined to move ahead with the establishment of the industry anyway. 'It's all going so fast we really should stop and think it through,' says Charles Wanguhu from KCSPOG. One industry insider has a less forgiving view: 'This is being pushed through by an inexperienced government that is trying to do too much at once and wants oil production to happen before the next election [2016] so they can claim credit for it.'

Revenue management and sharing The proposed allocation of 20 per cent of national oil receipts to the Turkana region represents a significant sum that could go some way to addressing poverty and inequality. It is the highest regional share being proposed in any of the countries I visited, and some local leaders have even claimed that it should go up to 50 per cent. However, as yet there is no clear plan for how this will be implemented nor how to ensure that the local county authorities, established only a few years ago, are ready to absorb the influx of revenue. This presents very interesting questions about how devolution will work in practice in one of Kenya's most marginalised and isolated regions. 'A failure by Kenya to implement political devolution could be damaging to the timely development of the oil industry,' argues Luke Patey (2014b: 19).

The issue of how the government manages natural resource revenue for the benefit of the whole country – for example through a commitment to priority spending for development – does not currently appear to be on the agenda. It is important to remember that Kenya is one of Africa's largest economies, and the current predictions of some 600 million barrels in estimated reserves would make the country a reasonably small producer. At present, as we have seen in Ghana, oil does not look likely to provide the kind of 'shot in the arm' for public finances seen in Chad, nor does it look able to overwhelm the country's GDP. In terms of development, there is already a 'national long-term development blueprint' that was adopted by Mwai Kibaki's 'grand coalition' government of 2008. Known as Vision 2030, this document aims to chart a course for the country to achieve middle-income status by 2030, with a focus on achieving economic growth of 10 per cent per year. In addition to promoting industrialisation, it also proposes that central government money be used to achieve a set of developmental objectives, including recruiting 28,000 new teachers, providing education vouchers to the poorest families, restructuring and rehabilitating health services, building 200,000 new homes and establishing a social protection fund.

Many have argued that this document alone is enough to guarantee that oil revenues are absorbed into the greater economy and that it is simply not necessary for the government to legislate every single aspect of oil revenue management. 'Many of us have faith in our institutions,' says Wanjiku Manyara from the industry body Petroleum Institute of East Africa (PIEA). 'It's a good idea that decisions about spending should be made by the Treasury and not new bodies; we haven't got time to debate every single issue.' But civil society does not think the responsibility for development should be so lightly controlled. 'The government is happy to discuss the regional allocation question because it diverts attention away from the fact that there is no debate on what national government plans to do with the oil money,' says Charles Wanguhu. Interestingly, KCSPOG has been able to identify specific parallels with Chad's Law 001 and the Collège's attempts to monitor spending. The group's recent report argues that the failure of the World Bank project shows exactly why good laws need to be backed up with effective monitoring and with political will to enforce commitments.

> The lesson from Chad is that a revenue management model is a necessary, but not sufficient, condition to ensure the transformative effect of revenues. Transforming petroleum revenues into development also requires a sustained fiscal discipline and strong institutions capable of enforcing the restrictions (KCSPOG 2014: 26).

Local jobs for local people On the morning of 26 October 2013, a group of residents from Turkana South constituency gathered at the gates of Tullow Oil's Twiga well site, and stood in the hot sunshine to listen to local MP James Lomenen. Several people held parasols and listened attentively as the MP mounted a block and spoke passionately about how the oil company should be providing jobs and opportunities to local people. Apparently inflamed by the MP's comments, a group of around 400 people later returned to the site where they overwhelmed security guards and forced their way into buildings. Amateur video footage shows a small group of men, some of them wielding sticks, walking through what looks like a pristine dining hall, carrying bottles of water and pushing doors open. Tullow Oil immediately shut down drilling operations at the camp and staff were evacuated; local news reports claimed that damage amounting to US$90,000 had been caused.[19] Production restarted only after talks between the local community, government and the army and the signing of a memorandum of understanding that reaffirmed Tullow's commitment to creating local opportunities. Yet again the issue of local content was raising its head in one of Kenya's most marginalised and isolated regions.

Turkana, the largest and most north-westerly of Kenya's new counties created in 2010, is home to the Elmolo, Rendille, Samburu, Turkana, Dassanech, Ariaal and Gabbra peoples. It has one of the lowest population densities in Kenya, and many of the people who live there practise pastoralist or nomadic ways of life, or fish in the vast Lake Turkana. It is estimated that over 65 per cent of the population lives below the poverty line and illiteracy levels are assessed as being nearly 90 per cent (ibid.). It is an incredibly hot and dry region where communities such as the Turkana and the Pokot have clashed over grazing lands and scarce water sources. 'Tribal conflicts around cattle ownership are common among some ethnic groups, and cattle rustling is often associated with traditional rites of passage for young men' (Vasquez 2013: 30). According to a 2008 report by the Small Arms Survey, there is a proliferation of weapons in the region, partly due to its proximity to other conflict zones such as South Sudan and northern Uganda, and partly because, the report claims, Kenyan officials have turned a blind eye to ammunition being supplied to the region as the government is unable to fully secure the region itself (Wepundi et al. 2012).

As we have seen in Niger, Chad, Ghana and Uganda, oil is capital- and technology-intensive and rarely creates a large number of local jobs; in most cases, these jobs are for skilled workers who are more likely to come from more developed urban areas where appropriate engineering education is available. Kenya is no exception. So far, Tullow Oil's Kenya team is only about 200-strong, but encouragingly 88 per cent of those are Kenyan nationals, and around 3,000 indirect jobs have been created through contractors and US$3 million spent on acquiring services through local Turkana businesses. Following on from the protests, the company says that it is trying to address community grievances by offering scholarships and training schemes, and by opening community resource offices in Lodwar, Lokori and Lokichar. However, in the light of what happened in October 2013, executives have also pointed to what they say are the dangers of excessive legal requirements for local content (something civil society is very keen on) in areas where the skills shortage is so acute. This puts an interesting slant on an area that seems to have gained almost universal acceptance by the African oil producers profiled in this book. 'Local content rules can just be a form of protection and a barrier to trade,' said Simon Thomson, Tullow's Chairman, at a Chatham House event on Kenya's oil in October 2014. 'Local markets and skills bases are not big enough.' He argued that governments could be better placed to use tax revenue to diversify the economy.

The national oil company Another way of increasing local content is through promoting the participation of the National Oil Corporation of Kenya (NOCK) and Kenyan service companies in upstream activities. The NOCK first became active in 1984 at a time when there was little prospect of a big commercial find in Kenya, despite some drilling activities around Lamu and Mandera. When the 1986 Petroleum Act was passed, it gave the NOCK rights to an equity share in blocks, varying on a case-by-case basis; however, due to the perception that Kenya's oil production potential did not look promising, the NOCK focused its activities on regulation and downstream activities such as retail and distribution. Today, moves are being made to increase the NOCK's participation, including a commitment in the draft Energy Policy currently being debated to 'restructure and enhance NOCK's capacity and focus to conduct upstream business'. It already has one exploration block – 14T – and it is hoped that the corporation can find a commercial partner to develop the block if finds are made.

The NOCK faces some considerable hurdles, such as a lack of equipment and resources, and only a small number of trained graduate scientists. Environmental issues have already arisen in block 14T, with protests about potential damage to wetlands and grazing lands breaking out recently. However, the NOCK has a number of unique advantages, including a long history of collecting valuable data such as seismic results from previous exploration work, and it is hoped that this could be used to generate revenue. Kivuti Nyagah, a consultant for the NOCK, is keen for Kenyans to play a leading role in the sector: 'We're expecting US$9.8 billion investment in the sector over the next eight years. There are a lot of enthusiastic and well-trained people working in the corporation today who want to work out how to capture value from this opportunity.'

Kenya's considerable benefits as a regional economic leader also mean that it is well placed to take advantage of any upcoming commercial opportunities. As the Adam Smith International report notes: 'Kenya is a regional leader. It has the best infrastructure and it is ready ... to engage with a sector in its infancy' (Adam Smith International 2013). Already before a drop of oil has been extracted, a number of professional bodies and training organisations have sprung up. The Kenyan Oil and Gas Association, a professional body representing nine companies involved in upstream exploration, was formed in April 2014, and private firms are looking at a number of opportunities, including expanding drilling potential. Oil and Energy Services is a private consultancy that was set up to provide advisory and research services to the industry as well as tailored training courses for hopefuls looking for jobs in the industry; its mission statement reads: 'Our objective is raising the participation of Eastern Africa people and entrepreneurs in the Oil and Gas industry.' The PIEA (see above) has also arranged a number of bespoke professional training courses and discussion forums, and Tullow Oil has provided scholarships for talented locals. For Wanjiku Manyara, General Manager of the PIEA, promoting business opportunities and freeing up the private sector is the way to get things done in

Kenya: 'Government has too many other things on their plate; they need to get direction from the private sector which understands the sector and its requirements.'

Environmental and social concerns Ikal Angelei is a dynamic young woman whose father was a prominent MP in the Turkana region who made his name in the 1980s opposing the construction of the Turkwel Dam. In 2012 she won the prestigious Goldman Environmental Prize for the work that Friends of Lake Turkana – the group she founded – has done to educate the local community about plans for a new dam (the giant Gibe 3). Somewhat reluctantly she ended up taking the oil brief after she began to be concerned about the impact the new oil drilling and exploration could have on the vulnerable Lake Turkana. 'I really wanted to avoid getting into this after all the other battles I've been engaged in,' she told me with a rueful smile over espresso one chilly April morning in Nairobi, 'but I soon realised it was another enormous threat to our precious lake.'

Ikal's main concern is the threat from oil to livelihoods that already exist in the region, believing that the focus on new job creation and CSR spending is misplaced given past experience in other African countries. 'Everyone wants to work in oil, but agriculture, fishing and the pastoral way of life will have to continue, possibly long after the last drop of oil has been taken,' she argues. There have already been reports of complaints from local herders that some traditional dry season grazing areas have been fenced off.

Ikal is also worried about the quality of the EIAs that are being carried out. 'Lake Turkana has protected areas and that is not being taken into consideration. It's worrying,' she says. In fact, the Adam Smith International research notes that EIAs were often too narrow in scope and warns that 'NEMA is under-staffed and underfunded and does not have the full capacity needed for monitoring and assessment of oil and gas developments, particularly in environmentally and socially sensitive areas' (ibid.), highlighting the fact that the body has already said it needs another 700 staff. KCSPOG also says that there is a danger that EIAs could end up being a 'box-ticking exercise' if community consultations are not done effectively; its 2014 report draws attention to NEMA's own admission that it lacks capacity (KCSPOG 2014: 46). There are further concerns about the possible inadequacy of compensation plans for any land to be expropriated and that oil extraction could lead to more stresses on the region's limited water supply. In response, Tullow Oil says that it has not yet drilled near Lake Turkana, and there are no plans to drill within the protected area. The company says that the EIAs should be publicly available from NEMA, although I was unable to find them on the body's website.

Ultimately, for Ikal, the greatest challenge is to focus on what is already there and to help protect and develop that, rather than dreaming about unrealistic expectations of how oil could deliver transformational development and job creation in the Turkana region. In this respect she believes the learning from Chad's oil project has been explicit:

> What we saw there was that some people's livelihoods have been permanently disrupted by the construction of the Kribi pipeline. They never recovered. For me this is much more important than questions of revenue sharing or revenue management because this region has always had to look after itself and will again in the future.

Women

The idea to include a brief section on the role women play in the African oil industry – whether as civil society activists, employees, journalists or as people affected by oil development projects in communities – came to me after visiting Niger, Chad and Ghana and realising that I had met only one woman. I began to wonder why women were so absent from the debate, especially in civil society organisations in West Africa, which by and large tend to be fairly gender balanced. Is there something intrinsic to the oil industry that puts women off? Thankfully, my own frustrations at seeming to be a woman in a man's world myself were somewhat alleviated after visiting East Africa. As this chapter has shown, women are much better represented at all levels of engagement with the oil industry in Kenya and Uganda, as civil society activists and as executives and heads of professional bodies.

I was particularly impressed by the activities of groups such as Winnie Ngarbiiwe's Global Rights Alert (GRA), which has worked hard to make sure that women's voices are being heard in the debates about compensation and resettlement in the Hoima district of Uganda. Winnie herself became interested in the issues surrounding oil after working on access to healthcare in communities and realising the potential for oil money to be spent on improving health services:

> It very quickly dawned on me that if oil is a blessing it will be women who benefit – from improved schools, healthcare and farming support. If oil is a curse it will be women who suffer – they will lose their land or see it polluted and destroyed, their children could fall sick, they may end up living in slums. What can we do to mitigate those risks? Women must be at the table.

Our Land is Our Bank and *Sleepless Nights*, GRA's reports on the resettlement process in Hoima, get to the heart of the issues affecting women and how women have been absent from decision making and interactions with SFI, the company contracted to develop and implement the RAP. 'When we first starting holding meetings only a handful out of perhaps a hundred participants were women,' says Winnie, pointing to traditional gender roles that have tended to exclude women from decision making on land ownership, choosing the best land for relocation and managing family finances (Global Rights Alert 2013a: 7). The reports are invaluable for getting the voices of women out to a wider audience. One woman in Hoima, Kizza, told GRA: 'Our joy has turned to sorrow because of the refinery. They made us promises like those in thatched houses would be moved to permanent houses. We fell into the trap of promises.' Another, Harriet, said: 'They were threatened that if they didn't sign the compensation agreements, they would not get anything at all. People signed out of fear. People signed out of ignorance.'

Despite great strides in improving girls' access to education and affirmative action in politics, domestic violence is still a problem and women's property rights in marriage are still ambiguous (ibid.: 10). Winnie is frustrated that, although Uganda has a high proportion of female MPs, they have not been able to act firmly on this issue. 'We even have a female Minister of Energy [Irene Muloni]; surely that must count for something?' she says with an ironic smile. Of particular concern with regards to the RAP has been a failure to include a 'spousal consent' section on compensation forms, the absence of which has allowed men to set up bank accounts for the receipt of compensation monies in their names only. The report calls for education for both men and women concerning title rights for new pieces of land, and increased access to justice for women seeking redress. This is an issue that is also beginning to gain importance in Kenya, even though the plans for expropriation of land or grazing areas are much less well-developed. 'The marginalisation of women is particularly acute in the exploration stage of the development of the oil and gas sector,' argues the KCSPOG report. 'If women are left out at this stage it is unlikely that they will be included at later stages' (KCSPOG 2014: 43).

Equally important is the low level of representation of women working in the oil industry, from unskilled workers in indirect jobs, right up to the top level of management in IOCs. Rosie Pinnington, a British researcher working for International Alert in the Hoima district of Uganda, has observed that already people have begun making their way to the region to look for jobs. While in some ways this represents opportunities for women in 'the provision of food to camps and local hotels, but also if the right training is provided, [in] services such as catering, tailoring and hospitality', her research also found women were in danger of being held back by:

> their changing economic role and conflict between male and female partners. There were strong perceptions of insecurity

among male respondents whose female partners were engaged in income-generating activities, which was considered to threaten their role as 'providers' ... The inability of local men to find work in the sector, alongside the introduction of oil workers from elsewhere, constituted a significant threat to their sense of masculinity.

She also identified the risk of women and girls getting into prostitution and the dangers of increased sexual activity taking place in bars associated with oil workers, hearing testimony from girls who had fallen pregnant by oil workers and had been forced to drop out of school.

In his 2012 book on the resource curse, academic Michael L. Ross looked at how oil wealth affects the wider opportunities for women's participation in the labour force: 'As countries get richer, women typically gain more opportunities, both economic opportunities in the workplace and political opportunities to serve in government. Yet this has not occurred in countries that get rich by selling petroleum' (Ross 2012: 111). He found that this effect was strongest in Middle Eastern oil-producing countries, and interestingly he argues that this is because of the oil and not due to pre-existing cultural stereotypes. He blames the fact that oil does not generally benefit the wider economy, citing phenomena relating to the 'Dutch disease', which is often associated with the resource curse theory. This is where alternative economic sectors such as manufacturing and services, which would normally tend to offer opportunities to women, are not developed because oil makes the national currency appreciate and the sectors become less competitive. He also argues that oil-rich rulers with cash to spare can make direct transfers to households, reducing the incentives for impoverished women to go out to work.

The situation for women is perhaps even worse higher up the employment chain. 'From the outside the oil industry does look like a man's world. There seems little attraction and there are few role models for women,' says Wanjiku Manyara, General Manager of the PIEA, a powerful woman at the head of the trade body representing oil companies in Kenya. She talks of her own experience when visiting Aberdeen in the UK to renew her energy certificate; she was the only woman. She wonders if the image of dirty, intensely physical work in isolated places might put a lot of women off. This is certainly the impression I had of the oil industry before I began serious research for this book.

Overall, industry figures are depressing. For example, only 29 per cent of Tullow Oil's total workforce is female and only six out of forty-nine senior managers are women, yet women themselves in the company seem to prefer not to push for gender-specific affirmative action. 'Discussions on diversity have focused more on nationalisation programmes than gender balance,' says George Cazenove. 'Our hunch is that the lack of women in the industry is directly linked to the small numbers of women choosing engineering, geology and geophysics at university.' In the US, it is estimated that only 19 per cent of the workforce in oil and gas is female (IHS 2014b: 1), with many of those jobs in skilled, unskilled or administrative positions. However, the same report projected that some 70,000 jobs for women could be created in the industry in professional, technical and management positions by 2030.

There is some good news for Africa's oil women. Kenya offers a very encouraging example as it has one of Africa's first female CEOs of an NOC, Sumayya Hassan-Athami, who is also the Managing Director. She rose to this prominent position in 2011 after serving for several years as the NOCK's legal manager and developing the corporation's National Oil Strategic Plan for 2008–13. Nigeria has also made important strides in gender equality in the industry, with female heads of several local oil and service companies, and a female Oil Minister, Diezani Alison-Madueke. 'The fact that two of the biggest cabinet positions in Nigeria, petroleum and finance, are held by women shows how far we have come,' she was recently quoted as saying.[20]

Rebecca Ponton worked as a petroleum 'landman' (she recognises the irony), tracking down records of land titles for several years, and is now writing a book about gender and the oil industry called *Breaking the Gas Ceiling*. She says she has encountered negative attitudes towards women working in oil throughout her career. 'It has been perceived as a man's world and even a "good ol' boys" club,' she says, and complains that women in the industry do not get the recognition they deserve. But she believes that things are beginning to change. She points to women who have had success in the sector, such as Maria das Graças Silva Foster, the head of Petrobras, Brazil's NOC, and the first female CEO of a major global oil company, and Sara Akbar, the CEO of Kuwait Energy. There are also a number of new industry initiatives such as Pink Petro,[21] an online forum and chatroom dedicated to supporting women in the industry. 'Many of the major oil and gas companies now have diversity and inclusion departments as part of their commitment to women and minorities, and there is a movement in the US to encourage girls to excel in maths and science, which later may lead them into traditionally male-dominated fields such as engineering,' she says.

Kenya versus Uganda: will they or won't they?

In conclusion, much has been written on the so-called rivalry between Kenya and Uganda when it comes to producing oil first. The Africa Report has talked of a 'race' between the two countries.[22] With Tullow's Chief Operating Officer's frank comments to the Wall Street Journal that the company would be willing to consider selling some of its stake in Uganda to focus on operations in Kenya, the reader can be forgiven for thinking that Kenya could soon be emerging as the winner. In fact, Tullow Oil's George Cazenove estimates that because Kenya is closer to the coast and the government seems to want to move forward, 'Kenya can happen without Uganda, but Uganda cannot happen without Kenya'.

However, Tullow is not the only player in East Africa. CNOOC is quietly getting on with building up towards production in the Kingfisher field at the southern end of the Albertine Basin in Uganda, where it was granted a licence in September 2013. Total, which also has concessions in Uganda, has been more cautious. 'Detailed discussions will soon take place between the government of Uganda and the partners to identify the concrete steps and actions to be taken to ensure a smooth implementation of the memorandum,' Total Uganda's Corporate Affairs Manager Ahlem Friga Noy told the Africa Report in response to Tullow's possible Kenya refocus. Even if the Kenyan government wants to move ahead more quickly and has made those intentions clear to Tullow in private, the outstanding issue of the export pipeline has yet to be resolved. With fears over terrorism and no firm commitments from Uganda or South Sudan, it is hard to see this project moving forward within the kind of timescale necessary to facilitate production by 2016.

As Kenya comes to terms with the enormity of the challenge it faces on oil, Uganda's go-slow approach – no matter how frustrating it is for those IOCs with money at stake and local businesses raring to go – may begin to be seen as a better way of ensuring that the country is ready to make oil wealth work for the benefit of all. As my research from all five countries has shown, having a good legal and policy framework in place before oil is exploited has consistently helped countries avoid the worst effects of the resource curse. As George Boden from Global Witness succinctly puts it: 'Going slow is OK.'

Conclusion

As we have seen throughout this book, there is an unprecedented amount of interest and focus on new African oil. In each country I visited there was a lively debate about every aspect of setting up natural resource extraction projects, from contract transparency to environmental concerns, from creating local jobs to ensuring that the money is spent on development. African oil projects are no longer being written off as environmental and social failures in the same way as they once were in countries such as Nigeria, Angola and Equatorial Guinea, and there is active civil society, campaign group and public engagement on the issues. Despite industry shocks such as the crash in the global oil price in late 2014, which may lead to a more cautious approach by some to investments in African oil, there is still a very high level of interest, particularly from Asian companies.

In the eleven years since the World Bank Chad project launched, the idea of breaking the resource curse and making oil money work for development has undergone a major test in the 'laboratory' of Chad, and now seems to be a prerequisite for starting any new oil production operation. Uganda's 2008 National Oil and Gas Policy sets out its goals for the establishment of a national oil industry on the front cover: 'To use the country's oil and gas resources to contribute to early achievement of poverty eradication and create lasting value to society.' The 2013 annual report of Tullow Oil, the UK oil company that is keen to surge ahead with production in Uganda and Kenya, captures the new way of thinking perfectly, with a large section dedicated to 'creating shared prosperity'.

This new wave of optimism seems to suggest that oil might no longer inevitably end up being a 'curse' – the 'devil's excrement', as OPEC's founder Juan Pablo Pérez Alfonzo once described it (Shaxson 2008: 5) – and that oil rigs might no longer be seen only as 'giant metal mosquitoes, standing on the skin of the earth … drilling down with steel probosces to suck out the fluid that is the lifeblood of the world economy' (ibid.: 6). Instead, today there is a good chance that oil extraction projects could be considered a 'blessing' and an answer to a country's economic woes. The academic literature on the resource curse theory has also moved on in recent years, with some academics now recognising that more up-to-date economic figures suggest that, rather than oil causing economic catastrophe, the real issue is that 'oil has not typically been harmful but has also not created the economic boost that we might expect – it is more of a missed opportunity' (Ross 2012: 221).

Breaking the resource curse: an evaluation

This book has provided an introduction to a wide variety of measures that can be employed in the attempt to break the resource curse, and has shown how they have been implemented practically in Chad, Niger and Ghana. For Kenya and Uganda, we have seen the impact of these ideas on the oil debate as the countries gear up to production.

What has been especially interesting has been how each country has taken a unique approach, in effect trying to select which of the proposed 'solutions' to the resource curse would work best for them. In many cases, this is because of the specific political context of each of the countries; we recall again Michael L. Ross's statement that 'oil does not affect all counties equally' (ibid.: 229). There are clear examples of countries deliberately choosing *not* to consider a certain step, often for reasons of political expediency. For example, it appears that the Ugandan government does not want to cede control of its negotiating powers by publishing contracts or signing up to the EITI, and civil society there has argued that this is because the government is facing financial woes after a number of apparently anti-democratic laws have alienated foreign donors. The Chadian government clearly disliked the restrictions imposed on its freedom to spend by the World Bank when it was desperate to use oil money to fight the rebellion, and Idriss Déby Itno's remarkable grip on power allowed him to push through changes to the law with barely a ripple of dissent from parliament. Although the government of Mahamadou Issoufou in Niger has tried to reposition itself as a less autocratic version of the military dictatorships that preceded it, the decision to increase military spending, the refusal to publish contracts and the arrest of civil society activists show how far it really has to go to truly reform itself and to guarantee that natural resource wealth benefits all. Conversely, it can be argued that Ghana's approach to oil has been more open because of the country's stronger democratic credentials.

However, it is also important to appreciate that some of the more theoretical ideas seem to have had little resonance, in particular questions about saving for the future or setting spending restrictions. As we have seen in Uganda, the proposals to create a 'future generations fund' have run into conflict with what the government feels is the country's immediate need to address poverty and a lack of development. In Kenya, the debate has focused on the regional revenue share in the light of the devolution process, rather than on national spending priorities that the government appears to think can be solved using existing policies. Indeed, some of the best moves that have been taken towards combating the resource curse have actually been locally inspired: for example, the Chadians' rigorous adoption of Esso's high environmental standards vis-à-vis the CNPCIC, the declarations about natural resource ownership in the new Nigerien constitution of 2010, and Ghana's dedication of an entire new piece of legislation to promoting 'local content'.

In the Introduction, I introduced five broad areas into which the current thinking on combating the resource curse can be organised: namely, exploration and production rights and contract transparency, revenue management and sharing, local content, environmental and social protection, and transparency and accountability. What follows is a brief résumé of how these ideas have been implemented in the five countries surveyed and how useful they have been.

Exploration and production rights and contract transparency Up until now, only Ghana has made any real progress in publishing contracts, having been praised for putting several of the Jubilee field contracts with Tullow Oil on the government website; Kenya's President Kenyatta has made encouraging indications that he is in favour of disclosure. However, Chad's contracts with Esso were conceived in secrecy long before the CCDP began; Niger has committed to publishing contracts but has failed to do so and has recently rounded up civil society activists for planning a protest on the issue; and Uganda has been ambivalent on whether it will publish all details. Negotiations over the TEN development in Ghana, the Agadem 2 development in Niger and the Kingfisher licence in Uganda have all been going on in secret despite civil society pressure for openness. None of the countries profiled has made much progress towards increasing transparency in tendering and procurement processes, including for national infrastructure projects such as road building, hospitals and schools. While transparency campaigners agree on the value to society of being able to see whether a government has got a good deal through an open tender process, it seems that the commercial imperative and the countries' desires to be in a powerful bargaining position – plus perhaps the benefits to government insiders of keeping things under wraps – have somewhat stymied the potential of contract transparency so far.

Revenue management
SPECIAL FUNDS Collier and Stiglitz have both written about the value of creating stabilisation (or savings) funds to smooth out spending problems associated with volatile commodities markets (Collier 2010; Humphreys et al. 2007). Collier has developed ideas on the 'ethics of custody', and there has been much written on the value of 'future generations funds'. However, none of these concepts has proved particularly popular in the five African countries

profiled. Notoriously, in Chad the Future Generations Fund was the first thing to go when President Déby needed money to fight the rebels; a stabilisation fund was not considered, although two serious crashes in the oil price in 2008 and 2014 have shown how valuable it could have been. Only Ghana has actually established a future generations fund and a stabilisation fund, neither of which has so far performed particularly well. In fact, there has been considerable focus on the failings of sovereign wealth funds from civil society activist groups in recent years. PWYP, for example, argues that solving governance issues is more important; this view was backed up by research from the NRGI, which found that their performance was affected by an 'absence of transparency, found in half of the funds identified [which] presents significant obstacles to good governance and sustainable development'.[1] In terms of sharing revenues with oil-producing regions, no clear consensus has emerged: while Chad's 5 per cent grant to the Doba region continues, Ghana has refused to pay compensation to Sekondi-Takoradi because the oil project is offshore, and Niger has angered the Zinder region by paying for the Agadem project but not for the Soraz refinery.

SPENDING PRIORITIES AND RESTRICTIONS It should now be clear that the attempt to impose spending restrictions on Chad by the World Bank was not a success, with even the Bank's own evaluation reports concluding that dividing the revenue flows into strict percentages backed up by the law was too inflexible an approach. Seemingly based in part on that experience, the other countries profiled in this book have been more cautious about committing themselves to 'priority sectors'. Ghana and Niger have committed in principle but implementation has been lax; the 2012 PIAC report shows that Ghana identified thirteen sectors instead of the permitted four, and in the last four years Niger has quadrupled its defence spending, which was not identified as a priority sector. Fledgling moves to establish Kenya's oil production industry seem to have dismissed the need to set special targets, assuming rather that existing structures and national development plans can deliver the desired developmental objectives. Chad's difficulties in absorbing the vast influx of cash, managing disastrous oil price volatility and ensuring the quality of investment have been clearly highlighted, and although the other countries profiled have not yet earned enough money to practically make a difference in this area, it is likely that good fiscal management will continue to be a challenge for each of them.

Local content The idea that local people should benefit from jobs and economic opportunities has proved popular with transparency campaigners, and the Natural Resource Charter has advocated the value of creating 'commercially viable national oil companies' to help countries add their own value to exploitation. However, these provisions may be less popular with investors as they can be seen as restrictive trade practices. As we have seen, oil is a capital-intensive industry and all of the operating production projects profiled (in Chad, Niger and Ghana) have created relatively low levels of local employment and the underlying skills base has often been low. However, the good news is that the oil projects in four of the countries are now majority staffed by nationals; the exception is the CNPC's Soraz refinery in Zinder, where the ratio is still only about 50:50. Steps are being taken in Ghana, Uganda and Kenya to develop the capacity of NOCs, and the SHT in Chad has recently acquired a powerful 25 per cent stake in the Doba consortium that runs the oilfields. There is also still considerable debate over the refinery question; so far, the evidence that they can help maximise local value through job creation and the production of cheap domestically produced fuel is scant, and they may even be detrimental in slowing down the development of lucrative export potential.

Environmental and social protection All of the countries profiled in this book seemed at pains to avoid the environmental disaster seen in the Niger Delta, and some have taken steps to implement new, specific legislation. Chad in particular has extremely high standards for environmental protection that it is continuing to implement rigorously, and there are several impressive layers of local and international monitoring of these rules. However, questions remain about whether Chad's willingness to pick fights over environmental issues reflects a genuine commitment to environmental protection or whether it is simply another tool in the ongoing arm-wrestling match with foreign players. Uganda's track record in protecting Murchison Falls national park is more worrying, and it is still too early to assess whether Kenya will succeed in protecting Lake Turkana. Steps are being taken in Kenya to consider ways to protect pastoral and fishing livelihoods, and fishing communities in Ghana have increased engagement with the oil companies in looking for ways to protect the sector.

Transparency and accountability The importance of revenue transparency to all the countries profiled in this book is clear, as all of them have either joined or made commitments to join the EITI. Chad, Niger and Ghana have now achieved compliant status. Each country also has a local chapter of PWYP. As we have seen with revenue streams in Niger and Chad, the EITI reports really do make it quite easy to work out what a country has earned. All the countries except Kenya have discussed the idea of creating a separate 'petroleum account', and Chad and Ghana have done precisely that. Chad and Ghana have also established important civil society monitoring bodies that are charged with verifying the official figures – the Collège de Contrôle and the PIAC; these are making good progress in tracking revenue expenditure, although they both suffer from a lack of funding. Unfortunately, similar ideas in Niger and Uganda have not taken off.

Chad: lessons learned

This book's primary aim has been to shed light on the real impact of oil and to establish a factual picture of how well each of the five countries profiled is doing in guarding against the resource curse and harnessing its oil wealth for development. It has also strived to demonstrate the influential role Chad has played in all these countries' experiences.

Conclusion

After eleven years of experience in practical revenue management systems, a great deal of frustration remains in Chad about just how much has been earned and the perceived 'missed opportunity' for development. Only a small proportion of the US$10 billion the country has received has gone on development projects, and as much as US$4 billion may have been spent on the military. The country has failed to move off the bottom rung of a range of indexes measuring development and poverty reduction, and the average Chadian's life has barely changed. Nevertheless, there is still a number of positives from this experience, including the establishment of several innovative systems that survive today: the traceable escrow account, civil society monitoring of spending projects and, significantly, a high standard of environmental protection that has ensured that the project has caused nowhere near the level of damage and pollution seen in the notorious case of the Niger Delta. These high standards have allowed Chad to flex its muscles in demanding higher environmental standards from the CNPCIC.

Academic Peter Rosenblum was quoted in the Introduction to this book suggesting that Chad was the 'laboratory' for much of the thinking on tackling the resource curse that has developed over the last ten years. Certainly, it seems unlikely to be just a coincidence that a lot of the initiatives, such as PWYP and the NRGI, were born in the early 2000s, at exactly the same time as the heated debates on the parameters of the World Bank deal were taking place. As we have seen after visiting the other countries profiled, Chad's systems have been studied and evaluated by many in civil society and campaign groups looking for workable solutions to the resource curse. Eleven years on, it is remarkably easy – with the help of EITI reports – to see how much Chad has earned. The important work civil society groups such as PWYP and GRAMP-TC have played in helping Chad reach its goal of achieving compliance with the EITI must be acknowledged, and crucially the Chadian government has chosen not to close down all avenues leading to the continuation of civil society monitoring of revenue. 'One positive outcome of the entire effort was that it brought to the fore the fundamental need for civil society oversight and participation in the ... industry ... and the management of resulting revenue flows,' concluded a PWYP report on Chad. For Emmanuel Kuyole, from the NRGI in Ghana, the Collège has been an excellent example to learn from:

> Citizen oversight is something which everyone is interested in creating now. But we've seen how if government feels threatened by the body it can severely hamper its activities. For this reason we learnt from Chad that any civil society monitoring body needs to have its own independent source of funding.

Of course, that same issue has yet to be resolved with the PIAC monitoring body in Ghana. A report by the KCSPOG also explicitly mentions Chad's revenue management law and notes how its legal provisions were severely undermined by the lack of political will to enforce them.

In Ghana, Kenya and Uganda, several civil society actors were especially interested in the issue of a rigorous, independently verified environmental monitoring and compensation plan, such as the one agreed under the EMP of the CCDP. They believed that it was significant that there had been sustained negotiation between the architects of the oil project and the local communities in and around Doba about what they were being offered in compensation, and that some serious thinking had gone into restoring livelihoods and training people in sensibly managing huge one-off compensation payouts. 'We should all refer back to the way it was done in Chad. Rather than vague words like "fair and adequate" [compensation] there would be a set rate that people would agree to. The local institutions in Uganda were just unprepared for the amount of work they would have to do to value all this land,' says Paul Bagabo from Revenue Watch Uganda, referring to the way in which compensation has been worked out in the Hoima refinery scheme. Furthermore, Chad's pugnacious approach to China described in Chapter 3 has been noticed by civil society groups elsewhere. In Niger, I found that even small civil society organisations in Zinder were aware of the ongoing battles between the Chadian state and the CNPCIC over both the price of petrol and the allegedly lax environmental standards.

In my view, Chad's key contribution has been in showing that it is possible to attempt a 'cradle to grave' approach to managing the resource curse. What cannot be gleaned from its successes can certainly be surmised from its failures. The decision to scrap the Future Generations Fund when the World Bank pulled out in 2006 foreshadowed much current thinking on the real value of savings funds when development needs today are so urgent (see below). As discussed in Chapter 1, even the World Bank's own evaluation report concluded that the spending priorities in Law 001 were just too 'inflexible' and that future attempts to manage revenue must take that into account. I have also described the frustration with the fact that Chad's original contracts with Esso have never been published, and that open tendering – today considered by transparency campaigners as one of the most fundamental early steps – was never considered.

The experience has clearly demonstrated that it takes much more than a good set of written laws to guarantee that the money earned is spent on effective domestic investment that really does lead to development. Significant steps have been taken towards achieving that goal in Chad, where civil society has been allowed to continue monitoring spending, and new ideas such as the EITI have been introduced to complement what was left of the original World Bank deal. Nevertheless, while the unprecedented focus on the way in which things were set up in Chad at the beginning of the CCDP has undoubtedly prevented it becoming a resource-cursed basket case, so far there have not been sufficient accompanying improvements in governance and accountability to ensure that the enormous sums earned do not simply constitute a colossal missed opportunity. Good laws need political will to back them up.

Similar problems have started to emerge in Ghana and Niger, which have begun production in recent years, and are salutary for Kenya and Uganda as they embark on their own projects. In Niger, the government has taken important steps towards committing to transparency on paper, but so far implementation has been slow. With no immediate plans for exporting and not particularly encouraging results from the country's new refinery, it remains to be seen how transformative the CNPC operations in the east will turn out to be. Ghana has been hailed as a moderate success story; it doubtless has some of the best legislation and is notable for the ease of access to documents, reports and figures on the oil sector and its decision to publish certain contracts. The establishment of the oil industry has been quick and has already yielded results, even if production has yet to reach a peak. However, the country still has work to do to fully implement its new laws and to increase the participation of Ghanaians and Ghanaian businesses in the sector.

In the same vein, Uganda has created a good set of petroleum laws so far and is currently debating important measures about revenue transparency and spending plans. But what has been described as excessive political control and slow progress on getting these legislative frameworks off the ground risk alienating investors; taken together with the priority attached to building a refinery, with its attendant problems of land and resettlement, this could mean that the country is still some way off seeing any material benefit from its natural endowments.

Beyond transparency

Civil society advocacy and accountability movements, both local and international, have come a long way since the early days of discussing the resource curse at the start of the 2000s. Grassroots movements such as PWYP sprung up from a conviction that the secrecy surrounding how much IOCs were paying governments for the rights to natural resource extraction was at the root of the problems experienced in many resource-rich nations. Today, the debate has moved on to recognising that transparency needs to occur throughout the 'value chain'. 'The main change has been that we recognise it's not just about what companies pay,' says Alice Powell from the PWYP Secretariat in London. 'For example, if you don't pay attention at the contracts stage you've already lost out – it may be too late.' She adds that, although the idea of choosing *not* to extract at all if it seems that the project could harm the environment and livelihoods is generally unpopular in Africa, there are some places, such as Costa Rica, where views like this are starting to be taken seriously. 'These decisions need to be made at the community level. There needs to be more informed consent,' says Powell.

The EITI itself was one of the first to suggest that there could be limitations to the ability of transparency as an objective on its own to deliver a 'lasting benefit' to society from natural resource extraction. The sixth global EITI conference, which took place in Sydney, Australia in May 2013, was entitled 'Beyond Transparency', as was the organisation's 2013 progress report. Writing in the 2013 report, the Chair of the EITI, Clare Short, stated that 'the EITI is not yet generating informed public debate, and the public debate is not yet driving the reform that is needed to bring lasting benefits to the people' (EITI 2013b: 4).

At issue seemed to be the question of what civil society and ordinary people should actually do with the pages of excellent data and figures produced in the now more than 160 reports that have been completed by EITI teams globally. How could those revenue figures actually be used to generate debate? In fact, is it reasonable to expect ordinary people or civil society to engage on the issue of revenue management to such an extent? Many of the EITI reports are prepared meticulously but are quite difficult to understand for those without an accountancy or economics background. The 2013 EITI conference recognised that the reports: 'Have often been difficult to read and interpret ... and require that readers have technical experience about the extractives sector' (ibid.: 8). Certainly, it is easy to see the difficulties of getting the EITI message across in countries such as Chad and Niger, where literacy rates are below 30 per cent and only a fraction of the population has access to the internet, where they might be able to read the reports.

A similar problem has been identified in Ghana, which is proud of its status as an EITI-compliant country through its reporting on oil production as well as mining. Franklin Ashiadey from the EITI Steering Committee was frank:

> EITI is just the first step. We make the information available but civil society needs to do more to actually use the reports, to hold to account the policy makers. After all, it's a voluntary process; EITI is not a magic bullet.

This reflects some of the thinking behind new developments such as the Dodd–Frank Act (Chapter 6), which recognise that some form of mandatory disclosure for companies and governments may also be necessary. In Uganda, groups such as PWYP have been suggesting that some of the EITI principles could be integrated into law, in effect transforming the EITI reports from a standalone document to a more comprehensive national approach. Ghana has also made some impressive steps towards making revenue figures useful and accessible; the PIAC reports explain the numbers clearly and measure them against the commitments and laws made by the government – the 2012 report details precise 'lifts' of oil shipments from the Jubilee field, royalty and tax payments, the total allocation of those receipts by the Ministry of Finance, and even the investment performance of the holding and future funds. The Collège in Chad has also produced a number of similar reports. However, in both countries the question of who bears responsibility for acting upon that information and taking the government to task has not been fully resolved. 'Parliament should be the one to examine these reports and monitor what's being done but they don't have the capacity,' says Emmanuel Kuyole from NRGI in Ghana. 'The real problem is that neither the EITI nor the PIAC has any sanction power to change the government approach.'

What this new body of thinking appears to be saying is that without strong and accountable parliaments and democratic reforms, transparency runs the risk of becoming what the Open Society has called 'an end in itself'. I would also argue that there is still ample scope for all of the international campaign groups and organisations working on natural resource extraction and

Conclusion

transparency to better coordinate their work to prevent dupli-cated effort in areas such as transparency indexes, value chains and the various recommendations. Although these duplications have come about because many of the initiatives profiled in this book (PWYP, EITI, and so on) developed in an ad hoc and open environment, it is difficult for an outsider not to wonder if money and resources could be put to use more efficiently if a more consolidated approach could be found.

In conclusion, we return to the issue of governance, or effective-ly ensuring that leadership is accountable to the people. We have already seen the poor performance of Chad in the Mo Ibrahim Index of African Governance: in 2014 it came forty-eighth out of fifty-two countries (Niger came twenty-eighth, Kenya twenty-first and Uganda eighteenth, but Ghana did rather better at seventh).[2] The bottom of the list is littered with resource-rich countries including DRC, Equatorial Guinea, Guinea, Nigeria, Angola and Libya. Better governance in all the countries profiled in this book is needed so that every carefully created step towards effective natural resource governance – whether it be revenue management systems, stabilisation funds, spending priorities or commitments to publish contracts – is followed to the letter and that local populations feel empowered to challenge what governments are doing in their names. What has been abundantly clear in my research is that it is ultimately governments that decide how far it is in their interests to implement the many transparency measures profiled in this book. Civil society – campaign groups, journalists, ordinary people and opposition voices – has an important role to play, but if leaders decide against a step on whatever grounds, protest is often powerless. When Chad rewrote Law 001, when the Nigerien government directed resources to its defence budget and arrested transparency campaigners, when Uganda rejected plans for a civil society monitoring group and the reinstatement of clause 9, these were all fundamentally 'top-down' decisions. And when Ghana voted in its laudable revenue management law, this was the government's own initiative.

In addition, we have seen how opaque deals made with

Chinese companies have seemed to offer African governments fewer reasons to be accountable and transparent – at least in the early stages – challenging progress made elsewhere. However, this book has hopefully shown that, despite concern in the Chad and Niger projects that the Chinese approach would inevitably lead to a new wave of imperialism, African countries can and do stand up to China when the deals they have signed appear not to deliver what was promised. It has been a steep learning curve for the CNPC, which may now be beginning to adjust its approach – despite initial secrecy over the contracts agreed with Niger and Chad, the company has now become broadly supportive and compliant with initiatives such as the EITI.

Fantastic progress has been made in the last ten years. We have gone from a virtual acceptance that natural resource abundance would lead to poor economic growth, corruption and environmental destruction on the scale of the Niger Delta, to a situation today where vibrant debate on how to prevent the resource curse and deliver lasting benefits to the people seems to be at the heart of establishing oil extraction programmes across Africa. 'We've seen remarkable change even in the last three years. Civil society didn't even know how to engage on the issues and was completely outside the debate, but today we get invited to meetings and we are able to take part in the dialogue,' says Paul Bagabo from the NRGI. The next step, which will hopefully end for ever the wasting of billions of dollars in precious oil revenues, is to make sure that governments are listening.

Notes

Introduction

1 'Nigeria's Ventures magazine lists 55 billionaires', BBC News, 7 October 2013: www.bbc.co.uk/news/world-africa-24433996.

2 'The life of Ken Saro-Wiwa', Remember Saro-Wiwa: http://remembersarowiwa.com/background/the-life-of-ken-saro-wiwa/.

3 'Isabel dos Santos: "First African female billionaire"', BBC News, 25 January 2013: www.bbc.co.uk/news/world-africa-21184854.

4 See www.resourcegovernance.org/issues/natural-resource-charter.

5 Interview, 18 October 2013.

2 A model project

1 See IMF.

2 Interview with anonymous US academic, May 2014.

3 Phone interview, 18 October 2013.

4 See http://country.eiu.com/chad.

5 Calculations based on figures in the 2007–11 EITI reports.

6 Telephone interview, 18 October 2013.

7 See www.smallarms-survey sudan.org/fileadmin/docs/documents/HSBA-Sec-Gen-2009-562.pdf.

8 'Chad: top brass defectors protest Deby rule', IRIN, 12 December 2005: www.irinnews.org/report/57544/chad-top-brass-defectors-protest-deby-rule.

9 'Chad orders foreign oil firms out', BBC News, 27 August 2006: http://news.bbc.co.uk/1/hi/world/africa/5289580.stm.

10 'Chad: civil society disappointed by World Bank oil pull-out', IRIN, 14 September 2009: www.irinnews.org/report/80338/chad-civil-society-disappointed-by-world-bank-oil-pull-out.

11 'World Bank suspends loans to Chad – "model" oil project on the rocks', Oxfam, 6 January 2006: www.publishwhatyoupay.org/resources/world-bank-suspends-loans-chad-%E2%80%93-%E2%80%9Cmodel%E2%80%9D-oil-project-rocks.

12 Interview, 18 October 2013.

13 Interview with the Alternative Research Group on Oil Monitoring, 2009, and calculations based on IMF reports and EITI reports. See the figures on page 7 of the IMF Country Report No. 13/87 on Chad at www.imf.org/external/pubs/ft/scr/2013/cr1387.pdf. In 2009, GRAMP-TC estimated spending of US$600

million for the period 2003–09; and EITI estimated US$500 million for spending on the Mali intervention of 2013.

14 Author's interviews, 18 October 2013.

2 The aftermath

1 '2010 human rights report: Chad', US Department of State: www.state.gov/j/drl/rls/hrrpt/2010/af/154338.htm.

2 'Griffiths to pay millions in African bribery case', *The Globe and Mail*, 22 January 2103: www.theglobeandmail.com/report-on-business/industry-news/energy-and-resources/griffiths-to-pay-millions-in-african-bribery-case/article7622364/.

3 Interview with Mauricio Villafuerte, IMF economist on Chad, October 2013.

4 See http://eiti.org/eiti/history.

5 See http://international budget.org/.

6 'Chad recognised as compliant with EITI transparency standard', EITI website, 15 October 2014: https://eiti.org/news/chad-recognised-compliant-eiti-transparency-standard.

7 US$2,467,059,299 or 1190,672,497,355 CFA, of which US$1,597,751,772 or 771,606,930,743 CFA was spent on priority sectors. Figures from the Collège's annual report for 2012.

8 Interview with Alan Gelb, former Chief Economist for Africa at the World Bank, 20 October 2013.

9 Interview, June 2009.

10 Interview, 15 July 2013.

11 Interview with Mauricio Villafuerte, IMF economist on Chad, October 2013.

12 Follow-up email with Mauricio Villafuerte, IMF economist on Chad, October 2013.

13 'Chad backs out of hosting AU summit', eNews Channel Africa, 11 January 2015: www.enca.com/africa/chad-backs-out-hosting-au-summit.

14 See www.publishwhatyoupay.org/about/history.

15 Interview, 9 July 2013.

16 Email from Steve Coll, author of *Private Empire*, 13 March 2014.

17 Interview, 4 July 2013.

18 'Glencore to finance Chad's $1.3 bln oil assets purchase', Reuters, 16 June 2014: www.reuters.com/article/2014/06/16/chad-oil-glencore-idUSL5N0OX3MN20140616.

19 'Millennium development goals: big ideas, broken promises?', *Guardian*, 24 September 2013: www.theguardian.com/global-development/interactive/2013/sep/24/millennium-development-goals-data-interactive and World Data Bank: http://databank.worldbank.org/data/views/reports/tableview.aspx.

3 Lessons learned for China?

1 CNPC information from staff at Ronier site, July 2013.

2 Author's interview with Dou Lirong, 8 July 2013.

3 'EnCana sells all of its interests in Chad', EnCana, 12 January

2007: www.encana.com/news-stories/news-releases/details.html?release=609901.

4 'Chad says suspends CNPC refinery deal', Reuters, 24 January 2012: http://mobile.reuters.com/article/rbssOilGasRefiningMarketing/idUSL5E8CO3BR201 20124.

5 'Darfur: new weapons from China and Russia fuelling conflict', Amnesty International, 8 February 2012: www.amnesty.org/en/news/darfur-new-weapons-china-and-russia-fuelling-conflict-2012-02-08.

6 'China's oil fears over South Sudan fighting', BBC News, 8 January 2014: www.bbc.co.uk/news/world-africa-25654155.

7 'Chad: country analysis note': www.eia.gov/countries/country-data.cfm?fips=CD&trk=p1.

8 Sources from EITI.

9 'Chad suspends China's CNPC unit over environment', Reuters, 14 August 2013: http://uk.reuters.com/article/2013/08/14/us-chad-china-cnpc-idUKBRE97D0VN20130814.

10 Interview with anonymous US academic, July 2013.

11 Josef Skoldeberg, Lead Communications Officer, IFC Infrastructure and Natural Resources, 23 January 2014.

12 'Glencore to finance Chad's $1.3 bln oil assets purchase', Reuters, 16 June 2014: www.reuters.com/article/2014/06/16/chad-oil-glencore-id USL5N0OX3MN20140616.

13 'In Chad, elephants make a comeback', Aljazeera America, 5 September 2014: http://america.aljazeera.com/articles/2014/9/5/in-chad-elephantsmakeacomeback.html.

4 Resource nationalism in Niger

1 Interview, 21 February 2014.

2 Figures from February 2014.

3 Interview, 21 February 2014.

4 'Special report: Areva and Niger's uranium fight', Reuters, 5 February 2014: www.reuters.com/article/2014/02/05/us-niger-areva-specialreport-id USBREA140AA20140205.

5 'Niger activists arrested over Areva protest before François Hollande visit', Guardian, 18 July 2014: www.theguardian.com/global-development/2014/jul/18/niger-activists-arrested-areva-francois-hollande-france-uranium.

6 'Niger's Hama Amadou flees over baby-trafficking scandal', BBC News, 28 August 2014: www.bbc.co.uk/news/world-africa-28966966.

7 Preview version of the 2012 EITI report from the secretariat in Niamey.

8 Interview with Ali Idrissa, 20 February 2014.

9 Interview with Sergei Boeke, International Centre for Counter-Terrorism, 10 May 2014.

5 Civil society in Ghana

1 'Ghana "will be an African tiger"', BBC News, 19 June 2007: http://news.bbc.co.uk/1/hi/world/africa/6766527.stm.

2 'Why many of Ghana's gold

miners are giving up', BBC News, 30 December 2013: www.bbc.co.uk/news/business-25417492.

3 Ghana Oil Almanac: http://wiki.openoil.net/index.php?title=Ghana.

4 Interview, 22 January 2014.

5 Interview, London HQ, 25 April 2014.

6 Resource Governance Index, Natural Resource Governance Institute: www.resourcegovernance.org/rgi.

7 'Ghana lacks "capacity" to tackle oil spills, report shows', Bloomberg, 8 October 2010: www.bloomberg.com/news/2010-10-08/ghana-lacks-the-capacity-to-tackle-spills-from-oil-wells-report-shows.html.

8 'Mystery of Ghana whale deaths', BBC News, 6 September 2013: www.bbc.co.uk/news/world-africa-23992933.

9 Bank of Ghana: www.bog.gov.gh.

10 'Ghana limits dollar transactions to protect Cedi', BBC News, 6 February 2014: www.bbc.co.uk/news/world-africa-26064127.

11 International Monetary Fund: www.imf.org.

12 MDG 1: Eradicate extreme hunger and poverty, United Nations Development Programme: www.gh.undp.org/content/ghana/en/home/mdgoverview/overview/mdg1/.

13 'Introduction to UNICEF's work on statistics and monitoring', UNICEF: www.unicef.org/statistics.

14 'Ghana: the best mix of power sources – the way forward for Ghana', All Africa, 12 March 2014: http://allafrica.com/stories/201403120940.html.

15 Interview, 22 January 2014.

16 'Ghana: to flare or not to flare Jubilee gas', All Africa, 1 February 2014: http://allafrica.com/stories/201402031931.html.

17 'Natural resource-rich countries hampered by sovereign wealth fund opacity and mismanagement', Natural Resource Governance Institute, 8 April 2014: www.resourcegovernance.org/news/press_releases/natural-resource-rich-countries-hampered-sovereign-wealth-fund-opacity-and-misma.

6 East African miracle?

1 Oxfam US at Chatham House, 8 October 2014.

2 'Tullow may sell part of stake in Ugandan oil field: chief operating officer says focus may switch to Kenyan project', *Wall Street Journal*, 12 February 2014: http://online.wsj.com/news/articles/SB10001424052702304888404579378581273550024.

3 'Uganda: high stakes in the oil debates', Think Africa Press, 6 September 2012: http://thinkafricapress.com/uganda/oil-revenue-management-and-president-musevenis-exit.

4 President Museveni's speech to the Ugandan parliament, 13 December 2012.

5 'Uganda donors cut aid after president passes anti-gay law', *Guardian*, 25 February 2014:

Notes

www.theguardian.com/global-development/2014/feb/25/uganda-donors-cut-aid-anti-gay-law.

6 'East Africa: Kenya or Uganda, who gets oil first?', The Africa Report, 25 April 2014: www.the africareport.com/East-Horn-Africa/east-africa-kenya-or-uganda-who-gets-oil-first.html.

7 'Tullow's tax disclosures torpedo Big Oil's campaign for secrecy', Global Witness, 24 March 2014: www.globalwitness.org/library/tullow%E2%80%99s-tax-disclosures-torpedo-big-oil%E2%80%99s-campaign-secrecy.

8 President Museveni's speech to the Ugandan parliament, 13 December 2012.

9 '6 firms shortlisted for oil refinery deal', The Observer, 17 December 2013: http://observer. ug/index. php? option=com_content &view= article&id=29179:6-firms-shortlisted-for-oil-refinery-deal& catid=38:business&Itemid=68.

10 'Refinery compensation exercise behind schedule', Oil in Uganda, 2 July 2014: www. oilinuganda.org/features/land/refinery-compensation-exercise-behind-schedule.html.

11 'DRC and Uganda ease oil tensions', BBC News, 8 September 2007: http://news.bbc.co.uk/1/hi/world/africa/6984758.stm.

12 'Uganda: oil will not create jobs – Prof Collier', The Observer, 22 December 2013: http://allafrica.com/stories/201312230081.html.

13 'Tourism earnings hike to $400m', *New Vision*, 4 Nov-ember 2010: www.newvision.co.ug/D/8/220/737091.

14 'Uganda's environmental impact assessment process under fire', Oil in Uganda, 13 September 2012: www.oilinuganda.org/features/environment/ugandas-environmental-impact-assessment-process-under-fire.html.

15 George Cazenove, Tullow Oil spokesman, 21 April 2014.

16 'Tullow Oil's Sunderland AFC sponsorship ends amid controversy', Platform, 11 April 2013: http://platformlondon.org/2013/04/11/tullow-oils-sunderland-afc-sponsorship-ends-amid-controversy/.

17 'Kenya oil discovery after Tullow Oil drilling', BBC News, 26 March 2012: www.bbc.co.uk/news/world-africa-17513488.

18 '"Absolutely" – Kenya President backs full oil contract disclosure', GOXI, 27 August 2014: http://goxi.org/profiles/blogs/absolutely-kenya-president-backs-full-oil-contract-disclosure.

19 'Kenya MP accused of inciting protests against oil firm Tullow', Reuters, 31 October 2013: http://uk.reuters.com/article/2013/10/31/uk-kenya-tullow-idUKBRE99U11N20131031.

20 'Nigeria's growing number of female oil bosses', BBC News, 11 September 2014: www.bbc.co.uk/news/business-29127436.

21 Pink Petro: www.pinkpetro.com.

22 'East Africa: Kenya or Uganda, who gets oil first?',

The Africa Report, 25 April 2014: www.theafricareport.com/East-Horn-Africa/east-africa-kenya-or-uganda-who-gets-oil-first.html.

Conclusion

1 'Natural resource-rich countries hampered by sovereign wealth fund opacity and mis-management', Natural Resource Governance Institute, 8 April 2014: www.resourcegovernance. org/news/press_releases/ natural-resource-rich-countries-hampered-sovereign-wealth-fund-opacity-and-misma.

2 See www.moibrahim foundation.org/interact/.

Bibliography

Books and reports

ACEP (2013) *Between a Blessing and a Curse: The state of oil governance in Ghana*. ACEP Policy Paper 1. Accra: Africa Centre for Energy Policy (ACEP).

Adam Smith International (2013) *Recommendations for the Development of Kenya's Extractive Industries Based on Inclusive Multi-stakeholder Consultation*. Nairobi: Adam Smith International Africa and UK Department for International Development. Available at: http://ices.or.ke/wp-content/uploads/2014/05/Recommendations-for-the-Development-of-Kenyas-Extractive-Industries-v2-...-copy.pdf.

Ajugwo, A. O. (2013) 'Negative effects of gas flaring: the Nigerian experience'. *Journal of Environment Pollution and Human Health* 1(1): 6–8.

Alden, C. (2007) *China in Africa*. African Arguments. London: Zed Books.

APP (2013) *Equity in Extractives: Stewarding Africa's natural resources for all. Africa progress report 2013*. Geneva: Africa Progress Panel.

Barkan, J. D. (2011) *Uganda: Assessing risks to stability. A report*

of the CSIS Africa Program. Washington DC: Center for Strategic and International Studies (CSIS).

BP (2014) *BP Energy Outlook 2035*. London: BP. Available at: www.bp.com/content/dam/bp/pdf/Energy-economics/Energy-Outlook/Energy_Outlook_2035_booklet.pdf.

Calderisi, R. (2006) *The Trouble with Africa: Why foreign aid isn't working*. New Haven CT: Yale University Press.

Coll, S. (2013) *Private Empire: ExxonMobil and American power*. London: Penguin.

Collier, P. (2010) *The Plundered Planet: How to reconcile prosperity with nature*. London: Allen Lane.

Copnall, J. (2014) *A Poisonous Thorn in Our Hearts: Sudan and South Sudan's bitter and incomplete divorce*. London: C. Hurst.

ECMG (2012) *Report of the External Compliance Monitoring Group: Chad Export Project*. Genoa: D'Appolonia for the International Finance Corporation.

EITI (2013a) *République du Tchad / Initiative pour la Transparence des Industries Extractives: Rapport de l'Administrateur indépendant de l'ITIE pour les revenus de l'année 2011*. Paris: Fair Links for Extractive Industries Transparency Initiative (EITI). Available at: www.itie-tchad.org/publication/rapport/FairLinks_ITIETchad_Rapport_2011.pdf.

— (2013b) *Progress Report 2013: Beyond transparency*. Oslo: Extractive Industries Transparency Initiative (EITI) International Secretariat. Available at: https://eiti.org/document/progressreport.

— (2014) *République du Tchad / Initiative pour la Transparence des Industries Extractives: Rapport ITIE 2012*. Paris: Fair Links for Extractive Industries Transparency Initiative (EITI). Available at: www.itie-tchad.org/publication/rapport/FairLinks_ITIETchad_Rapport_2012.pdf.

Esso (2012) Chad/Cameroon Development Project: Project update no. 33. Year end report 2012. Houston TX: Esso Exploration and Production Chad Inc.

Gary, I. and N. Reisch (2004) *Chad's Oil: Miracle or mirage? Following the money in Africa's newest petro-state*. Baltimore MD: Catholic Relief Services.

Ghazvinian, J. (2007) *Untapped: The scramble for Africa's oil*. Orlando FL: Harcourt.

Global Communities (2013) 'Fuelling the future of an oil city: a tale of Sekondi-Takoradi in Ghana'. Accra and Sekondi-Takoradi: Global Communities Ghana.

Global Rights Alert (2013a) *'Our Land is Our Bank': Gender issues in Uganda's resettlement action plan*. Kampala: Global Rights Alert.

— (2013b) *Sleepless Nights: The fears and dilemmas of oil refinery project communities in the face of Government of Uganda's resettlement action plan*. Kampala: Global Rights Alert.

Goldman, A. (2014) 'Nigeria forum: what happens when oil prices fall?', African Arguments, 1 December. Available at: http://africanarguments.org/2014/12/01/nigeria-forum-what-happens-when-oil-prices-fall-by-anthony-goldman/.

Humphreys, M., J. D. Sachs and J. E. Stiglitz (2007) *Escaping the Resource Curse*. New York NY: Columbia University Press.

IBP (2012) *Open Budget Survey 2012*. Washington DC: International Budget Partnership (IBP). Available at: http://internationalbudget.org/wp-content/uploads/OBI2012-Report-English.pdf.

ICG (2009) 'Chad: Escaping the oil trap'. Africa Briefing 65. Brussels: International Crisis Group (ICG).

— (2013) 'Kenya after the elections'. Africa Briefing 94. Nairobi and Brussels: International Crisis Group (ICG).

IEA (2013) *Key World Energy Statistics*. Paris: International Energy Agency (IEA).

IHS (2014a) 'Chadian government's environmental dispute

with CNPC escalates'. Engle-
wood CO and London: IHS Oil
and Gas Risk Service.

— (2014b) *Minority and Female
Employment in the Oil & Gas
and Petrochemical Industries*.
Washington DC: IHS Global
Inc. Available at: www.api.
org/~/media/Files/Policy/Jobs/
IHS-Minority-and-Female-
Employment-Report.pdf.

ILPI (2013) 'Political economy
analysis of the oil sector in
Uganda'. Oslo: International
Law and Policy Institute (ILPI).

IMF (2014) 'Chad: IMF Country
Report No. 14/100'. Washington
DC: International Monetary
Fund (IMF). Available at:
www.imf.org/external/pubs/ft/
scr/2014/cr14100.pdf.

International Alert (2011) 'Oil and
gas laws in Uganda: a legislators' guide'. Oil Discussion
Paper 1. Kampala: International Alert Uganda.

Katsouris, C. and A. Sayne (2013)
*Nigeria's Criminal Crude:
International options to combat
the export of stolen oil*. London:
Chatham House.

KCSPOG (2014) *Setting the Agenda
for the Development of Kenya's
Oil and Gas Resources: The
perspectives of civil society*.
Nairobi: Kenya Civil Society
Platform on Oil and Gas.

KPMG (2013) *Oil and Gas in Africa:
Africa's reserves, potential
and prospects.* Johannesburg:
KPMG. Available at: www.
kpmg.com/Africa/en/IssuesAnd
Insights/Articles-Publications/

Documents/Oil%20and%20
Gas%20in%20Africa.pdf.

Lujala, P. and S. A. Rustad (eds)
(2012) *High-value Natural
Resources and Post-conflict
Peacebuilding*. Abingdon:
Earthscan.

Matisoff, A. (2012) *Crude Beginnings: An assessment of China
National Petroleum Corporation's
environmental and social performance abroad*. San Francisco
CA: Friends of the Earth.

Michel, S. and M. Beuret (2009)
*China Safari: On the trail of
China's expansion in Africa*.
New York NY: Nation Books.

MINES ParisTech (2012) *Analysis of
the Environmental Situation in
the Bongor West Permit, Chad*.
Geo2012 series. Paris: École
des Mines de Paris (MINES
ParisTech).

Ministry of Finance and Economic Planning (2013) *Final
Report on the Aggregation/Rec-
onciliation of Mining Sector Payments And Receipts: 2010–2011*.
Accra: Ministry of Finance and
Economic Planning and Ghana
Extractive Industries Transparency Initiative. Available at:
https://eiti.org/files/Ghana-
2010-2011-EITI-Report_0.pdf.

Mitchell, T. (2013) *Carbon Democracy: Political power in the age
of oil*. London: Verso.

Oxfam (2013) *Niger: À qui profite
l'uranium? (Who benefits from
Niger's uranium?)*. Paris: Oxfam
France.

Patey, L. (2012) 'Lurking beneath
the surface: oil, environmental

degradation, and armed conflict in Sudan'. In Lujala, P. and S. A. Rustad (eds) *High-value Natural Resources and Post-conflict Peacebuilding*. Abingdon: Earthscan.

— (2014a) *The New Kings of Crude: China, India, and the global struggle for oil in Sudan and South Sudan*. London: C. Hurst.

— (2014b) *Kenya: An African oil upstart in transition*. OIES paper WPM 53. Oxford: Oxford Institute for Energy Studies (OIES). Available at: www.oxfordenergy.org/wpcms/wp-content/uploads/2014/10/WPM-53.pdf.

PIAC (2012) *Report on Management of Petroleum Revenues for Year 2012: Annual report*. Accra: Public Interest and Accountability Committee, Ghana (PIAC).

Republic of Kenya (2014) *Draft National Energy Policy*. Nairobi: Republic of Kenya, Ministry of Energy and Petroleum. Available at: www.energy.go.ke/downloads/National%20Energy%20Policy%20-%20Final%20Draft.pdf.

Republic of Uganda (2008) *National Oil and Gas Policy for Uganda*. Kampala: Republic of Uganda, Ministry of Energy and Mineral Development. Available at: www.acode-u.org/documents/oildocs/oil&gas_policy.pdf.

Republique du Niger and ITIE Niger (2013) *Rapport de Mission de Collecte et de Réconciliation des Revenus Miniers et Pétroliers (Annee 2011)*. Niamey: République du Niger and ITIE Niger. Available at: https://eiti.org/files/4eme_rapport_itie_niger_2011_0.pdf.

Ross, M. (2012) *The Oil Curse: How petroleum wealth shapes the development of nations*. Princeton NJ: Princeton University Press.

Shaxson, N. (2008) *Poisoned Wells: The dirty politics of African oil*. Basingstoke: Palgrave Macmillan.

Southall, R. and H. Melber (eds) (2009) *The New Scramble for Africa?: Imperialism, investment and development*. Scottsville, South Africa: University of KwaZulu-Natal Press.

Taylor, I. (2006) 'China's oil diplomacy in Africa'. *International Affairs* 82(5): 937–59.

Tsalik, S. and A. Schiffrin (eds) (2005) *Covering Oil: A reporter's guide to energy and development*. New York NY: Open Society Institute.

Tullow Oil (2013) *Creating Shared Prosperity in Partnership: Tullow Oil plc 2013 corporate responsibility report*. London: Tullow Oil. Available at: www.tullowoil.com/files/pdf/reports/TLW_CR_2013.pdf.

— (2014) *Africa's Leading Independent Oil Comapny: Tullow Oil plc 2013 annual report & accounts*. London: Tullow Oil. Available at: www.tullowoil.com/files/pdf/tullow_ar_report_2013.pdf.

UN Panel of Experts (2009) 'Report of the Panel of Experts established pursuant to resolution 1591 (2005) concerning the Sudan'. Geneva: UN Panel of Experts on Darfur Arms Embargo. Available at: www.smallarmssurveysudan.org/fileadmin/docs/documents/HSBA-Sec-Gen-2009-562.pdf.

UNDP (2013) *Human Development Report 2013. The rise of the South: Human progress in a diverse world.* New York NY: United Nations Development Programme (UNDP).

US Department of State (2011) *Chad: 2010 human rights report.* Washington DC: US Department of State. Available at: www.state.gov/j/drl/rls/hrrpt/2010/af/154338.htm.

van Oranje, M. and H. Parham (2009) *Publishing What We Learned: An Assessment of the Publish What You Pay Coalition.* London: Publish What You Pay.

van Vliet, G. and G. Magrin (eds) (2012) *The Environmental Challenges Facing a Chinese Oil Company in Chad.* Focales 09. Paris: Agence Française de Développement.

Vasquez, P. I. (2013) 'Kenya at a crossroads: hopes and fears concerning the development of oil and gas reserves'. Articles and Debates 4.3. Geneva: Graduate Institute Geneva.

WBG (2009) *The World Bank Group Program of Support for the Chad–Cameroon Petroleum Development and Pipeline Construction: Program performance assessment report.* Washington DC: World Bank Group (WBG), Independent Evaluation Group. Available at: www.oecd.org/derec/worldbankgroup/44392731.pdf.

Wepundi, M., E. Nthiga, E. Kabuu, R. Murray and A. Alvazzi del Frate (2012) *Availability of Small Arms and Perceptions of Security in Kenya: An assessment.* Geneva: Small Arms Survey.

World Bank (2010) *Silent and Lethal: How quiet corruption undermines Africa's development efforts. Africa Development Indicators 2010.* Washington DC: World Bank.

Yankson, P. W. K. (2010) 'Gold mining and corporate social responsibility in the Wassa West district, Ghana'. *Development in Practice* 20(3): 354–66.

Online news articles

'6 firms shortlisted for oil refinery deal', The Observer, 17 December 2013: http://observer.ug/index.php?option=com_content&view=article&id=29179:6-firms-shortlisted-for-oil-refinery-deal&catid=38:business&Itemid=68.

'"Absolutely" – Kenya President backs full oil contract disclosure', GOXI, 27 August 2014: http://goxi.org/profiles/blogs/absolutely-kenya-president-backs-full-oil-contract-disclosure.

'Chad backs out of hosting AU

summit', eNews Channel Africa, 11 January 2015: www.enca.com/africa/chad-backs-out-hosting-au-summit.

'Chad: civil society disappointed by World Bank oil pull-out', IRIN News, 14 September 2008: www.irinnews.org/report/80338/chad-civil-society-disappointed-by-world-bank-oil-pull-out.

'Chad orders foreign oil firms out', BBC News, 27 August 2006: http://news.bbc.co.uk/1/hi/world/africa/5289580.stm.

'Chad says suspends CNPC refinery deal', Reuters, 24 January 2012: http://mobile.reuters.com/article/rbssOilGasRefiningMarketing/idUSL5E8CO3BR20120124.

'Chad suspends China's CNPC unit over environment', Reuters, 14 August 2013: http://uk.reuters.com/article/2013/08/14/us-chad-china-cnpc-idUKBRE97DoVN20130814.

'Chad: top brass defectors protest Deby rule', IRIN News, 12 December 2005: www.irinnews.org/report/57544/chad-top-brass-defectors-protest-deby-rule.

'China's oil fears over South Sudan fighting', BBC News, 8 January 2014: www.bbc.co.uk/news/world-africa-25654155.

'Darfur: new weapons from China and Russia fuelling conflict', Amnesty International, 8 February 2012: www.amnesty.org/en/news/darfur-new-weapons-china-and-russia-fuelling-conflict-2012-02-08.

'DRC and Uganda ease oil tensions', BBC News, 8 September 2007: http://news.bbc.co.uk/1/hi/world/africa/6984758.stm.

'East Africa: Kenya or Uganda, who gets oil first?', The Africa Report, 25 April 2014: www.theafricareport.com/East-Horn-Africa/east-africa-kenya-or-uganda-who-gets-oil-first.html.

'EnCana sells all of its interests in Chad', EnCana, 12 January 2007: www.encana.com/news-stories/news-releases/details.html?release=609901.

'Ghana lacks "capacity" to tackle oil spills, report shows', Bloomberg, 8 October 2010: www.bloomberg.com/news/2010-10-08/ghana-lacks-the-capacity-to-tackle-spills-from-oil-wells-report-shows.html.

'Ghana limits dollar transactions to protect Cedi', BBC News, 6 February 2014: www.bbc.co.uk/news/world-africa-26064127.

'Ghana: the best mix of power sources – the way forward for Ghana', All Africa, 12 March 2014: http://allafrica.com/stories/201403120940.html.

'Ghana: to flare or not to flare Jubilee gas', All Africa, 1 February 2014: http://allafrica.com/stories/201402031931.html.

'Ghana "will be an African tiger"', BBC News, 19 June 2007: http://news.bbc.co.uk/1/hi/world/africa/6766527.stm.

'Glencore to finance Chad's $1.3 bln oil assets purchase',

Reuters, 16 June 2014: www.reuters.com/article/2014/06/16/chad-oil-glencore-idUSL5N0OX3MN20140616.

'Griffiths to pay millions in African bribery case', *The Globe and Mail*, 22 January 2013. www.theglobeandmail.com/report-on-business/industry-news/energy-and-resources/griffiths-to-pay-millions-in-african-bribery-case/article7622364/.

'In Chad, elephants make a comeback', Aljazeera America, 5 September 2014: http://america.aljazeera.com/articles/2014/9/5/in-chad-elephantsmakea comeback.html.

'Isabel dos Santos: "First African female billionaire"', BBC News, 25 January 2013: www.bbc.co.uk/news/world-africa-21184854.

'Kenya MP accused of inciting protests against oil firm Tullow', Reuters, 31 October 2013: http://uk.reuters.com/ article/2013/10/31/uk-kenya-tullow-idUKBRE99U11N20131031.

'Kenya oil discovery after Tullow Oil drilling', BBC News, 26 March 2012: www.bbc.co.uk/news/world-africa-17513488.

'Mystery of Ghana whale deaths', BBC News, 6 September 2013: www.bbc.co.uk/news/world-africa-23992933.

'Natural resource-rich countries hampered by sovereign wealth fund opacity and mismanagement', Natural Resource Governance Institute, 8 April 2014: www.resourcegovernance.org/news/press_releases/natural-resource-rich-countries-hampered-sovereign-wealth-fund-opacity-and-misma.

'Niger activists arrested over Areva protest before François Hollande visit', *Guardian*, 18 July 2014: www.theguardian.com/global-development/2014/jul/18/niger-activists-arrested-areva-francois-hollande-france-uranium.

'Niger's Hama Amadou flees over baby-trafficking scandal', BBC News, 28 August 2014: www.bbc.co.uk/news/world-africa-28966966.

'Nigeria's growing number of female oil bosses', BBC News, 11 September 2014: www.bbc.co.uk/news/business-29127436.

'Nigeria's Ventures magazine lists 55 billionaires', BBC News, 7 October 2013: www.bbc.co.uk/news/world-africa-24433996.

'Refinery compensation exercise behind schedule', Oil in Uganda, 2 July 2014: www.oilinuganda.org/features/land/refinery-compensation-exercise-behind-schedule.html.

'Special report: Areva and Niger's uranium fight', Reuters, 5 February 2014: www.reuters.com/article/2014/02/05/us-niger-areva-specialreport-idUSBREA140AA20140205.

'The life of Ken Saro-Wiwa', Remember Saro-Wiwa: http://remembersarowiwa.com/background/the-life-of-ken-saro-wiwa/.

'Tourism earnings hike to $400m', *New Vision*, 4 November 2010: www.newvision.co.ug/D/8/220/737091.

'Tullow may sell part of stake in Ugandan oil field: chief operating officer says focus may switch to Kenyan project', *Wall Street Journal*, 12 February 2014: http://online.wsj.com/news/articles/SB10001424052702304888404579378581273550024.

'Tullow Oil sets new standard for transparency', ONE.org, 24 March 2014: www.one.org/international/press/tullow-oil-sets-new-standard-for-transparency/.

'Tullow Oil's Sunderland AFC sponsorship ends amid controversy', Platform, 11 April 2013: http://platformlondon.org/2013/04/11/tullow-oils-sunderland-afc-sponsorship-ends-amid-controversy/.

'Tullow's tax disclosures torpedo Big Oil's campaign for secrecy', Global Witness, 24 March 2014: www.globalwitness.org/library/tullow%E2%80%99s-tax-disclosures-torpedo-big-oil%E2%80%99s-campaign-secrecy.

'Uganda donors cut aid after president passes anti-gay law', *Guardian*, 25 February 2014: www.theguardian.com/global-development/2014/feb/25/uganda-donors-cut-aid-anti-gay-law.

'Uganda: high stakes in the oil debates', Think Africa Press, 6 September 2012: http://thinkafricapress.com/uganda/oil-revenue-management-and-president-musevenis-exit.

'Uganda: oil will not create jobs – Prof Collier', *The Observer*, 22 December 2013: http://allafrica.com/stories/201312230081.html.

'Uganda's environmental impact assessment process under fire', Oil in Uganda, 13 September 2012: www.oilinuganda.org/features/environment/ugandas-environmental-impact-assessment-process-under-fire.html.

'Why many of Ghana's gold miners are giving up', BBC News, 30 December 2013: www.bbc.co.uk/news/business-25417492.

'World Bank suspends loans to Chad – "model" oil project on the rocks', Oxfam, 6 January 2006: www.publishwhatyoupay.org/resources/world-bank-suspends-loans-chad-%E2%80%93-%E2%80%9Cmodel%E2%80%80%9D-oil-project-rocks.

Websites

Bank of Ghana: www.bog.gov.gh.

'Chad', *The Economist* Intelligence Unit: http://country.eiu.com/chad.

Ghana Oil Almanac: http://wiki.openoil.net/index.php?title=Ghana.

'History of EITI', Extractive Industries Transparency Initiative: http://eiti.org/eiti/history.

'History', Publish What You Pay:

www.publishwhatyoupay.org/about/history.

International Monetary Fund: www.imf.org.

'Introduction to UNICEF's work on statistics and monitoring', UNICEF: www.unicef.org/statistics.

MDG 1: Eradicate extreme hunger and poverty, United Nations Development Programme: www.gh.undp.org/content/ghana/en/home/mdgoverview/overview/mdg1/.

Mo Ibrahim Index of African Governance (2014): www.moibrahimfoundation.org/interact/.

Natural Resource Charter, Natural Resource Governance Institute: www.resourcegovernance.org/issues/natural-resource-charter.

Pink Petro: www.pinkpetro.com.

'Promoting the sustainable development of Kenya's extractive industries', Adam Smith International: www.adamsmithinternational.com/explore-our-work/east-africa/kenya/the-sustainable-development-of-kenyas-extractive-industries-scoping-study-a.

Resource Governance Index, Natural Resource Governance Institute: www.resourcegovernance.org/rgi.

Interviews

Alan Gelb, former Chief Economist for Africa at the World Bank: telephone interview, 20 October 2013.

Alice Powell, Communications Officer at the Publish What You Pay secretariat, London: face-to-face interview, March 2014; follow-up telephone interview, 2 September 2014.

Ann Pettitt, Director of Safer Birth in Chad: email questions, 19 July 2013.

Anonymous source, CNPCIC: various email contacts from July 2014 onwards.

Anonymous US academic: various telephone interviews from October 2013 onwards.

Bady Mamadou Balde, EITI officer responsible for Chad: telephone interview, 26 May 2014 and various email questions.

Franklin Cudjoe, Director of the Imani Institute, Accra: 23 January 2014.

George Boden, Uganda campaigner for Global Witness: various email interviews from October 2013 onwards.

George Cazenove, Tullow Oil press officer, London headquarters: face-to-face interview, 25 April 2014.

Geraud Magrin, author of *The Environmental Challenges Facing a Chinese Oil Company in Chad*: various email conversations from December 2013 onwards.

Josef Skoldeberg, Lead Communications Officer at the IFC's Infrastructure and Natural Resources Group: email, 23 January 2014.

Mahaman Laouan Gaya, former Secretary General at the Nigerien Ministry of Mines:

face-to-face interview, 20 February 2014; follow-up email questions.

Mauricio Villafuerte, IMF economist for Chad: telephone interview, 18 October 2013; various follow-up email questions.

Peter Rosenblum, Columbia Law School (involved in the early days of civil society activism in Chad in the 2000s): telephone interview, 18 October 2013.

Rebecca Ponton, author of *Breaking the Gas Ceiling*: various email interviews from June 2014 onwards.

Robert Calderisi, author of *The Trouble with Africa* and former World Bank Country Director for Central Africa: telephone interview, 18 October 2013.

Sergei Boeke, senior analyst at International Centre for Counter-terrorism: telephone interview, 10 May 2014.

Stephanie Hancock, BBC correspondent in Chad from 2005 to 2008: face-to-face interview, 15 October 2013.

Steve Coll, author of *Private Empire*: email questions, 13 March 2014.

Index